A Dolores Huerta Reader

A DOLORES HUERTA

READER

Edited by Mario T. García

UNIVERSITY OF NEW MEXICO PRESS
ALBUQUERQUE

14 13 12 11 10 09   2 3 4 5 6 7

Library of Congress Cataloging-in-Publication Data

A Dolores Huerta reader / edited by Mario T. García.
    p. cm.
Includes bibliographical references.
ISBN 978-0-8263-4513-4 (pbk. : alk. paper)
1. Huerta, Dolores, 1930–
2. Mexican American women labor leaders—United States.
3. Agricultural laborers—Labor unions—Organizing—United States.
I. García, Mario T.
HD6509.H84D65 2008
331.88´13092—dc22
        2008026302

Designed and typeset by Mina Yamashita.
Text composed in Utopia Std, a typeface designed
by Robert Slimbach for Adobe in 1989.
Display composed in Frutiger 77 Black Condensed,
designed by Adrian Frutiger in 1976.
Printed by Thomson-Shore, Inc. on 55# Natures Natural.

To Dolores Huerta,

whose commitment to the

struggle for social justice

and a more democratic

America inspired this book.

Contents

Part Two: DOLORES HUERTA SPEAKS

Acknowledgments

I want to first thank Dolores Huerta and her longtime struggle for social justice as the inspiration for this book. Lisa Pacheco at the University of New Mexico Press immediately saw the importance of this project and without hesitation embraced it at our wonderful and productive lunch in Santa Fe in the early winter of 2006. Lisa has skillfully and with commitment shepherded the manuscript through the various phases of review and production. As part of this process, I want to also express gratitude to the anonymous reviewer who likewise appreciated the value of this anthology and provided not only support but also very useful suggestions to improve it. Of course, an anthology or collection is only as good as the contributors to it. This book in part is a collection of published journal articles, book chapters, newspaper articles, and interviews on Dolores Huerta written by historians and journalists who provided thoughtful and well-researched portraits and views of Huerta concerning her history and struggles at different times of her life. These writers include Margaret Rose, Richard Griswold del Castillo, Richard A. García, Jean Murphy, Barbara L. Baer, Glenna Matthews, Eileen Foley, Judith Coburn, Nelda Clemmons, Scott Forter, Aurora Camacho de Schmidt, Ruth Carranza, Lisa Genasci, Julie Felner, James Rainey, María Luisa Torres, Ryan Floersheim, Vincent Harding, Julia Bencomo Lobaco, Samuel Orozco, and Frances Ortega. Besides acknowledging these writers and interviewers, I also want to thank the different publishers who provided us with permission to reproduce the articles, interviews, and documents that compose the volume. These particular acknowledgments are provided in the book itself.

For the photos used in the book, I want to thank LeRoy Chatfield and the Farmworker Movement Documentation Project for the assistance in locating photos and the photographers. I also want to thank Matt Herron and Take Stock Photos for further assistance and permission in use of photos. The individual photographer and sources of the photos are noted in the book itself.

For her research assistance in the early phases of this project, I am grateful to Monica García.

Finally, I wish to pay special thanks to my other research assistant, Colleen Ho, whose work in the last year of the project was crucial in scanning the different articles and documents into a workable manuscript, helping to edit the manuscript, word processing the various drafts, and communicating with publishers for the permissions. Throughout this process, she has been totally reliable and professional in her work. It has been a pleasure to work with such a hardworking and talented graduate student who undoubtedly will go on to a stellar career as a medieval historian. ■

Dolores Huerta, Delano, 1965.
Courtesy of Harvey Richards.

Introduction

La Pasionaria Chicana

Dolores Huerta is one of the great women of twentieth-century American history. Her role as coleader of the farm workers' struggles alongside César Chávez, her work as a civil rights advocate, her leadership in the feminist movement, her championing of peace and environmental issues, and her role as a model for several generations of Chicana and Latina women, are all tributes to her significant place in history. For six decades La Pasionaria (the passionate one), as she is also referred to, has personified leadership, courage, commitment to the cause of the downtrodden and powerless, and, yes, passion for social justice. Still active at age seventy-eight, Dolores Huerta has rightfully gained a major place in Chicano and American history.

Yet despite her important historical role, Dolores Huerta has not received the same type of coverage from historians and journalists as has César Chávez. The literature on Chávez is voluminous, and even though no major biography has yet been written on the great farm worker and spiritual leader, there are many books and articles about him.[1] The same is not true of Huerta. Not only has no biography been written about her, but the literature on her is quite scant. As a result, her role in history is much less appreciated.

Recognizing this deficiency, I have edited this volume precisely to help correct this and to bring attention to her importance and the need for scholars to turn their attention to her. This volume by no means replaces the need for a significant biography of Huerta, but until that occurs, it will fill a gap in the literature for scholars and for students. I have researched and brought together two important sets of documents that help reveal Huerta's place in history as well as her own views and reflections on her work and on herself. Part One is a collection of what I consider to be among the best primary and secondary literature on her in the form of journal articles, book chapters, and journalistic pieces. Part Two is a collection of interviews, speeches, public statements, conference dialogues, and correspondence by Huerta herself. This section is the closest to an autobiography by Dolores Huerta. Hopefully, this volume about her and by her will reinforce her standing among knowledgeable scholars and, at the same time, introduce her and her importance to many others.

Section One clearly brings forth Dolores Huerta's story. Because several of the articles in this section cover her life and work in some detail, I will only summarize her history here. Although associated with California due to her role in the farm labor movement of that state, Huerta (her married name) was born in the northern mining town of Dawson, New Mexico, on April 10, 1930. Her parents bridged the historical connection between the U.S.-born and immigrants. Her mother, Alicia Chávez, descended from several generations of Hispanos in New Mexico. Her father, Juan Fernández, was the son of Mexican immigrants. Her parents divorced when Huerta was still a young girl and she left New Mexico with her mother and other siblings for California. Settling in Stockton, her mother worked in the canneries and as a waitress until she owned and operated a restaurant and later acquired a hotel. As a result of this mobility, Dolores Huerta grew up in a more middle-class household, which was further solidified by two additional marriages by her mother. There is no question that Huerta was significantly influenced and shaped by her strong and socially conscious mother. At the same time, she was also affected by her father and what contact she had with him over the years. Her father, who remained in New Mexico, became a key labor union organizer with the CIO during the 1930s and later served in the New Mexico state legislature. Her mother represented a role model of an independent and strong female while her father provided a lesson in labor and political leadership. Dolores Huerta would go on to embody both sets of influences.

Experiencing two marriages and eventually having eleven children with three men, Huerta refused to be subordinated as a woman to the role of wife and mother. She achieved more education than other Chicanas or, for that matter, Chicanos of her generation. After high school, she attended the local community college in Stockton where she earned an AA degree and later pursued a teaching career. But teaching was not her main interest. Community and political involvement proved to be her passion. In the mid-1950s she met and was influenced by Fred Ross, the head of the Community Service Organization (CSO) in California, an offshoot of the Industrial Areas Foundation in Chicago led by Saul Alinsky.[2] Ross saw in the already charismatic Huerta the potential for her to become a significant community organizer in the Mexican American community where CSO was focusing its efforts. Huerta joined the civil rights and community self-help organization and quickly, as Ross predicted, emerged as a key leader on voter registration and other community issues such as education, health care, and police abuse. At the same time, Ross had also met and recruited César Chávez to CSO from his home in San Jose. Chávez went on to become the director of CSO in California. When Huerta first met Chávez, she notes that she was not initially impressed. Unlike herself, Chávez was much more shy, quiet, and physically unimposing. Despite this initial encounter, both would later make history together and complement one another.

Chávez, as a son of farm workers and one himself as a youth, possessed a dream of successfully organizing farm workers. Although he had succeeded as an urban community organizer with CSO, he wanted to go back into the fields and organize. However, he failed to convince the organization to support such an effort. Consequently, Chávez left CSO in 1962 and started his own National Farm Workers Association (NFWA) operating out of Delano in the Central Valley with Helen, his wife, and other members of his family and a few close associates. César wanted Dolores Huerta to join him. He succeeded and soon Huerta also found herself in Delano. After three years of house meetings with workers and their families, the association was able to recruit a number of workers. However, its biggest challenge came in the fall of 1965 when a largely Filipino farm labor union, the Agricultural Workers' Organizing Committee affiliated with the AFL-CIO, went on strike against some of the large grape growers in the San Joaquin Valley. They approached Chávez and the NFWA to join them. Despite some initial hesitancy, Chávez and Huerta and the other leaders of the fledgling union agreed to do so. Using the symbolic date of Mexican Independence Day, September 16, the mostly Mexican American workers voted to join the strike. This commenced the historic five-year grape strike led by Chávez and Huerta and laid the foundation for the late 1960s merger of the United Farm Workers (UFW) union and the AFL-CIO.

While Chávez represented the public and spiritual face of the farm workers' struggle symbolized by marches or what he called *peregrinaciónes* or pilgrimages and physical fasts, Huerta represented the nuts and bolts of the movement. Huerta proved indispensable on the picket line and in keeping up the morale of the workers. She was especially critical in getting more women involved in the strike and through their influence keeping the struggle focused on Chávez's key principle of nonviolence. Moreover, when the union increased the pressure on the growers by launching a national and international boycott of table grapes, Huerta spearheaded this effort by organizing the boycott outside California, especially by spending a considerable amount of time in New York City and the East where she successfully managed boycott efforts. Returning to California by the late 1960s, she assumed additional responsibilities as vice president of the UFW by becoming its chief negotiator with the growers when they finally agreed to talk to the union. Her courage, tenacity, and unwillingness to be intimidated by the all-male growers led to the final victory of the union and the signing of contracts with the agribusiness. This marked the first successful unionization drive by agricultural workers in U.S. history. There is little doubt that César Chávez and Dolores Huerta's leadership was the key to this success.

However, neither could afford to rest on their laurels. Within three years, the growers refused to extend the union contracts and instead opted to sign "sweetheart contracts" with the Teamsters Union. The result was intense and confrontational competition between the UFW and the Teamsters that at times led to the use of violence by the latter. It also led to the resumption of the grape boycott and the addition of a lettuce one. Dolores Huerta again led in these efforts and more. In the end, the UFW and the Teamsters agreed to split unionization efforts. The Teamsters would organize packinghouse workers while the UFW would organize the larger population of field workers. Additionally, in 1975 in efforts further spearheaded by Huerta, the union achieved the establishment of the Agricultural Labor Relations Act to deal with future labor disputes in the fields. Within a ten-year period César Chávez and Dolores Huerta had made history.

But the struggles and the plight of farm workers continued. Growers in California and elsewhere still refused to negotiate with the UFW and more strikes and boycotts followed for the next two decades. Throughout all these ups and downs, the leadership of Dolores Huerta remained steady and unwavering. When César Chávez died in 1993, physically weakened after many years of sacrifice and engaging in fasts, Dolores Huerta remained as the living embodiment of the movement. Her leadership and influence kept the union going until new leadership in the form of Arturo Rodríguez took over. However, as vice president emeritus of the UFW since the late 1990s, Huerta has never abandoned the farm workers and continues to be a voice for them and their families.

Like César Chávez, Dolores Huerta's work has been multifaceted. She supported and participated in Mexican American civil rights struggles as part of the 1960s and 1970s Chicano Movement. Indeed, she has never stopped working on civil rights, not only for Latinos but also for any discriminated community. Already possessing feminist traits in her early years, including the initial period of the UFW, Huerta became a more pronounced feminist and advocate for women's rights, especially for minority women, by the 1970s. In addition, she, like Chávez, became an early environmentalist due to the harmful effects of pesticides in the fields. Farm workers and their families suffered many illnesses and physical problems due to their contact with pesticides sprayed as they worked. The UFW documented the existence of cancer clusters in many farm worker communities in the San Joaquin Valley. Moreover, Huerta linked her farm labor activism with electoral politics, especially within the Democratic Party. She understood that the UFW needed outside support, in addition to labor and religious support, and that some of it could come from the more liberal wing of the Democratic Party. For example, in 1968, she and Chávez openly campaigned for Senator Robert Kennedy in his effort to win the Democratic nomination for president. Huerta stood alongside Bobby Kennedy at the Ambassador Hotel in Los Angeles after he won the crucial Democratic primary, assisted by an impressive turnout of Mexican American voters. At the podium that tragic evening, Kennedy expressed his support to Dolores Huerta and the farm workers. Within minutes, he lay dying in the pantry of the hotel, shot down by an assassin. But Kennedy's death would not deter or discourage Huerta, and through the years she has worked for and supported many candidates for office as long as they in turn supported the farm workers. Finally, the multidimensional Huerta has supported many other causes for peace, human rights, nuclear disarmament, and the end to U.S. military interventions such as in Iraq.

With this short summary of Dolores Huerta's life and work, I want to now comment and reflect on some of the key aspects of her story that the documents in this reader bring to light. I do so here without any particular order of importance.

First of all, Huerta's life tells us something about the condition of farm workers. Her work with César Chávez and the efforts begun in 1962 to unionize in the fields focused on the difficult and exploitive conditions of these workers and their families. Huerta always observed how farm workers were treated inhumanely and with a lack of human dignity. Growers and the public gave them little concern and, even worse, no recognition. The farm workers' working and living conditions attested to this treatment. They worked for the lowest wages of all workers; they worked long hours with little relief; they had no toilet facilities in the fields; they were exposed to harmful pesticides; they lived in run-down company camps; their children were deprived of education due to migrant life and lack of educational facilities in the agricultural areas; they possessed no health insurance; they received no social security benefits; they were cheated and exploited by labor contractors; and they faced seasonal unemployment due to the agricultural cycle. They truly reaped what famed journalist Edward R. Murrow called the "harvest of shame."

As a farm labor leader Huerta experienced some of these forms of degradation. But more importantly, her vocal and charismatic leadership as vice president of the UFW and chief negotiator with the growers brought local, state, national, and even international attention to the poverty and powerlessness of farm laborers, predominantly Mexican and minority in character.

Huerta's history reveals her to be an atypical labor organizer. First and foremost her gender distinguished her role. In general, very few women served as labor leaders in U.S. unions and certainly few held top positions. For these reasons, Huerta's emergence as César

Chávez's top lieutenant and coleader of the UFW makes her unique. However, it is not just her anomaly as a woman that distinguished her leadership; her persona, characterized by her toughness and her lack of intimidation by men, set her apart as well. Huerta would never take a backseat to any man, not even Chávez. The growers did not refer to her as the "Dragon Lady" for nothing. Huerta was and is a woman and a leader of strength who refuses to compromise her core principles of social justice and equality for all.

While Huerta is an atypical labor leader, she is also part of a tradition of strong Chicana/Latina labor and community leaders of the twentieth century. This includes Luisa Moreno, a key organizer for UCAPAWA (United Cannery, Agricultural, Packing, and Allied Workers of America), who in the 1930s and 1940s led a successful drive to unionize Mexican American cannery workers in Los Angeles and elsewhere. Josefina Fierro, a protégé of Moreno, proved to be a charismatic and significant civil rights leader in Los Angeles and southern California as the executive secretary of the National Congress of Spanish-Speaking Peoples (El Congreso). Finally, in Texas as a young teenager, Emma Tenayuca, equally as charismatic as Fierro, successfully organized Mexican American pecan shellers in San Antonio.[3] These women possessed many if not all of the same strong qualities as Dolores Huerta.

One of the more fascinating aspects of Huerta's life is her relationship with Chávez. Tied together in struggle for the farm worker cause, they developed a symbiotic yet somewhat competitive relationship. Their personalities were strikingly different. Where Huerta was outspoken and openly aggressive, Chávez was soft-spoken and calm. Yet both were thoroughly committed to La Causa—the struggle. Huerta accepted Chávez as the titular leader of the movement and yet, as some of her early correspondence with Chávez reproduced in this volume reveals, she more than any other figure was not timid about challenging his views or asserting her own. While Chávez often teased Huerta about her style of leadership and even her opinions, he conceded how much he appreciated and valued her questioning in order to help him make decisions. On the other side of this relationship, Huerta needed and appreciated Chávez's patience with her; his willingness to give her latitude of action; and his ability to help her focus. They were close friends, even brotherly and sisterly, and were able to have fun together and help each other relax and put things in perspective during the long and difficult years of organizing.[4]

Another interesting feature of Huerta's life, discussed in both sections of this volume, is her family. Here again she proved to be atypical. Twice divorced and later openly living with Richard Chávez, César's brother, and having children from all three, Huerta was a far cry from the more traditional Mexican wife and mother. Her need to be herself and to assert herself represented traits she inherited from her own independent-minded mother, herself a businesswoman and twice divorced. Dolores Huerta did not believe that the proper and respectful place for a woman—any woman—was at home taking care of children and her husband. She believed that women also belonged in the public sphere and she followed that belief first in her role in CSO, where she learned her organizing skills, and later within the farm worker movement, where she expanded those skills.

At the same time, Huerta believed in family and motherhood, but in a modified form and on her terms. She loved children and had eleven sons and daughters. She believed that having children filled a special need for her and other women. In this sense, she conveyed a certain traditionalism, but only to an extent. She did not believe that having children should curtail her need to be politically active. Juggling children with relatives and friends and taking care of them while working, she somehow managed to be both mother and activist. She often observed that the best example she could give her children was a sense of public responsibility and involvement and of sacrifice for others. All of her children, with the exception of one physically disabled daughter, at one time or another worked for the union and have gone on to different careers characterized by helping others. Probably without recognizing it, in a sense Dolores Huerta redefined family and motherhood, certainly within a Chicana/Latina context.

Is Dolores Huerta a feminist? She certainly considers herself a feminist, but with the caveat that this also is on her own terms and not something prescribed. She acknowledges that the 1960s Second Wave of feminism, and in particular leaders such as Gloria Steinem, influenced her to openly embrace feminism. However, feminism for Huerta meant adapting it to her own life. This included not personally supporting abortion and birth control. She personally broke with these feminist-supported issues, but only privately. She did not publicly oppose abortion or birth control because she respected other women's choices and she would not impose her views on others. For Huerta, feminism meant struggling to achieve total and equal rights for all women, but in her own personal life being selective of certain feminist issues. In this way, she defied the stereotypical and monolithic view of American feminists.

Dolores Huerta also personifies the bridging of gender and ethnicity. As a strong female leader and as a feminist, she has deep pride in her New Mexican Hispano and Mexican American roots and ethnicity. Like most other Chicana feminists of her time, she first became politically active about her ethnicity. As a result, she involved herself in Mexican American civil rights issues when she joined CSO. When César Chávez invited her to help organize a farm workers union, she accepted, recognizing the Mexican American background of the majority of workers. But as an assertive woman, Huerta came to combine ethnic consciousness with gender and feminist awareness. Indeed, her sense of self-identity went beyond this duality—it was in fact a multiple identity. Besides ethnicity and gender, Huerta, especially through her work with farm workers, conveyed class-consciousness rooted in support of working-class struggles against growers and other representatives of the capitalist class. She was not a Marxist or socialist, but an American social democrat. She was not a supporter of American capitalism, but she pragmatically understood that revolutionary conditions did not exist. One had to force changes within the system by exposing the contradictions of American democracy that excluded so many from its benefits. Based on her CSO training, Huerta believed that you work within the system, but not with it. Huerta understood what Chicana scholars called the triple oppression of Chicanas and other minority women: race, class, and gender. She understood that Chicanas, especially in farm labor, suffered from racism, class exploitation, and gender discrimination.[5]

In her own close relationship with César Chávez, Dolores Huerta shared many common principles, including an adherence to nonviolence. Chávez, influenced by his knowledge of Gandhi and St. Francis and his learning from Dr. Martin Luther King Jr., centered his farm workers' movement on nonviolence. If there is any one principle or value that most Americans associate with Chávez, as they do with King, it is nonviolence. The same is also true of Dolores Huerta. Although more publicly combative than Chávez, she embraced the concept of nonviolence and practiced it for philosophical as well as practical reasons. She understood the power of nonviolence and that farm workers and their supporters could not resort to violence because it was antihuman and antichristian. If life was precious and if the farm workers were struggling for human dignity, they could not be violent. It would be a contradiction. Nonviolence was also practical. Huerta understood that violence would result in counterviolence by the growers and their supporters. It would be suicidal and counterproductive for her and the farm workers to resort to violent tactics. Moreover, nonviolence was a more effective way of reaching out to other Americans of different backgrounds who would respond to such a principle and, in turn, support the farm workers. Huerta knew that this struggle, including the grape strike and the subsequent grape boycott, could not possibly succeed without support from Americans of all walks of life. Nonviolence was the key to that support.[6]

The theme of nonviolence and its importance in reaching out to a diverse group of supporters likewise brings attention to Huerta's secular ecumenism. Although she supported the more ethnic or cultural nationalism of the Chicano Movement of the late 1960s and early 1970s, neither she nor Chávez represented hard-core nationalists. Both used ethnic symbols, such as the eagle of the Mexican flag on the UFW banner, Spanish terms such as *huelga* (strike) and La Causa, and appealed to Our Lady of Guadalupe among other Mexican-origin symbols to assist in organizing the majority of Mexican American workers. However, as noted earlier, they also recognized that the farm workers could not win their struggle by only appealing to other Mexican Americans. They needed allies from other ethnic groups and mainstream Americans. Consequently, Huerta pursued alliances and contacts with people who responded to the farm workers' messages not in ethnic terms, but in human. Huerta and Chávez's power lay in their ability to motivate everyman and everywoman.

One also cannot help but be impressed with Dolores Huerta's self-sacrifice. Like César Chávez, she possessed the talent and, in her case, the education to have pursued a more lucrative career. Instead they chose to work with farm workers at a high personal price. This choice meant accepting poverty for themselves and sacrifice for their families. Yet neither was concerned with material acquisitions and personal security. For Huerta and Chávez, self-sacrifice was a higher virtue with greater rewards. Huerta often notes in these documents that she, like the others in the union, received only $5 a week and had to rely on donations of food and clothes in order to survive. Very few could engage in this type of sacrifice, but she never thought twice about it despite her large family. For her, it was a way of life and one that she wanted to pass on to her children.

At the same time, self-sacrifice was coupled with a sense of community. Without community, Huerta, Chávez, and the others in the union could not have succeeded. By supporting one another and, in turn, being supported by outside followers, the union was able to survive and provide enough for its members to offset the limited monetary conditions. The bonding of the union that Huerta refers to in this reader is almost religious in nature; that may not be a coincidence since both Huerta and Chávez were highly religious and spiritual. This unity and solidarity is further characteristic of a Catholic religious order such as the Franciscans with their vow of poverty. The Franciscans come to mind especially since Chávez had a strong devotion to St. Francis and had close ties to the Franciscan order. Dolores Huerta contributed to this sense of community by her commitment to building that solidarity and mutual support. Never thinking in individualistic terms but rather in communal ones, Huerta exemplified collective leadership and collective struggle.

I come away from Dolores Huerta's story appreciating her critical leadership in the farm workers' struggle and in the building of the UFW much more than I had before. People have to remember what a David and Goliath story this was in the 1960s. Organize farm workers into a union? This had never been done before and everything mitigated against it, including the migratory nature of the workers and their powerlessness. On the other side stood the great power of agribusiness and its allies both in Sacramento and Washington, to say nothing of local politicians and police forces. Yet César Chávez and Dolores Huerta achieved something never accomplished before. They built a farm labor union—the UFW—out of nothing but their vision, courage, perseverance, and faith that they could win. They believed that right was on their side—indeed that God was on their side—and that history was also with them. They could not lose. And they didn't. There is no question that Chávez was the motivating and inspirational leader of this unprecedented movement, but Dolores Huerta was right there as well. Her drive, spirit as a fighter, and willingness to get down in the trenches, recruiting union members, being on the picket line, leading the boycott in faraway places such as New York, and her verbal arm wrestling with the growers as the union's chief negotiator were all indispensable for the movement's success. As La Pasionaria—the outwardly passionate leader of the union—Dolores Huerta willed and fought to achieve victory. Her role alone in this success story is enough to solidify her rightful place in history.

Huerta's story also reveals the many sides to her public life. As noted earlier, there is the civil rights worker, the farm labor leader, the feminist, the environmentalist, and the peace advocate. Following the death of César Chávez, there was the second coming of Dolores Huerta in the UFW as she resurrected her activism to help fill the lack of leadership caused by Chávez's death. Retiring from the union at the turn of the twenty-first century, Dolores has spearheaded her own Dolores Huerta Foundation, aimed at building a new generation of Latino community leaders who will carry on her work and that of César Chávez. There have certainly been many sides to Huerta, but one thing has remained constant: her unquestioning belief in social justice and the ability of the poor and oppressed to achieve it. "Sí Se Puede," the mantra of the farm workers' struggle, is not only a slogan for Dolores Huerta—it is a way of life.

Still another impressive attribute of Huerta concerns her public rhetoric—her rhetorical ability to address the plight of the farm workers and the goals of the movement. She possesses a natural speaking ability more so than did César Chávez. Even as a young child she was very verbal and outspoken. In fact, her grandfather called her "Seven Tongues" because she liked to talk so much. Bilingual and equally as powerful in English and Spanish, Huerta could reach out to different audiences and connect with them. But what made her rhetoric particularly potent was her conviction that the struggle was a just one. Sincerely believing in the struggle, she effectively transmitted her message to her audiences. She converted them into believers in La Causa. The farm workers' struggle was not just a physical one but a discursive one as well. In this effort, the voice of Dolores Huerta was crucial.

I want to conclude these reflections on what I believe are some key aspects of Dolores Huerta that we learn from this collection of documents by bringing attention to still one more side of her that is much overlooked. This has to do with her deep spirituality. As with nonviolence, spirituality is a characteristic more often associated with César Chávez than Dolores Huerta. Chávez is often pictured as almost a mystic due to his fasting, meditations, retreats, and pilgrimages (peregrinaciónes), while our view of Dolores is as the more secular, combative, and feisty labor and civil rights leader willing to go toe-to-toe with anyone.[7]

Yet I was fascinated to go beyond these common images. I believed there was this aspect to her life. As a result, I interviewed Dolores specifically about her spirituality (see chapter 35). I was not disappointed. She is a very devout and religious person. This goes back to her New Mexican Catholic background and her mother's belief that Dolores and her siblings had to grow up with moral and Catholic values. As Dolores matured and became politically active these values focused on what can be called the liberationist aspects of her Catholic faith. As an instinctive liberationist rather than an intellectual one, Huerta saw her faith through the lens of social justice, especially for the poor and the powerless. She and Chávez did not study what in Latin America came to be called Liberation Theology, but they lived it. Like liberationists in Latin America, she believes that the historic and proper role for the Catholic Church and for Catholics is to be on the side of the poor and marginalized. This is the Jesus story and contemporary Catholics should emulate it. Huerta has clung to this side of her faith throughout her life. Despite her divorces and her criticisms of the hypocrisy of the institutional Church over the recent sexual scandals, abortion, birth control, gay rights, and women as priests, she has not abandoned her faith or her Church. But it is a faith and a vision of the Church rooted in the liberation of the soul and the body. It stresses what is called the incarnational side of faith, that is, Christ becoming man and the Church in the modern world. This liberation is achieved not only through prayer but also through the struggle for justice and freedom for all: farm workers, the poor, minorities, women, gays, and any others facing prejudice, exploitation, injustice, and discrimination. She believes that this is where God (Jesus) and La Virgen (Mary) are and where she needs to be. Like her fellow missionary César Chávez, Dolores Huerta in her struggles over so many years has been sustained first and foremost by her faith. Her persona—La Pasionaria—is shaped by her spirituality.

This reader cannot replace the much-needed biography of this fascinating and powerful figure, but my hope is that it will fill a large void and lay the inspiration for the kind of historical treatment that this great American and Chicana/Latina so rightfully deserves. I am honored to do my bit in this effort.

I want to say a word about the documents themselves. The reader will notice that there is some repetition of material. This is unavoidable since each writer, or Dolores Huerta herself, felt the need to refer to common information, especially about her life. The importance of organizing a collection of material on Dolores Huerta overrode any concerns on my part about repetition, although I have chosen these documents in an effort to keep this repetition to a minimum. However, despite the repetition, each document inevitably contains some new information or insights. Some documents were edited, but many I decided to leave as they were originally published or transcribed in order to retain their originality.

Santa Barbara, California
September 2007

Notes

1. See, for example, Jacques Levy, *César Chávez: Autobiography of La Causa* (New York: W. W. Norton & Company, 1975); Mark Day, *Forty Acres: César Chávez and the Farm Workers* (New York: Praeger Publishers, 1971); Susan Ferriss and Ricardo Sandoval, *The Fight in the Fields: César Chávez and the Farmworkers Movement* (New York: Harcourt Brace & Company, 1997); David Goodwin, *César Chávez: Hope for the People* (New York: Fawcett Columbine, 1991); Richard Griswold del Castillo and Richard A. García, *César Chávez: A Triumph of Spirit* (Norman: University of Oklahoma Press, 1995); John C. Hammerback and Richard L. Jensen, *The Rhetorical Career of César Chávez* (College Station: Texas A&M University Press, 1998); Peter Matthiessen, *Sal Sí Puedes: César Chávez and the New American Revolution* (New York: Random House, 1969); Ronald B. Taylor, *Chávez and the Farm Workers* (Boston: Beacon Press, 1975); Winthrop Yinger, *César Chávez: The Rhetoric of Nonviolence* (Hicksville, N.Y.: Exposition Press, 1975); Frederick John Dalton, *The Moral Vision of César Chávez* (Maryknoll, N.Y.: Orbis Books, 2003); Mario T. García, ed., *The Gospel of César Chávez: My Faith In Action* (Lanham, Md.: Sheed & Ward, 2007).

2. See Fred Ross, *Conquering Goliath: César Chávez at the Beginning* (Keene, Calif.: El Taller Grafico Press Book, 1989).

3. On Luisa Moreno, see Vicki L. Ruiz, *Cannery Women, Cannery Lives: Mexican Women, Unionization, and the California Food Processing Industry, 1930-1950* (Albuquerque: University of New Mexico Press, 1987); on Fierro, see Mario T. García, *Mexican Americans: Leadership, Ideology, and Identity, 1930-1960* (New Haven: Yale University Press, 1989), 145-74; on Tenayuca, see Zaragosa Vargas, "Tejana Radical: Emma Tenayuca and the San Antonio Labor Movement during the Great Depression," *Pacific Historical Review*, 66 (Nov. 1997), 553-80.

4. On the correspondence between Huerta and Chávez, see Margaret Rose, "César Chávez and Dolores Huerta: Partners in 'La Causa,'" in Richard W. Etulain, ed., *César Chávez: A Brief Biography with Documents* (Boston: Bedford/St. Martin's, 2002), 95-106.

5. On the concept of triple oppression, see Denise Segura, "Chicanas and Triple Oppression in the Labor Force," in National Association for Chicana and Chicano Studies, ed., *Chicana Voices: Intersection of Class, Race, and Gender* (1990) and reprinted in Mario T. García, ed., *Bridging Cultures: An Introduction to Chicano/Latino Studies* (Dubuque, Iowa: Kendall/Hunt Publishing Company, 2000), 85-96. Also see Alma M. García, *Chicana Feminist Thought: The Basic Historical Writings* (New York: Routledge, 1997).

6. See García, *Gospel of César Chávez* and Dalton, *Moral Vision of César Chávez*.

7. Ibid.

Part One

ON DOLORES HUERTA

Dolores Huerta and César Chávez, "Profiles of Courage." Courtesy of Jon Lewis.

1

Dolores Huerta

The United Farm Workers Union

Margaret Rose

Since 1848, people have crossed back and forth over the porous U.S.-Mexico border. Residents from both countries have sought adventure, vacations, and visits with families and friends. The American Southwest has also served as a powerful magnet for Mexican workers headed for the fields and orchards and later the factories and railroads in search of employment. Although intending to stay a short time before returning home, many joined their Mexican American "cousins" and established permanent homes in the United States.

In the nineteenth century the traffic across the border was informal and largely unchecked. Before 1917, Mexican workers entered the United States with little difficulty, and refugees fleeing the political turmoil of the Mexican Revolution sought safety across the border. With laws passed in the early twentieth century, however, border crossings became increasingly more regulated, and an elaborate bureaucracy grew up to monitor comings and goings. The Immigration Act of 1917 instituted requirements of literacy and the payment of a head tax. Growers in the Southwest immediately protested that the new law would cause severe labor shortages.

The involvement of the United States in World War I effectively suspended the enforcement of the act, temporarily permitting the immigration of Mexican workers. After the war the temporary admissions program was extended, and even upon its expiration in 1922 the enforcement of the Immigration Act became so lax that growers' access to Mexican labor was virtually unimpeded. Further encouragement

Originally published in Eric Arnesen, ed., *The Human Tradition in American Labor History* (Wilmington: SR Books, an imprint of Rowman & Littlefield Publishers, Inc., 2004), 211–29.

of Mexican entry for menial labor resulted from the passage of the comprehensive Immigration Act of 1924. Although the act imposed quotas for the first time on certain nationalities, the classification of all Mexicans as "white" circumvented restrictions that prohibited the entry of anyone with "more than 50 percent Indian blood." During the 1920s, estimates of the proportion of Mexican farm laborers in the California agricultural work force of 200,000 ranged from 50 to 75 percent.

In the 1930s, however, when unemployed workers and Dust Bowl migrants sought work in the fields, Mexican and, in some cases, Mexican American workers were herded up and deported by federal officials. Governmental protections of due process were suspended during the Depression decade. Then, during World War II, the government of the United States drew up specific agreements with Mexico to control the importation of workers. The "bracero" program officially began in 1942 as a wartime measure and, although there were protests by Mexican workers and the Mexican government concerning employer violations of the agreement, it continued after the war. Successful lobbying by large-scale growers and their political allies kept the law in place until 1964. It was finally defeated by a coalition of labor, ethnic organizations, Democratic legislators, and church and philanthropic groups.

Throughout the years, workers have ignored authorities and evaded official measures to limit movement across the border. Subject to political uncertainty and shifting economic fortunes, laborers of Mexican heritage, particularly those at the margins of society, have found their working conditions to be precarious. Politically powerful and well-connected growers have been able to keep labor costs down. Consequently, agricultural workers are among the lowest-paid segments of the work force. Attempts to provide them with better wages and protections have ranged from efforts by religious associations, community organizations, and charitable groups to demands for civil rights and unionization. In the first half of the twentieth century, such actions were short-lived and ameliorative. After World War II serious and sustained attempts to organize workers, especially farm laborers or "campesinos," coalesced. For years agribusiness managed to keep wages down and union organizers out. But in the 1960s, a decade of social and political activism, the founding of the National Farm Workers Association (NFWA)—precursor of the United Farm Workers—signaled the beginning of many confrontations on behalf of these most marginal of workers.

The lack of legislation covering agricultural labor proved a formidable obstacle to the NFWA, as it had for other union organizers in the twentieth century. Because of the overwhelming influence of large-scale agribusiness, farm laborers had been exempted from the protections provided by both the Wagner Act, a 1935 law that encouraged collective bargaining for industrial and other workers and established the National Labor Relations Board, which supervised elections and adjudicated labor grievances. Consequently, there was no legal mechanism at the federal or state level through which agricultural workers could petition for elections or union recognition. Their only recourse was to strike or boycott.

With no laws to protect them, the working conditions and standard of living of agricultural laborers were among the lowest in the nation. Their wages in the late 1950s and early 1960s ranged from seventy-five cents to $1.00 per hour, forcing most families to live below the poverty level. To make ends meet, many families took their children out of school, thereby contributing to a vicious cycle of poverty. Working conditions in the fields were deplorable. Employers did not provide toilets, hand-washing facilities, or drinking water. During the summer harvests, temperatures in the inland valleys rose to over 100 degrees. Workers were exposed to pesticides without adequate warning or protective coverings. The job-injury rate was three times that of U.S. workers in the nonagricultural sectors. Malnutrition and the poor diet of impoverished field workers had severe health ramifications. The death rate of migrant laborers' babies and mothers was 125 percent higher than the rate among other Americans. Agricultural workers were twice as likely to get flu or pneumonia and even more likely to suffer from tuberculosis. Their life expectancy was forty-nine years; other Americans lived to the age of seventy on average.

Beginning in the early 1960s the NFWA championed the rights of farmworkers to organize for improved wages and working conditions. The association was very effective at communicating the plight of this sector of the American economy to the larger population and fought to represent these laborers in collective bargaining with employers. At a time when the nation was experiencing the social upheavals of the civil rights movement, the NFWA was launching its crusade on behalf of field workers. Increased awareness of inequity and prejudice directed at African Americans heightened public consciousness of injustice and racism against Mexican-heritage workers. The strategies of nonviolence, coalition building, and grassroots protests demonstrated by such leaders as Martin Luther King Jr. served the farmworker cause as well. Leaders and supporters in both camps became allies in the struggle for civil, economic, and political rights for their constituencies.

One leader in this daunting challenge to the combined power of agricultural employers and their political allies is Dolores Huerta—sometimes referred to as Dolores "Huelga" (strike)—the most prominent Chicana labor leader of her generation in the United States. For more than forty years she has dedicated her life to the struggle for justice, dignity, and a decent standard of living for one of the country's most exploited groups: the women and men who toil in the fields. Proud of her Latina heritage, Huerta is an admirable representative of an ethnic, female, and working-class tradition of protest. As a middle-class Chicana and mother of eleven children, however, she does not neatly fit the typical mold of a labor organizer. Resisting mid-twentieth-century ideals of female behavior, she chafed against the conventions for Mexican American women coming of age in the 1950s. Surmounting ethnic, gender, and class expectations, she brought her considerable skills as an organizer, picket captain, union official, contract negotiator, boycott leader, and spokeswoman to the campaign to unionize farmworkers. Historians, perhaps misled by the focus on César Chávez in early accounts of the union, have missed the importance of the Huerta-Chávez collaboration.

"Abajo con opresión! Down with oppression! Abajo con racismo! Down with racism! Abajo con sexismo! Down with sexism!" At the conclusion of her speeches, Dolores Huerta invited her audiences to join her in these exhortations on behalf of the farmworkers' movement. "Viva la union! Viva la causa!" she continued. "Long live the union! Long live the cause!"[1] Whether addressing field workers, religious groups, political gatherings, ethnic assemblies, unionists, students, antiwar activists, or women's groups, the diminutive, energetic, and charismatic Huerta was a compelling and fiery advocate whose passion won many adherents for the UFWA's battle against the entrenched interests of agribusiness.

Huerta developed a social conscience as a teenager but gravitated toward activism as a young mother in her late twenties. A native of New Mexico, she had moved as a youngster to California with her mother and two brothers. A bright, articulate, and active child, she did not seem destined to become a highly regarded social reformer and labor leader. Although sharing an ethnic background, culture, and religion with the campesinos whose cause she so eloquently and ardently championed, Huerta differed from them in significant ways. She was bilingual; she graduated from high school and attended college. With only limited experience in field labor, she had career options unavailable to farmworkers. Although raised a Catholic, she married and divorced several times. She enjoyed motherhood but adamantly rejected the restrictions that idealized the role of woman as a homemaker. Defying conventional attitudes, she invaded the male-dominated arena of union organizing. Her association with the union provided an affirmation of her "own life's worth. . . . Before I joined the union," she related in an interview, "I was having a hard time really swallowing that I would be a teacher living in a suburb. . . . My longings for my own life were answered by being able to participate in the building of the union."[2]

Despite her youth and feminine appearance, when she dedicated herself to "la causa" in the early 1960s, Huerta earned the respect of union rank-and-file members because of her unrelenting dedication to farmworkers. Some may have expressed reservations about her casual attitude toward her family and her personal life-style, but they admired her for her all-consuming commitment, picket-line work, personal sacrifices, arrests, and the life-threatening injury she endured in her work for the union. She was also a very effective advocate for the cause in her frequent travels and appearances across the nation on behalf of "el movimiento." Her middle-class upbringing gave her the ability to appeal to mainstream America and to engage consumers, largely women, in supporting the union's powerful boycott strategy. Her advocacy of farmworkers' rights also earned her the wrath of opponents of unionization. Reacting to her uncompromising and forceful manner, one grower exclaimed, "Dolores Huerta is crazy. She is a violent woman, where women, especially Mexican women, are usually peaceful and calm."[3] High-spirited, tough, and outspoken, she confronted gender and ethnic stereotyping in improving the lives of farmworkers.

Although she is celebrated in the Mexican American community, in labor halls, and in feminist circles, Huerta's early history—her family life and transformation to labor activist—is little known. What in her background foreshadowed the emergence of an important labor leader? How did she possess the fortitude to disdain sentimental motherhood and domestic responsibility at a time when the proper role for a middle-class mother was in the home?

Huerta's story began in the small mining town of Dawson in the mountains of northern New Mexico where she was born on April 10, 1930. Dolores Fernández was the second child and only daughter of Juan and Alicia (Chávez) Fernández. On the maternal side of her family, Huerta was a third-generation New Mexican. Her father was also born in Dawson but to a Mexican immigrant family. The young couple's marriage was troubled early on, and when Huerta was a toddler, her parents divorced. Determined to start her life anew, her mother moved her three children—John, Dolores, and Marshall—first to Las Vegas, New Mexico, and then to Stockton, California, where the family had relatives.

As a single parent in Depression-era California, Alicia Chávez Fernández endured hardships to support her young family. To make ends meet, she labored at a cannery at night and as a waitress during the day. "My mother was very quiet," Huerta recalled, "and she was very effective at whatever she did, and very ambitious." For child care, Alicia Fernández relied on her father, Herculano Chávez, who had followed her to Stockton. "My grandfather," Huerta noted, "kind of raised us. My grandfather's influence was really the male influence in my family." The outgoing Dolores enjoyed this warm relationship in a contented childhood with attentive supervision, respect for one's elders, Mexican corridos (ballads), and Rosary recitations. Judging herself a dutiful but playful child, Huerta reminisced, "My grandfather

used to call me Seven Tongues . . . because I always talked so much."
Verbal dexterity would serve her well in later life.[4]

The family's economic circumstances improved during the war
years. Alicia Fernández managed a restaurant and then acquired
a hotel in Stockton with her second husband, James Richards, with
whom she had another daughter. During the summers, Dolores and
her siblings helped run these businesses located on the edges of skid
row, catering to multicultural urban working-class and farmworker
patrons. Huerta relished the exposure to the vibrant cultural mix of
Chinese restaurants, Filipino pool halls, and Mexican bakeries. Her
home life, however, was disrupted when her mother's second marriage ended in divorce.

The postwar years proved more satisfying. In the early 1950s her
mother married for a third time. This happy union with Juan Silva
produced another daughter and endured until her mother's death.
Huerta looked back fondly on her mother's energy and expectations
for her children. "My mother was always pushing me to get involved
in all these youth activities. . . . We took violin lessons. I took piano lessons. I took dancing lessons. I belonged to the church choir. . . . And
I was a very active Girl Scout from the time I was eight to the time I
was eighteen."[5] As a youngster growing up in Stockton and especially
after her mother's improved financial outlook and remarriage, Huerta
experienced a more middle-class upbringing. After graduation from
Stockton High School, she continued her education at Stockton
College with her mother's support. Following a not uncommon period
of teenage rebellion, mother and daughter shared a caring relationship that extended into Huerta's adult years.

After her parents' divorce, Huerta had only sporadic contacts
with her father. Nevertheless, his work history and activities influenced her. Like most people in Dawson, Juan Fernández worked in
the coal mines and, to augment his wages there, joined the migrant
labor force, traveling to Colorado, Nebraska, and Wyoming for the
beet harvests. Outraged over inferior working conditions, frequent
accidents, and meager wages, Fernández became interested in labor
issues. Leaving Dawson after the disintegration of his marriage, he
continued his labor activism by becoming secretary-treasurer of the
Congress of Industrial Organizations (CIO) local at the Terrero Camp of

the American Metals Company in Las Vegas. Using this predominately Hispanic local union as a springboard, he won election to the New Mexico state legislature in 1938, representing San Miguel County. He worked with like-minded colleagues to pass a labor program, including New Mexico's "Little Wagner Act" and a wages-and-hours bill to empower industrial workers and improve their lives. Yet because of his outspoken demeanor and intemperate personality, he served only one term in the statehouse.[6] Although their relationship remained distant until the end of his life, Huerta was proud of her father's union activism and political achievements. Always supportive of her union organizing, he was less approving of her disordered personal life and failed marriages.

Huerta did not marry as young as many Chicanas of her generation but temporarily interrupted her college studies when she wed her high-school sweetheart, Ralph Head, in an elaborate church ceremony. The marriage lasted only a few years. After her divorce she held a number of clerical and secretarial positions. Then, with the financial and emotional support of her mother in rearing her two daughters, Celeste and Lori, she returned to school to pursue a career in teaching and earned an A.A. degree.

Huerta's plans for a conventional life and comfortable career in education changed when she got caught up in the wave of civic activism that swept through Mexican American communities after World War II. Earlier involved in Catholic relief activities and in the Club Azul y Oro, a Latina women's social group, she was politicized by the establishment of a chapter of the Community Service Organization (CSO) in Stockton in the mid-1950s. The original association, a Mexican American self-help group, had emerged under the auspices of the Industrial Areas Foundation located in Chicago and headed by Saul Alinsky. The aim of the CSO was to promote increased civic participation by the Spanish speaking community. The group focused on the political concerns and social problems of working-class Mexican American families in urban areas, principally in California and Arizona. Achieving success in Los Angeles, where the CSO was instrumental in electing Edward Roybal (the first Hispanic member of the Los Angeles City Council in the twentieth century), West Coast organizer Fred Ross took his recruiting efforts to other parts of California and the Southwest. In Stockton, Huerta, along with her mother and an aunt, became active in the program. The thrust of the women's activities consisted of registering voters in the barrio, teaching citizenship and naturalization classes, pressuring for neighborhood improvements such as better streets, lighting, parks, and playgrounds, and engaging in the typical behind-the-scenes tasks of preparation for local and regional CSO meetings.

During this time, Huerta married her second husband, Ventura Huerta, also a CSO member. This union ultimately produced five more children: Fidel, Emilio, Vincent, Alicia, and Angela. Their mother's zeal for community activism caused problems at home, and her marriage began to deteriorate when her husband objected to the increasing intrusion of CSO work into their home life. "I knew I wasn't comfortable in a wife's role," she acknowledged, "but I wasn't clearly facing the issue. I hedged, I made excuses, I didn't come out and tell my husband that I cared more about helping other people than cleaning our house and doing my hair."[7] Despite the growing domestic tensions, Huerta deepened her commitment to the CSO. Her interests also expanded when several of her Stockton CSO colleagues formed the Agricultural Workers' Association (AWA) in 1958. These socially conscious citizens advocated a separate effort to deal with the abject poverty and exploitation of local farmworkers, as distinct from the problems faced by Mexican American families in the cities. This local interest group dissolved when the AFL-CIO–sponsored Agricultural Workers' Organizing Committee (AWOC) emerged a year later. Former AWA members enlisted in the campaign, and Huerta became secretary-treasurer. However, the AWOC officials, veteran organizers who had earned their experience with industrial workers, were entirely unfamiliar with agriculture and with the ethnic workers who toiled in the fields. She soon grew disenchanted with the group's leadership, direction, and top-down policies and resigned.[8]

By the late 1950s, Huerta had completely abandoned the ranks of female volunteers and emerged as a political activist. Her intense dedication and abilities had attracted the attention of CSO associates, who offered her the position of lobbyist, traditionally a post held only by men. Responsible to the general director of the organization, César Chávez, she worked at the Los Angeles CSO headquarters and in Sacramento during the legislative session. Chávez had gained a reputation as a masterful organizer; Huerta's recognition derived from her skills as a forceful and articulate communicator and advocate. "Everyone knows her," observed Chávez following a trip to the state capital in the early 1960s, "and the usual remark is that she is a fighter."[9]

Huerta's absorption in social activism had contributed to trial separations from her husband, and their alienation intensified when she weighed an invitation by Chávez to commit herself exclusively to the farmworker cause. United by a common outrage at the exploitation and poverty of farm laborers, Huerta and Chávez shared profound disappointment over the CSO's decision not to support a proposed campaign of improving their conditions. The CSO was reluctant to embrace the risky proposition of fighting for a marginal group—some of whom were not U.S. citizens, some who were in the country illegally, some who were non-English speakers, some who annually migrated from farm to farm following the crops—against a Goliath of agricultural corporations. Agonizing over this rejection, Chávez dramatically resigned his position in 1962 and asked Huerta to join him in launching the National Farm Workers Association (NFWA). With her characteristic optimism, Huerta enthusiastically embraced the challenge to unionize California's agricultural workers.

Aware of the financial strain and emotional stress that establishing an independent organization would entail, Chávez persuaded Huerta to remain on the CSO payroll until the prospects of the NFWA improved. As the group was getting off the ground, Huerta lived and worked in Stockton while Chávez was setting up the headquarters in Delano, California. From 1962 until 1964 the two communicated frequently by mail. Their letters indicate Huerta's central role in the founding and management of the organization. While discussing goals, strategies, obstacles, disagreements, and family concerns, they continually commiserated over their limited resources and lack of funds to do the job adequately.

In her thirties, with six children and a seventh on the way and an estranged second husband (whom she later divorced), Huerta juggled a considerable financial and domestic burden. She harbored serious reservations about Chávez's plans for her continued employment at the CSO, given his own disagreement with and sudden departure from the organization. "I feel there will be a lot of criticism," she explained to him frankly. "If I did not have to work for the CSO, but could have an independent income, then no one could say anything about what I do."[10] Coaxed by Chávez, she endured as long as she could her "killer schedule" of working in the office during the day and organizing at night. But her initial misgivings proved justified, and she was eventually terminated for her overriding interest in farmworker organizing over CSO business.

With no regular salary and with her unemployment checks soon exhausted, Huerta survived with temporary translation assignments, substitute teaching, and even a brief backbreaking stint in the onion harvest, in addition to her work for the NFWA. Support from her two former husbands was not reliable and inadequate when paid, barely enough to keep her in groceries and utilities. "Any help I get from my two exes has to go for grub for my seven hungry mouths," she bluntly wrote Chávez, "and I am keeping one jump ahead of PG and E [Pacific Gas & Electric] and the Water Dragons who close off water for nonpayment."[11] Her mother, other relatives, and friends helped from time to time, and an anonymous donation of food appeared on her doorstep when funds were particularly low, but during those struggles of the early years, Huerta recollected, "we really operated totally on faith."[12]

The only other source of income came from union dues. Huerta labored long days and nights publicizing the new organization, setting up meetings, calling on workers in their homes, and visiting labor camps in farmworker towns such as Acampo, Woodbridge, Manteca, Victor, Linden, and Lodi as well as Stockton. She recognized that the $3.50 monthly fee was not easy for workers to commit to, given their meager wages, their fear of employers' retaliation, competition from other unions, the unpredictable nature of agricultural employment, unexpected illness, or family emergencies. "I have been rustling dues," Huerta repeatedly conveyed in her letters from 1962 to 1964. Normally, the totals ranged from $10 to $30.[13] Huerta and Chávez shared the slender proceeds. "César was very fair about that," she forthrightly asserted.[14]

The lack of simple organizer's tools—a functioning car, gas money, and a working telephone—further complicated dues collection and organizing. "It makes me sick of the time I have lost because of my junkie cars," she once noted, "yet I hate to get in debt for a better car when I am not sure where my next month's check is coming from."[15] Chávez readily sympathized; he too, had experienced setbacks and delays on account of car troubles. She was equally exasperated by canceled meetings and worker apathy, sometimes caused by resistance to female organizers. Workers were unaccustomed to an assertive woman labor leader who often traveled alone and called evening meetings. In Stockton she had outlasted this reluctance, but the issue reappeared when she targeted new areas. She recounted incidents when meetings, attended primarily by men, were abruptly canceled when she arrived at the appointed hour. Still, dismissing such opposition as routine for a professional organizer, she persisted in her efforts. Although women's issues were gaining attention in the 1960s, gender consciousness was not as widespread as it would later become. Huerta herself only gradually became aware of this additional barrier that female labor activists faced.

Huerta coped with an ever greater obstacle in her work with the NFWA: as a divorced, full-time working mother, she had family obligations that exceeded those of men. It was not the customary organizer's challenges but child care that habitually impeded her progress. To deal with her irregular night and weekend schedule, Huerta relied on her mother for assistance and then, after Alicia's death, on a steady succession of relatives and live-in help. Although she took great pride in her large family, the continual juggling frequently exasperated her and forced her to cancel, reorganize, and postpone plans. "So help me, César, without someone to watch my kids," she lamented, "I just can't find enough time to work, especially in the evenings when it counts."[16] Arranging for child care caused her considerable stress throughout her long career.

Despite her difficult balancing act, Huerta persisted in her commitment to the NFWA. She and Chávez collaborated on its incorporation, constitution, organizing strategies, group insurance plan, credit union, fund-raising, and political tactics. Repeatedly, Huerta sought advice from her networks of contacts in northern California and conveyed information and made recommendations to Chávez. She regularly traveled to Delano for board meetings.

Huerta and Chávez had developed a dynamic partnership. Although disagreements arose, they had a comfortable working relationship, displayed mutual respect, and shared an unshakable commitment to unionizing farmworkers. Over the three years that Huerta remained in Stockton, from time to time Chávez broached the subject of her relocation to Delano to work with him, Manuel Chávez, Gilbert Padilla, Anthony Orendain, and others. Initially resisting, she finally agreed that the union's success required a more intensive effort in the southern San Joaquin Valley. Huerta waited until summer.[17] Even then she found it difficult to leave her extended family and social network in Stockton to start the search for housing and child care and to resettle her children. The family lived temporarily in the crowded Chávez household until she found her own accommodations.

With the shift to Delano promising greater efficiency, direction, and focus for building the NFWA, Chávez and Huerta and a small core of loyal supporters prepared to launch a coordinated drive to change the lives of farmworkers—a moment that arrived much sooner than they had dreamed possible. The turning point came when the rival AFL-CIO–sponsored AWOC, recently established in California with a predominantly Filipino membership, went on strike and asked the NFWA to honor its actions. The consequent cooperation resulted in the now famous Delano grape strike of 1965, the subsequent creation of the United Farm Workers' Organizing Committee, and the beginning of new era in the life of Dolores Huerta.[18]

Her years of work had prepared Huerta to assume a highly visible role in the farmworkers' struggle. "Virtually all observers on the scene at that time," wrote a news reporter who followed events, "were convinced that next to Chávez, Dolores Huerta . . . was the top leader of the union."[19] As vice president of the organization and the only female elected official, she participated in all policymaking and strategy sessions and also helped to implement decisions. Her talents and energy and the critical need for leadership, as the fledgling union was thrust into national headlines, outweighed conventional gender expectations.

With apparent disregard for personal comfort and for the impact of her absences on her family, she plunged into a whirlwind of activities organizing workers, leading picket lines, participating in marches, and undergoing arrest (not only in 1965 but during more than a decade of the social upheavals of the civil rights era). Along with these activities, Huerta kept the grape strike before a public increasingly receptive to the message of social justice and reform. Her heavy speaking schedule necessitated frequent separations from her children, whom she left with family, friends, or union supporters—usually without advance notice. Like Chávez, she was in constant demand as a speaker. Her facility with language, fast talking, and quick thinking made her a natural choice. Her uniqueness as a Mexican American woman in a male-dominated movement attracted additional public attention from the press—a case where gender operated to her advantage. The photogenic Huerta, with her dynamic and intense personality, recruited many dedicated supporters for the union and generated needed funds for the strained union budget.

When months of picketing resulted in recognition of the union by one local grower, Huerta assumed an additional responsibility. While the strike continued against the majority of grape ranches, Huerta engaged in the collective bargaining process. Contemporary observers on the scene noted that Chávez left the negotiations to her.[20] A protracted and grueling process, contract deliberations required her to put in long hours hammering out agreements with the highly experienced lawyers employed by agribusiness. As the union's first contract negotiator, founder of that department, and director in its early years, Huerta left a lasting contribution at a critical juncture in the union's history.

Against seemingly insurmountable odds, the NFWA had succeeded in bringing together in a union what some had considered an "unorganizable" work force. Such solidarity was especially astonishing because agricultural producers had often used racial and ethnic tensions to divide the Mexican American, Mexican-born, Filipino, Yemeni, and black workers who regularly traveled up and down the state following the harvest. Without the additional cooperation of socially conscious middle-class white supporters, to whom union leaders such as Huerta appealed, the political and economic power of growers might have thwarted this unionization effort.

Growers fought back, enlisting the support of federal and state governments to protect their interests. They employed high-priced lawyers to argue for injunctions against the union and limitations on picketing. To undermine the union's position further, they set up company unions and negotiated sweetheart contracts with the Teamsters. Union leaders and workers were not easily intimidated by growers' tactics, however.

The social movement origins of the NFWA in the 1960s and its cross-cultural, cross-race coalition set it apart from earlier, failed collective bargaining campaigns. The show of solidarity lent the union's cause important strength and visibility outside of California. As workers demonstrated growing confidence in the ability of the union to deliver on its promises by joining the effort, union contracts significantly altered the balance of power between agribusiness and agricultural labor. In addition to wage increases and the establishment of a seniority system, workers now received vacation, health, and pension benefits. The union health plan was named after the slain civil rights hero, Martin Luther King Jr.

Still, despite successful negotiations with some companies, including major wineries, many grape growers continued to resist union demands for contracts. To counter this intransigence, the union resorted to the boycott to pressure uncooperative producers. Huerta became a prominent player in this strategy when she assumed the directorship of the table-grape boycott in New York City, and then a position as the East Coast boycott coordinator. "When we got to New York," she vividly remembered, "it was something like four or five degrees above zero."[21] Undeterred, she and the busload of some forty farmworkers and a small group of student volunteers accustomed to the mild California climate immediately got to work. As Huerta delivered speeches to labor, church, student, civic, consumer, African American, Puerto Rican, and women's organizations, her colleagues passed around lists to recruit picketers and collected contributions. Gaining experience and confidence in the Big Apple, members of the initial contingent fanned out to other major cities across the East Coast and the nation.

In New York, Huerta also became increasingly aware of the power of the growing feminist movement through her contacts with Gloria Steinem and other activists who endorsed the farmworkers' cause. For years she had dismissed the women's liberation movement as a middle-class phenomenon. She had ignored comments and gender bias directed at her and other women by male colleagues. Increasingly, though, she became sensitized to the sexism in her own organization and directly challenged inappropriate remarks and stereotypes. She also began to voice her concerns regarding the absence of women from leadership positions in the organization and, further, questioned the clustering of women in traditional union work such as service centers and administration. She argued that women's opinions and issues, such as child care and sexual harassment, should be taken seriously by the union. Under the influence of feminist leaders, Huerta began to incorporate a feminist strand into her human rights philosophy.

Through Huerta's and her colleagues' work with women's groups, civil rights volunteers, ethnic organizations, church supporters, students, environmentalists, antiwar activists, and the labor community, the recognition of the farmworkers' movement grew. Five years after the Delano strike began, the power of this grassroots, cross-class, and cross-cultural coalition across the nation finally compelled the Delano and Coachella grape growers to negotiate the historic contracts of 1970. But the struggle against the entrenched power of agriculture was not over. Before the union could fully savor its accomplishment, it had to go through the lettuce, Gallo wine, and table-grape boycotts of the 1970s. Huerta's energy, organizing expertise, and legendary speaking abilities advanced the cause of the union (now officially known as the United Farm Workers of America—the UFW) when she returned to the East Coast to oversee the New York effort. The pressure of the renewed cross-class and cross-cultural cooperation in New York and in other major cities across the United States facilitated the passage of the Agricultural Labor Relations Act (ALRA) in 1975, the first law to recognize the collective bargaining rights of farm laborers in California.[22] It was during this decade that the UFW reached its highest level of union membership. According to union estimates, 100,000 workers became members.

In the midst of the boycott, the political campaign for the ALRA, a heavy travel itinerary, and an ambitious speaking schedule, Huerta began a relationship with Richard Chávez, César's brother. This liaison produced four more children—Juanita, María Elena, Ricky, and Camilla—bringing the total number of her children to eleven. Huerta not only faced criticism for her casual attitudes toward child-rearing but also for her unorthodox cohabitation arrangement with Richard. "I think had it not been for the women's movement," she conceded, "I never would have had the courage to do what I did to get involved with him."[23] Although family, friends, and union officials frowned on this unconventional relationship, it persisted.

Not even her new domestic responsibilities slowed Huerta down. During the late 1970s she accepted the directorship of the Citizenship Participation Day Department, the political arm of the UFW, and spearheaded the union's drive to protect the new farm labor law in the legislative arena in Sacramento. In the 1980s the UFW became even more involved in California politics when Republican governor George Deukmejian won election with the backing of corporate agriculture. During these difficult years, Huerta began devoting time to another ambitious UFW overture: the founding of Radio Campesina, the union's radio station, KUFW. But declining membership, a problem that the UFW shared with other unions in the antiunion environment of the Reagan era, frustrated leaders and supporters alike. Huerta maintained her ambitious schedule and accommodated numerous speaking engagements, fund-raising activities, publicity for the renewed grape boycott, and testimony before state and congressional committees on a wide range of matters including pesticides, wages, benefits, the health problems of agricultural workers, Mexican American political issues, and immigration policy.

Huerta's dedication to the UFW exacted a personal price. Not only was she arrested more than twenty times but she also suffered a life threatening injury in a 1988 peaceful demonstration against the priorities of presidential candidate George H. W. Bush, who was campaigning in San Francisco. Rushed to a local hospital after an assault by baton-wielding police officers, Huerta underwent emergency surgery in which her spleen was removed, then endured a protracted hospital stay recovering from the operation and six broken ribs. As reported in a 1991 story in the *Los Angeles Times*, the incident forced the police department to revise its rules regarding crowd control and police discipline. Another repercussion was the $825,000 financial settlement to Huerta as a consequence of the personal harm she sustained.[24]

Slowly recuperating from this serious impairment to her health, Huerta took a leave from the UFW to work on the Feminist Majority's Feminization of Power campaign. For two years she traveled around the United States encouraging Latinas to run for office, fulfilling a long delayed desire to increase ethnic women's visibility and representation in the political system. Though stunned by the premature death of César Chávez in 1993, she jumped back into union organizing. In addition to campaigning for California's strawberry workers, she resumed an active schedule of lecturing on college campuses, attending union conferences, participating in political rallies, and testifying before congressional committees.

Not until 2000, after nearly four decades of activism, did the 70-year old Huerta begin to moderate her intense involvement. She continued to speak on behalf of farm laborers, worked in the presidential campaign of Al Gore, and steadfastly advocated for women's needs, but she chose not to seek reelection as the UFW secretary-treasurer. Not long after making this decision, she was hospitalized in critical condition, diagnosed with an abdominal aneurysm that required massive blood transfusions. She underwent emergency surgery and was later transferred to Los Angeles for additional treatment. Her family cited her "fighting spirit" as a reason for her recovery.

Huerta's lifelong dedication to social change has earned her many tributes and awards from labor, women's, Hispanic, and political groups. She was named Outstanding Labor Leader by the California state senate in 1984. In 1998 she was celebrated as one of *Ms. Magazine's* "Women of the Year" and one of the *Ladies' Home Journal's* "100 Most Important Women of the 20th Century." Huerta received the prestigious Hispanic Heritage Award in 2000, and President Bill Clinton bestowed on her the Eleanor Roosevelt Award for Human Rights.

Always outspoken and frequently criticized for her unorthodox personal life, Huerta has left an indelible and complicated legacy to the farmworkers' movement. Often stung by Huerta's reproaches for gender bias, UFW leaders have nevertheless praised her single-minded devotion to social and economic change and hailed her as a model for others. "While few, if any, can fill her shoes," noted Paul Chávez, son of the late organizer, "many will follow in her footsteps."[25] For women, particularly Chicanas and Mexicanas in the union, Huerta has left a powerful example. "It was Dolores who showed us not to be afraid to fight for a better life for ourselves and our children," noted one farmworker woman in her fitting tribute to the retiring labor activist, "and she did it at a time when women didn't have a voice."[26]

Notes

1. Dolores Huerta, speech delivered at the University of California, Los Angeles, February 11, 1978, text held at the school's Chicano Studies Center.

2. Dolores Huerta, interview with author, February 26, 1985.

3. Quoted in Barbara L. Baer, "Stopping Traffic: One Woman's Cause," *The Progressive* 39, no. 9 (September 1975): 39–40.

4. Dolores Huerta, interview with author, March 16, 1984.

5. Ibid.

6. [State of New Mexico], New Mexico Blue Book, 1939–1940 (Las Vegas, NM: Optic Publishing Company, 1940).

7. Quoted in Baer, 39.

8. Dick Meister and Anne Loftis, *A Long Time Coming: The Struggle to Unionize America's Farm Workers* (New York: Macmillan Company, 1977), 92–96.

9. César Chávez to Fred Ross, December 14, 1962, folder 10, Ross Collection, Archives of Labor and Urban Affairs, Walter P. Reuther Library, Wayne State University, Detroit (hereafter ALUA).

10. Dolores Huerta to César Chávez, n.d. (circa 1962–1964), National Farm Workers Association, ALUA.

11. Ibid.

12. Dolores Huerta, interview with author, February 8, 1985.

13. Huerta to Chávez, n.d. (circa 1962–1964), ALUA.

14. Huerta interview, February 8, 1985.

15. Huerta to Chávez, n.d. (circa 1962–1964), ALUA.

16. Ibid.

17. Joan London and Henry Anderson, *So Shall Ye Reap* (New York: Thomas Crowell, 1970), 149.

18. Linda C. Majka and Theo J. Majka, *Farm Workers, Agribusiness, and the State* (Philadelphia: Temple University Press, 1982), 172–73.

19. Quoted in Sam Kushner, *Long Road to Delano* (New York: International Publishers, 1975), 157.

20. Ronald B. Taylor, *Chávez and the Farm Workers* (Boston: Beacon Press, 1975), 217.

21. Quoted in Jacques E. Levy, *César Chávez: Autobiography of La Causa* (New York: W. W. Norton, 1975), 267.

22. J. Craig Jenkins, *The Politics of Insurgency: The Farm Workers Movement in the 1960s* (New York: Columbia University Press, 1985), 195–200.

23. Huerta interview, February 26, 1985.

24. *Los Angeles Times*, January 25, 1991.

25. *Fresno Bee*, September 3, 2000.

26. Ibid.

2

Coleadership

The Strength of Dolores Huerta

**Richard Griswold del Castillo
and Richard A. García**

I am visible—see this Indian face—

Yet I am invisible.

To survive the Borderlands/You must live

Sin fronteras/be a crossroads.

—Gloria Anzaldúa

By 1960, César Chávez and Dolores Huerta had a symbiotic relationship. Chávez was the visible leader and Huerta was the "hidden" one. He functioned as the catalyst; she was the engine. Most people did not realize the qualities Huerta brought to the Farm Workers Association: personal strength, communication skills, an ethic of work, an intellectual approach, and a strong sense of self. In 1962, Chávez had asked Huerta to be cofounder of the Farm Workers Association because he recognized her leadership abilities, her powerful character, her intellectual toughness, and above all her self-assuredness. Farm workers listened to her; young Chicanas followed her. She placed the traces of her character on the union, just as Chávez placed the traces of his spirit, his soul, on the union. To understand Chávez and the union, we must also understand Huerta.

Originally published as "Coleadership: The Strength of Dolores Huerta" in *César Chávez: A Triumph of Spirit* by Richard Griswold del Castillo and Richard A. García, pp. 59–75.

Her role in shaping César Chávez's life and the farm-worker movement was crucial, especially during the early organizational years. To the farm workers she was La Pasionaria (the Passionate One) and a union leader. To César she was a key negotiator, a nontraditional Mexicana, and a loyal follower. While many books have been written about César Chávez, almost nothing has been written about Huerta. Her appearance is familiar, but not her persona. She is a woman, an organizer, and a symbol of justice and fairness, and she carries the aura of César Chávez and the United Farm Workers Union. During her adult life, she was the organizer who led the Chávez negotiating team against the powerful growers. She worked as a lobbyist for the union in Washington and Sacramento; and she innovated in using the management theories of Kenneth Blanchard to restructure the farm workers' union into an almost corporate-like structure. More than once she has risked her life for Chávez and the union.

Dolores Huerta has been an important influence on Chávez and the union. Like Chávez she has been a follower of Saul Alinsky's basic belief that the poor must determine their own issues and that a mass organizational drive for power is basic. Huerta has not been driven by ideological concerns but by a passion for justice and fairness. But she functioned like a corporate executive. To understand the inner strengths of the union is to understand the strength, drive, and the many personalities of Huerta.

Criticisms

Dolores Huerta is a very complicated woman. She was often at odds with César. As she has said: "César and I have a lot of personal fights, usually over strategy or personalities. I don't think César himself understands why he fights with me." Judith Coburn, writing in *Ms. Magazine*, said that "a book could be written on their complex relationship." Both were stubborn and opinionated, and Dolores was notorious in the union for her combativeness. She also has had frequent conflict with her two husbands—the price of a strong personality and her independence. For example, Dolores forced Ventura Huerta, her second husband, to quit his job and work with her in union activities because she was not being accepted as an organizer in the first few years. He would "front" for her as the organizer while she made the decisions. Ventura vigorously opposed her methods and also disagreed with Huerta's belief that family came second to her work in the union. Dolores's father opposed her "unconventional family and personal life."

Perhaps it is because of her independence and strong personality: Dolores has had two husbands and presently maintains a live-in arrangement with Richard Chávez, César's older brother. During these three relationships, she has borne eleven children, bringing responsibilities that have not compromised her union activity. As she acknowledges, "The time I spend with my kids is very limited." Sometimes she is separated for months at a time from her children. As several writers have pointed out, she is a tough, competitive, individualistic, and a very skilled woman. Because of her conflicts with men, her "neglect" of her children, and her aggressive role in the union many traditionalist Mexican women have berated her, although young Chicanas were attracted to her independent stand. In many ways, Huerta lives in the space between the traditional woman's role and the radical feminist one.

Huerta resembles the New Mestiza role Gloria Anzaldúa describes in her book, *Borderlands/La Frontera*, living on the border between tradition and nontradition, between the accepted and the unaccepted. Anzaldúa puts it: "Living on borders and in margins, deepening in fact one's shifting and multiple identity and integrity, is like trying to swim in a new element, an alien element." Many Mexican women, in addition to criticizing her conflict with men and her aggressive, almost manlike role in the union, berate Huerta for "neglect" of her children. At times, César Chávez, reacting to her independent personality, even said to her: "You're not a Mexican." She has replied: "I know it's true, I am a logical person. I went to school, and you learn that you have to weigh both sides and look at things objectively." Chávez is more dogmatic in his views than Huerta. She is able to move pragmatically through the limits of "lo Mexicano" and "lo Americano" without losing her sense of both.

Thus, Huerta diverges from the traditionally accepted model of the Mexican woman, especially women like César Chávez's wife Helen. Writing of this comparison, historian Margaret Rose has concluded that Huerta is a very nontraditional woman who is unlike the

majority of strong Mexican women, who are not combative or competitive. Within accepted Mexican tradition, a woman, according to
Rose, may be an activist, but she must still be a housewife. She can
be an organizer, but not a leader. Rose writes that "Huerta's union
activism is atypical. She rebelled against the conventional constraints
upon women's full participation in trade union activism, competing directly with male colleagues in the UFW." Rose also writes that
Huerta's "activism resembles that of other well-known Latina labor
leaders of earlier generations, such as Emma Tenayuca and Luisa
Moreno: it can only be labeled 'non-traditional.'" For Rose, the more
traditional activist is Helen Chávez, because she "juggles" not side-
steps the "demands of family life," the sexual division of labor, and
quietly protests behind her man. Huerta does not think of herself simply as a woman; nor does she conduct her life vis-à-vis men as did
1945 labor activist Josefina Fierro de Bright. She is different. She simply sees her work as a personal calling rather than as a woman's duty
to her man—or allegiance to ideological fervor, which was the case
with both Moreno and Tenayuca.

An Egalitarian Upbringing

Huerta's upbringing shaped her attitudes toward gender: her inner
strength and independent resourcefulness come from her mother.
As Huerta recalled in an interview, "My mother raised me and was a
dominant figure in my early years. At home, we all shared equally in
the household tasks. I never had to cook for my brothers or do their
clothes like many traditional Mexican families." Writer Ruth Carranza
further suggests that "Huerta's egalitarian family background has contributed to her leadership style. For Huerta there was no sexual discrimination in her home and consequently no sense of priority or no
encouragement to accept a sense of second role in her life and later in
her work with the union. Also, there was no contradictory masculine/
feminine messages by her mother."

Consequently, Huerta's assertiveness is predicated on her strong
sense of self. This character trait is what is appealing to modern-worker
women, to urban Mexican-American women, and young Chicanas. It
is her air of personal strength, of assertiveness, her disdain of feminine mystique that caused long-time organizer and labor leader Bert

Corona to call her too aggressive. Corona liked the fieriness of Luisa Moreno and sexuality of Josefina Fierro de Bright. Unlike these other union leaders, Huerta helped Chávez and the union by being a role model for young Chicanas.

Ironically, though Huerta in her family life and her organizational work is the "new woman" that the younger generation seems to be seeking, she has acted publicly as if she were the traditional woman behind the male leader Chávez. Chávez tried to keep a tight rein on his lieutenants, even on his equals like Huerta. But Dolores Huerta, by her strong, everyday example, broke from the image of the traditional mother and wife and the role of the traditional woman activist behind the scenes. Her behavior toward Chávez and other male farmworkers helped to break gender and sexual misperceptions of women. This allowed for equality within the union. Again, she exemplifies what Anzaldúa has written of the New Mestiza: "To live in the borderlands means you are neither hispana, india, negra, española, ni gabacha, eres mestiza, mulata, half-breed caught in the crossfire between camps while carrying all five races on your back not knowing which side to turn to from; to survive the Borderlands you must live sin fronteras, be a crossroads." Huerta as a woman lives at these crossroads of gender and ethnicity.

Huerta began to experience this life sin fronteras (without borders) as a child. She grew up assuming that women and men were equal because she constantly saw the strength and activism of her mother—a business entrepreneur, independent of men. She also saw and accepted the ideal of equality in a part of the United States where ethnicity was not a barrier. As she writes: "I was raised with two brothers and a mother, so there was no sexism. My mother was a strong woman and she did not favor my brothers. There was no idea that men were superior. I was also raised in Stockton in an integrated neighborhood. There were Chinese, Latinos, Native Americans, Blacks, Japanese, Italians, and others. We were all rather poor, but it was an integrated community so it was not racist for me in my childhood." Huerta perceived and interpreted the world as one of equality between men and women, regardless of ethnicity. She felt free to be herself and worked hard to succeed in school. She believed that she could participate in life as actively as her mother had. She especially saw how her mother, after her first divorce, had, without the help of a man, worked hard and started a successful restaurant and a hotel.

Her mother provided Dolores with a semblance of middle-class life, in values if not in fact. She gave Dolores both personal security and the financial foundation to pursue her education in an integrated high school and continue her education at a community college. As a result, Huerta grew up being active in the Girl Scouts, singing in a church choir, and aspiring to be a dancer. She learned the value of work, hope, perseverance, and independence. Huerta describes her mother as independent, ambitious, and a "Mexican-American Horatio Alger type." Her mother was her model, the United States was her teacher, and men were simply other people, not superiors, not bosses. Above all, Huerta saw herself and her friends as proof that Chicanos could succeed in the United States. She remembers that "all the Chicanos who went to school where I did are all making it. We grew up in Stockton, but weren't in a ghetto. As a result, we didn't have a whole bunch of hang-ups, like hating Anglos, or hating Blacks."

Clearly, Huerta grew up in a communal atmosphere of security and self-esteem, where ethnic differences were not insuperable barriers. Like Emma Tenayuca, she grew up with a middle-class mentality. She reflected such values of stability, tradition, and "Americanism" that, in her twenties, she briefly joined the Republican Party. In fact, her Americanism was so pronounced that, as she remembers, "I thought Fred Ross from the Community Service Organization . . . a Saul Alinsky organizer, was a Communist, so I went to the FBI and had him checked out. I really did that. I used to work for the Sheriff's Department. See how middle class I was. In fact, I was a registered Republican at the time [the late fifties]." However, in spite of her middle-class life, she remembers having friends who were pachucos and says: "I don't think I was ever really a cop-out."

But her life had many moments of ambiguity. For example, she later recollected that in elementary school the equality she had felt was tainted. "The teachers," she remembers, "treated us all equally mean." Later, in high school, underneath the world of lessons, A-grades, and clubs, there lurked a world of clear difference between rich and poor. "When I got into high school," she writes, "it was really segregated. There were the rich and the real poor. I later realized we were poor too, and I had got hit with a lot of racial discrimination." In spite of the racism, Huerta succeeded, but she was frustrated. As she yearned to succeed in college, she continued to notice the inequalities. She saw the poor on the streets and realized that most of the out-crowd of her high school clubs were "poor," too. She specifically remembers being crushed—her word—when she was questioned on the legitimacy of her high school essays, since they were so well written. The teacher thought someone else was writing them for her. "That really discouraged me," she said, "because I used to stay up all night and think, and try to make every paper different, and try to put words in there that I thought were nice."

Huerta consequently began to see life through a different lens, not because she felt an absence of freedom, or because of a personal sense of inequality, but because of widespread injustice—which applied to her, her Mexican friends, and other Americans. In short, she began to see the paradox between equality and justice, and equality and class. These disparities became more apparent to her after her mother took her, at age seventeen, to Mexico City. "This trip," she recalls, "opened my eyes to that fact that there was nothing wrong with Chicanos." The contrasts between Mexican and United States society made her acutely aware of two realities: societal injustices and her own lack of activism.

She remembered the other side of her mother's personality: her mother's commitment to helping poor Mexicano families; and she also felt her New Mexico traditions of Hispanidad. She became active in women's Hispanic groups, such as the Comité Honorifico Women's Club. She pursued the traditional elite Mexican woman's activist role: to serve in women's organizations, apart from men. But she soon discovered that "all of these organizations . . . didn't do anything but give dances and celebrate the Fiestas Patrias." This demonstration of civic virtue in the women's world did not satisfy her.

Simultaneously, her first marriage (in 1950 she had married an Irishman—her high school sweetheart) was failing and she found her role as a mother to several children to be unsatisfying. She also found that her two years of college no longer provided her with adequate intellectual or personal satisfaction. As she writes: "I felt I had all of these frustrations inside me. I had a fantastic complex because I seemed to be out of step with everybody and everything. You're try-ing to go to school and yet you see all of these injustices. It was just such a complex." Even teaching in the 1950s and helping children did not satisfy her. However, her awareness of racism, poverty, inequal-ity, and discrimination inflicted on the poor had not yet replaced her middle-class life: she was caught in her own world of children, motherhood, and wifely dependence; caught in the central tension of her life—between dreams of education and achievement on one hand and an acute awareness of injustice and unfairness on the other. Remembering her mother's constant advice—which would become an axiom—"Be yourself," she began to shift her view to a new life per-spective—a new gestalt.

"Be Yourself"

In 1955, armed with a community college background (which was more education than most women had in the 1950s) and bilingual skills, she began actively to change her life. She was driven by a strong belief that she could change her life and the lives of others. Hearing Saul Alinsky's call for radicalism in the voice of Fred Ross, she joined the Community Service Organization. As she would later say, she put herself at the service of others as an organizer and negotiator. As she entered the world of the 1950s, she held to an important belief: that, in any endeavor, "women have one advantage over men, their egos aren't so involved." She could "Be herself" and serve without feeling threatened by men. As she put it: "I think women are particularly good negotiators and organizers because we have a lot of patience, and no ego trips to overcome." She thus entered the world of power. The mes-sage from the Saul Alinsky Industrial Areas Foundation and the CSO was to gain reform for the poor by actively involving them in achiev-ing reform—and the emphasis of Alinsky's message coincided with hers: a practical, nonideological approach to life and change.

The world of the CSO and later the farm-workers union was no different from any other sector of the business world: they all needed good organizing executive managers who wanted to succeed. Dolores Huerta fit this to a tee. She was free of a sense of ethnic inferiority—a woman who felt equal to men in a world where women were still con-sidered to be the second sex.

The Organizer: "Pursuing Justice"

Huerta responded to Fred Ross's CSO in 1955 about her becoming an organizer because the job provided her with both an avenue to serve the poor and an avenue to "make it"—albeit not in mainstream America. The new challenge coincided with her philosophical axiom: "Be yourself." As she put it: "I like to organize and help people. I like social change. I feel humble because I've been very fortunate in my life. God has put me in the position and provided the opportunities and skills to get things done." In following a life of service, Huerta was making personal, moral, and political choices.

Huerta never changed her mind about her decision. She endured the criticism of her father (for failing in her wifely and motherly duties); she suffered through two failed marriages; she became the target of the anger of both middle-class and farm-working women (who berated her for neglecting her children, although she entrusted them to communal parents when she went on months-long organizing trips); and she endured the resentment of male farm workers and put up with Chávez's constant anger at her independence. Above all, she endured conditions of poverty for herself and her children: she often did not have money for milk or food. In 1962, she moved from a relatively comfortable administrative position with the Community Service Organization to work as the powerful, but still impoverished, first vice president and principal director of negotiations for the farmworkers organizing committee. Jean Murphy, writing in *Regeneración*, put Huerta's notable role and difficult choice in clear perspective:

"If César Chávez is the hero of the Farmworkers movement, Dolores Huerta is its unheralded heroine. Huerta plays a key organizing and leadership role. The role, however, is not easy. Eighteen hour days of planning boycotts, of speaking at rallies, of negotiating, of traveling, and of seeking public support for La Causa are more common than not. Nor is the work well paid. Like all other union officials and employees, she makes a minimal salary and a bare subsistence depending upon contributions of food and clothing. In her own humorous words Huerta has said of her choice: 'All of us have very exotic wardrobes. We get our clothes out of donations.'"

Huerta's egalitarianism and sense of justice also seem to be taken from America's trashcan. Out of discards she has fashioned a sense of hope and leadership, a hope based on the conviction that justice and fairness are the intellectual basis of a new society. As an organizer, Huerta still carries with her memories of youthful anomalies: the selfless elementary school girl selling war bonds; the girl working overtime to write papers that were considered suspect because they were written well; the child watching her mother help farm workers and braceros; the girl writing poems to capture a more sensitive world; or the teenager fighting for lower ticket prices to the poor at high school.

Her early experiences have helped shape her guiding manias; she seeks to balance differences between rich and poor. In the choices she made to establish a new life, Huerta took a pragmatic approach to her moral conflict. Her ideas were implicit guides to activity and behavior; and her knowledge of what was good and right was verified by her activism. She did not attempt intellectually to resolve her frustrations, her unorthodoxy, and her moral crisis. Stressing the power of moral choice, Huerta applied it to her work as an organizer and leader. She believes that the power for change is predicated on the power of individuals to make moral choices for justice over personal welfare. For Huerta, all individuals—farm workers, academics, and everyone else—must make a commitment, and the totality of commitment will either form a mass organization or establish a climate for a political movement.

Huerta believes that organizing is a creative process that gives her intellectual and personal fulfillment. She says: "My duties are policymaking like [those of] César Chávez. It is the creative part of the organization. I am in charge of political and legislative activity. Much of my work is in public relations." All her work, regardless of whether it is policymaking, political and legislative activity, or public relations, is always on four axioms: first, to establish a strong sense of identity; second, to develop a sense of pride; third, always to maintain the value of service to others; and fourth, to be self-reflective and true to oneself. For Huerta, all organizing and leadership work must be imbued with these principles. When Huerta described what she wanted her children to become, she summarized her major ideals: "Tough, political, responsible, and loving." Above all, she believes in psychological strength. She has always urged the Mexican community, the politician, and the poor in general not to be afraid to deal with issues. As she put it, "que no fueran miedosos" (do not be afraid of anything).

Huerta has remained selfless as an organizer, committed to a philosophy of service that she has pragmatically developed. Luis Valdez, artist, producer, and former head of the farm workers' teatro, perceptively captured Huerta's qualities as a woman and organizer in a 1990 newspaper article:

> Dolores was a 35 year old firebrand in 1965, and she was commanding crusty macho campesinos 20 years her senior. What dazzled my radicalized university-trained Chicano mind was that she led through persuasion and personal example, rather than intimidation, and that she was one hell of an organizer. People tend to forget that the 1960s were the sexist dark ages, even in the Chicano movement, as we called it, but Dolores was already way out in front. She was a woman, a Mexican-American, a Chicana cutting a swath of revolutionary action across the torpidity of the San Joaquin Valley.

Valdez adds: "The wonder of Dolores Huerta is that she has never given up struggling for what is right, decent and human in the world, and she never will."

This strong will and consciousness of egalitarianism are the underlying factors that maintain Huerta's sense of hope. They also established her style of intellectual leadership. As Huerta says: "To me a leader is someone who does things for people, and whom people will follow. It is not somebody who gets out there and imposes himself on people. I think people develop charisma in trying to reach people, in trying to get to them. Gradually and before you know it, you become a charismatic leader." Like Chávez, Huerta feels that a leader should get commitment from the workers—commitment to service for their own goals.

Huerta's Ideas

Through her early organizing years, Huerta did not consider herself to be a feminist or Chicana leader: she just followed her assumptions that equality is basic to life, and that justice, fairness, is the key. "I have been asked," she says,

Whether being a woman has made it difficult for me in my exercise of leadership. For years I never thought about that. We were too busy in organizing struggles. Now suddenly I am invited to speak here and there on different issues. The suggestion being that I am a symbol of the women's movement or that I speak for Hispanic women. And that has been difficult, I am a sort of born again feminist.

In spite of this recent consciousness of feminism, she has always realized the importance of women in building the union, and here being strong and independent women leaders and organizers. "I know," she says, "that the history of our union would have been quite different had it not been for my involvement. So I am trying to get more of our women to hang in there. The energy of women is important." Huerta speaks strong words for female leadership without overlooking the importance of male leadership in organization too.

She believes that the equal participation of women in an organization is vital. "The participation of women has helped keep the movement nonviolent," she says. For Huerta, women are more patient, less volatile than men. For Chávez the philosophical ideal on gender was for women to be separate but equal; for Huerta, women's leadership complemented men's, therefore gender equality and justice were not only to be pursued as goals but they must be nurtured and practiced in daily organizing activities. Equality, for Huerta, is intertwined with justice and gender, but the core of her philosophy remains the freedom of self through choice.

Dolores Huerta's ideas are rooted in numerous traditions. In many ways her conceptualization, "Be yourself," is very American, echoing the traditions of Emerson and Thoreau; that is, she stresses individual freedom and morality but ties them to communal responsibility. These notions were also espoused by the Mexican-American intellectual Octavio Romano in his 1960s and 1970s journal *El Grito*. In addition, her emphasis of the idea that organizers and leaders do not just give to the workers in the tradition of liberal-welfarism, or lead in the Marxist-Leninist tradition, coincides with Saul Alinsky's philosophy of organizing. Knowingly or not, she also mirrors John Rawls's idea that justice conveys a philosophical core of individual inviolability, a doctrine of fairness, and a method of compromise. Consequently, Huerta's simple message can function to deconstruct the utilitarian philosophy of justice that operates in the United States, calling for the greatest good for the greatest number. Huerta wants the poor to sit side by side with the rich and contractually agree to the choices of the primary goods and services to be distributed (i.e., liberties; economic, personal, intellectual, and political freedoms).

Huerta argues that there is a need for "mass organizations," "voter registration," "voter education," and for the people themselves to "identify the issues." "Our success," she continues, "is due to the New Deal tradition among older Americans" and the "younger generation which responds to César's charismatic leadership." Huerta clearly links the New Deal policies of justice and fairness with the 1960s youth rebellion for a new, Hobbesian contractualism and redistribution of society's primary goods and services.

While César Chávez was more directly concerned with building a union and getting people's commitment to such specific union activities as boycotts, Huerta was not always directly attempting to build a commitment to the farm workers union. She supported other causes, too. She reaches out to people with a simple message that can shape an alternative intellectual world. It is not an ideological message; nor is she calling for a structural revolution: she is simply demanding a new moral commitment based on a new sense of individual responsibility. Her vision of justice calls for this alternative intellectual world to be used as an ideal plan of action. Her thought is within the philosophical tradition of pragmatic self-discovery. For Huerta, ideas, action, and the individual are central to change, and gender is a core strength and energy. In her words: "The worst that I see is guys who say, 'man, they don't have any Chicanos up there [in places of power],' and they're not in there working to make sure that it happens. We [as Chicanos] criticize and separate ourselves from the process of change. We've got to jump in there with both feet to change conditions." For Huerta, ideas are vital, criticism is necessary—but it is action, through a responsible commitment and moral choice, that is the key to creating a just society.

A Symbol of Openness

As outlined above, Huerta represents many different ideas, but she always illustrates the ideas of fairness and justice, regardless of her audience. Because of this perception of her openness, César Chávez does not see her as he sees himself, strong and unwavering on certain ideas and ideals. Huerta points out that Chávez often referred to her as a "liberal." She said: "When he really wants to get me mad he says, 'you're not a Mexican,' because he says I have liberal hangups. And I know it's true. I am a logical person. I went to school and you learn that you have to weigh both sides and look at things objectively. But the farm workers, I believe, know that wrong is wrong. They know that there's evil in the world and that you have to fight evil."

Clearly, Huerta is more than just a unionist, an ethnic representative, or a liberal. We cannot rely on the familiar categories to characterize or understand Huerta. Although all of these, she retains her own distinctiveness. She exhibits all the personal and symbolic attributes applied to her—feminist, nationalist, humble, aggressive, nontraditional, and passionate. But her individuality is in their overlapping and their excesses as she responds to events and issues. It is difficult to place Huerta within one intellectual tradition because she works the constantly changing material of issues and crises as determined by people in different communities. She is continuously revitalized by, as well as revitalizing, temporal issues and discursive events.

Like other Latina women organizers such as Emma Tenayuca, Luisa Moreno, or Josefina Fierro de Bright, Huerta functions in her own space—a space at the crossroads of liberalism, conservatism, and radicalism. She speaks when others are still silent. For example, in April 1973, at the height of the nationalist ethnocentric Chicano movement, when nothing short of ideological purity was the required litmus test for all Chicanos, Dolores Huerta attended the seventy-fifth birthday of Paul Robeson, joining the likes of Angela Davis, Pete Seeger, Ramsey Clark, James Earl Jones, Ossie Davis, Sidney Poitier, Harry Belafonte, Mayor Richard G. Hatcher, Coretta Scott King, and multitudes of others who jammed Carnegie Hall. She joined in supporting Robeson's message, "dedicated to the worldwide cause of humanity," especially when she linked Robeson's humanism and universalism to the cause of the farm workers under the grito of "Viva Robeson! Viva la causa!"

At its core, then, Huerta's cause is societal openness, universal equality, and a new humanism based on justice. Obviously, Huerta is a symbol of openness—of not fixing knowledge to truths, of not dogmatizing life, of not establishing barriers by ethnicity. For her, justice is at the crossroads of freedom and equality. As she stated, "I would like to be remembered as a woman who cares for fellow humans. We must use our lives to make the world a better place to live, not just to acquire things. That is what we are put on the earth for." This simple but fundamentally radical message mirrors that of Chávez—that everyone should make a personal moral choice of commitment to and responsibility for justice.

Dolores Huerta, 1966. Courtesy
of Jon Lewis.

3

César Chávez and Dolores Huerta

Partners in "La Causa"

Margaret Rose

United Farm Workers (UFW) historians have located the origins of the movement to organize California's farmworkers in César Chávez's dramatic resignation from the directorship of the Community Service Organization (CSO) in March 1962 and the launching of the Farm Workers Association (FWA). As Chávez later revealed in an interview, Dolores Huerta contributed significantly to this effort: "Dolores and I were the architects of the National Farm Workers Association."[1] Huerta played a major role not only in designing the organization but also in running it. Although Chávez was chosen general director of the group, Huerta served as vice president and the only female elected official. In the early years of the group's existence, the two consulted frequently on basic decisions: the name, the incorporation of the FWA, its constitution, dues setting, group insurance benefits, credit union, fund-raising, organizing strategies, and political tactics. Repeatedly, Huerta sought advice from her network of contacts in northern California and conveyed legal information and made recommendations to Chávez.

Huerta's close collaboration with Chávez placed her in a unique position to observe and comment on him and his actions. On the way to explaining how she interpreted Chávez, this essay will also reveal her very important role in the emergence of the union. As a strong-willed and independent thinker, she felt intensely about issues of poverty, injustice, and exploitation. An articulate and educated woman, she did not hesitate to offer opinions. During the time the FWA was getting off the ground, Huerta lived and worked in Stockton, California, while Chávez set up its headquarters in Delano. This separation necessitated frequent communication by mail. The existence of the unique and detailed correspondence of more than fifty letters from Huerta to Chávez during the almost three years the two were establishing the FWA provides fascinating glimpses into her view of his leadership, the personal sacrifices they made, the tenuous nature of their early efforts, their disagreements, and their complex working relationship.[2] Perhaps misguided by early treatments of the farm workers movement that focused largely on Chávez, historians have missed the importance of this partnership. Scholars now have the opportunity to evaluate more accurately the relationship between these two social activists. These documents reveal how Chávez, and by extension the farmworkers, benefited from a dedicated confidante and an outspoken Chicana advocate.

Huerta's esteem for Chávez derived from her respect for his leadership of the CSO, the self-help association that emerged in Mexican American barrios in the post–World War II era throughout the Southwest. The CSO sparked Chávez's and Huerta's social consciences and provided an avenue to civic activism. Starting as a volunteer in San Jose, Chávez became an organizer and later general director of the group.[3] Huerta's entry into community involvement centered in Stockton, where she volunteered in voter registration drives, educational campaigns, and chapter fund-raising. Her abilities and passion for social justice attracted attention, so she was offered the position of lobbyist.[4]

Huerta's first reaction to Chávez was not promising. "I found César was very shy," she noted to a journalist. "The first two or three years I knew him it was difficult to have a conversation with him."[5] Increasingly, their paths crossed at numerous meetings, conventions, and campaigns. During this time, Huerta's interests broadened when several of her Stockton CSO colleagues and other socially conscious citizens formed the Agricultural Workers Association (AWA) in 1958. This local interest group dissolved when the AFL-CIO–sponsored Agricultural Workers Organizing Committee (AWOC) emerged a year later. Former AWA members enlisted in the campaign, including

Huerta, who became secretary-treasurer. She soon grew disenchanted with the leadership, direction, and policies, however, and resigned from the group.[6] As Huerta worked more closely with Chávez, a common bond developed. Their experiences, their unswerving commitment to the Mexican American community, a shared outrage for the abject conditions of farmworkers, and their impatience with the ineffectual policies of the past further united them. Frustrated by the failure of the CSO to support an internal initiative to organize farmworkers and by the misguided approaches of the AWOC, they turned their energies to the campesinos (farm laborers).

Swept up in the idealism and reform then associated with Lyndon Johnson's Great Society programs and civil rights movements, Chávez and Huerta embarked on a journey that would test their resolve and stress their families' financial and emotional lives. Exhibiting her characteristic optimism, Huerta enthusiastically embraced this challenge to unionize California's agricultural laborers. In Chávez, she had found a colleague willing to dedicate himself body and soul to a cause—a trait she identified in herself. Pleased and humbled, she wrote to him, "It looks like working for the Association is just the job I need. Whether my assistance will be of value, is another question."

Establishing the financial viability of the FWA proved to be a far more difficult task than either could have imagined. Eschewing outside assistance, Chávez and Huerta believed that the fledgling organization had to stand on its own. She admired his quiet strength, single-mindedness, and determination. Clearly, the personal costs of this decision were high. After depleting their unemployment insurance and savings, Chávez and his wife, Helen, along with their eight children, faced financial difficulties. "Helen," Chávez wrote his CSO mentor Fred Ross in August 1962, "is now working a few hours every day out in the fields. She is cutting grapes and works from about 6:00 in the morning till about 1 in the afternoon."[7] In the afternoons, Helen sought employment assembling cardboard boxes in a packing shed. When the grape season ended, she engaged in other piecework jobs. After school and during the summers, her older children joined her in the harvests. And at times when finances were particularly desperate, Chávez took time off from running the Delano office to work in the fields. Family illness further strained the household income.

Learning of Helen's illness, Huerta recommended hiring her after her recovery to assist with the FWA bookkeeping. "It would be a good way to get the work done," she thought, "and also help out your family." Given the limited FWA revenue, even these strategies were not sufficient to keep the family solvent. Both César's and Helen's families contributed groceries, clothes, and child care to supplement their insufficient income.[8]

Huerta shared in their reduced circumstances. Recognizing their bleak prospects, Chávez persuaded her to stay on the CSO payroll until the financial outlook of the FWA improved.[9] The Chávez family was not alone in their marginal existence. Huerta, in her thirties, with seven children and an estranged second husband (whom she later divorced), also shouldered considerable financial burdens. She harbored grave reservations about Chávez's plans for her continued employment with the CSO. Fred Ross endorsed the idea, but only if Huerta fulfilled her current duties for the Stockton chapter. This, in effect, meant that she had to work two jobs while receiving the salary of one. She reluctantly agreed to the arrangement but expressed misgivings. "Everyone seems to think I can take care of the [CSO] office and the farm worker project . . . and I'm not sure I can," she said frankly to Chávez. Her reservations centered not only on the "killer schedule" and the greater lack of control over her activities, but also on the conflict of interest created by her continuing relationship with an organization Chávez had left because of its failure to organize farmworkers. "I feel there will be a lot of criticism," she continued. "If I did not have to work for the CSO, but could have an independent income, then no one could say anything about what I do." Coaxed by Chávez, she endured as long as she could. But her initial apprehensions eventually proved justified. "I am to be terminated," she noted tersely to Chávez.

Huerta's correspondence with Chávez reveals a constant struggle to make ends meet. Her finances took a turn for the worse when her unemployment check from the CSO job ran out. She proposed a solution. "What I wanted to ask you," she wrote to Chávez, "was if I could charge $5.00 for some of the cases [dealing with members' immigration and welfare problems]. Not for everyone, but if I could get $15.00 per week . . . that would be enough. However, I believe it is much more important to get members plus loyalty, so don't feel bad in tell-ing me no. I will manage somehow." Chávez's response was no. He believed that working on such problems made people dependent—a view that contrasted with Huerta's more service-oriented approach and detracted from organizing efforts. Support, however irregular, came from her two former husbands, family members, and friends. She augmented these sources with temporary translation assign-ments, substitute teaching, and even a brief stint in the onion har-vest, in addition to her work for the FWA.

While Chávez concentrated on workers in the Delano area, Huerta organized workers from her base in Stockton. Her letters describe the long days and nights publicizing the new organization, setting up meetings, calling on workers in their homes, and visiting labor camps in farmworker towns such as Acampo, Woodbridge, Manteca, Victor, Linden, and Lodi, in addition to covering Stockton. Her correspon-dence also describes the frustrations endured as a result of the lack of basic needs for a farm labor organizer—reliable transportation and communication. Huerta and Chávez commiserated on the simple tools that most took for granted. "Right now I have three handicaps," she bluntly asserted to Chávez, "no car, no typewriter, no phone." A car in need of a mechanic and a delinquent phone bill brought her work to a standstill. Help from her brother and a family friend ended those temporary, but frequent, impediments. In response to simi-lar woes from Chávez, she immediately sympathized: "Sorry to hear about your car. Should we try to get some money for repairs?" She offered to take up a collection and send the money to Delano. Both were always scrambling for gas money and overextending the FWA credit card.

Huerta's financial problems continued. Even with a used car she purchased with a $100 auto loan, building up support for the group was slow and arduous because of the reluctance of some workers to get involved and because organizational meetings were often can-celed at the last minute because of a misunderstanding or other unexpected glitch. "Thursday night's meeting was also a fluke," she lamented in what was becoming a common complaint. "Only the fellow who would give the meeting was there, but he is going to try again. (Ain't this a bitch?)"

Canceled meetings and worker apathy were occupational hazards for both, but Huerta also had to contend with resistance to a female organizer. In Stockton, she ignored and outlasted this reluctance, but the issue arose again whenever she targeted a new area. A house meeting in Modesto, attended primarily by men, abruptly terminated when she appeared at the scheduled hour. The participants did not try to conceal their motives, stating openly their refusal to meet with a woman.[10] As in Stockton, she did not allow such hostility to deter her and doggedly persisted in her efforts. Although women's issues were emerging in this decade, gender consciousness was not yet as widespread as it would later become. Revealingly, Chávez did not consider this type of discrimination as a distinct obstacle for women. Huerta herself only gradually came to recognize this additional barrier female organizers confronted.

A functioning car, gas money, a working telephone, and a typewriter—mundane items, yet they were central to the operation of the FWA. These tools helped generate the dues that were critical to the survival of the effort. Huerta included dues in almost every letter she sent to Delano during these years. "I hope this letter finds you in the best of health," she wrote, "and not close to a nervous breakdown over the coming dues collections." As she well knew, the $3.50 monthly expense was not easy for workers to pledge because of their meager wages, their fear of employers' retaliation, competition from other unions, the unpredictable nature of agricultural employment, labor surpluses, and unexpected illnesses and family emergencies. As a result, union members frequently missed payments. They also moved around the state in search of work, leading to additional bookkeeping problems. Despite the disappointing, irregular, and inadequate collections, after deducting expenses, Chávez and Huerta shared the slim proceeds. Commenting in an interview, Huerta adamantly stated, "César was very fair about that. He would always divide it down the middle."[11]

Although Huerta shared with Chávez a deep commitment to unionizing field laborers, she differed with him on politics. When not organizing workers, Huerta lobbied political officials, an atypical avocation for a Mexican American woman at the time, but one at which she became unusually adept. "Everyone knows her," observed

Chávez following a trip to the state capital in December 1962, "and the usual remark is that she is a fighter."[12] He remained more ambivalent regarding the political arena as an effective avenue for achieving significant change.

Despite Chávez's reservations, Huerta maintained an avid interest in the political process. She had first gained exposure to lobbying as a legislative advocate for the CSO in the late 1950s. By the time of her association with the FWA, her skills had become almost legendary. Huerta took pride in her successful invasion of the male world of Sacramento politics, and she proved to be successful in her struggles on behalf of old-age pensions, a higher minimum wage for field workers, and aid to dependent children of unemployed agricultural workers.

Even though Chávez recognized Huerta's political talents, he did not encourage her lobbying efforts because they took time away from field organizing and perhaps also because he resented the public attention she received. To Huerta, the state capitol was a place where she was not only effective but also removed from the male workers whom she tried to organize and who resisted an independent female labor leader. The elected officials, by contrast, listened to and frequently voted for legislation she supported. Their greater openness offered her an opportunity to exercise more professional and political autonomy away from unreceptive farm laborers and from Chávez himself.

Huerta carried her lobbying efforts beyond California to the nation's capital. When Johnson's Great Society programs gained momentum in the 1960s, federal agencies tapped her expertise on the conditions of Mexican Americans in general and farmworkers in particular. She took advantage of her entrée to advance the interests of Mexican, Mexican American, and FWA workers testifying before committees and meeting with individual lawmakers. Among the issues of greatest concern was Public Law 78.[13] Enacted by Congress in 1951, the law extended a World War II program to regulate the annual importation of farm laborers from Mexico. In the late 1950s and early 1960s, opposition mounted against the legislation from labor, civic, ethnic, and religious groups, as well as from the leadership within the Democratic party. Huerta was among those attacking the program at the state and national levels. Congress eventually ended it in 1965.[14] Overall, Huerta's enthusiasm for legislative action caused friction with Chávez. "We probably should have made the decision," she contended, "that my work in the field was more important [than] the legislative work before I started." She remained more confident and more comfortable engaging the political system than he did.

Operating on a shoestring, making decisions on a trial and error basis, creating a union from the ground up, and adapting tactics from the civil rights movement, Chávez and Huerta were both dedicated and strong-willed individuals. Though exhibiting mutual respect, collaborating as closely as they did under difficult circumstances, they were bound to have misunderstandings, conflicting points of view, and arguments. But for the organization to survive, it was crucial to negotiate their differences.

Although Huerta may have felt deference toward Chávez initially, as the struggle to unionize farmworkers advanced, she did not hesitate to speak her mind. Many supporters within and outside the organization increasingly held Chávez in awe, but Huerta characteristically confronted him and questioned his ideas and decisions. "To further finish up my peeves," she wrote after a miscommunication during an FWA board meeting in Delano, "I also resent it when you are not honest with me . . . I do not mind playing the part of the heavy if I know why and when I am supposed to take on this role." To her credit, Huerta did not bear grudges and could move forward after venting her grievances. Having a trusted and forthright colleague who was willing to work behind the scenes to negotiate sensitive internal and personnel matters gave Chávez more room to maneuver. Huerta's candid assessments also expanded the range of options in developing strategies to combat agribusiness and its political allies.

As a forceful and self-assured person, Huerta could tolerate criticism. "I received your penitent letter, much to my surprise, and as the natives say, 'no hay fijon' [pay it no mind]," she responded to one reproach from Chávez. "I deserve the recriminations. Furthermore, I think I am still ahead when it comes to losing tempers." Although she appreciated Chávez's apology, Huerta preferred to work under pressure and accepted the tensions and strains that inevitably emerged under such circumstances. Obviously, Chávez benefited from her frankness and toughness. Her attitude created a more open environment for airing opinions, exchanging views, and arriving at a decision.

From 1962 to 1964, Huerta proved an integral part of the emergence and development of the FWA. From her Stockton base, she sought legal advice and assistance on the incorporation of the organization, conferred with various representatives to obtain information on group insurance policies, supported favorable legislative initiatives in Sacramento and Washington, D.C., recruited new members, collected dues from established supporters, traveled to Delano for board meetings, and regularly consulted with Chávez on the progress and direction of the group. She did all this while raising a family of seven children, eventually as a single parent. Her family would grow still larger in the 1970s.[15]

Huerta felt comfortable with this working relationship, she valued the cause, and she respected Chávez. Despite the hardships and their disagreements, she believed that she could work with him and make a difference in the lives of impoverished farmworkers. Perhaps this is why she finally succumbed to repeated pressures from Chávez to relocate to the southern San Joaquin Valley.

In 1964, Huerta finally agreed with Chávez's view that the FWA's success required a more concentrated effort in Delano and greater visibility of the organization's message through the dissemination of a newspaper. This decision required Huerta to uproot her family from Stockton and, when Chávez could find no one else suitable for the weekly paper, to add writing to her responsibilities. Huerta assented to the move but only after school was out.[16]

Even then, Huerta found it difficult to resettle her children, to leave her extended family and social network in Stockton, and to begin anew the tasks of locating child-care and housing. She lived temporarily in the crowded Chávez household until she could find and afford her own housing.[17] She also regretted having to curtail her political lobbying and relinquish the greater independence that the physical separation from the Delano headquarters had permitted. Yet the shift to the southern San Joaquin Valley offered greater efficiency, direction, and focus for building the FWA.

Chávez and Huerta, with a small core of supporters, now prepared for the time when they could launch a coordinated drive to change the lives of farmworkers—a contest that came far sooner than they had anticipated. The opportunity arose when the rival AFL-CIO–sponsored AWOC, with a predominantly Filipino membership, went on strike and asked for FWA support. The consequent cooperation resulted in the famous Delano grape strike of 1965, the subsequent creation of the United Farm Workers Organizing Committee (UFWOC), and the beginning of a new era in César Chávez's life, as well as in Dolores Huerta's.[18]

At the outset of their mission to improve the lives of farmworkers, Huerta questioned the value of her assistance to the cause. Clearly, she underestimated her impact and the vital importance of her presence for Chávez and the farmworkers movement. The years 1962 to 1964 tested her resolve. She proved to be a steadfast defender of the social, political, and economic rights of agricultural laborers. In addition to abandoning her personal life, Huerta also sacrificed the comfort and ease of her family. Although several opportunities for better-paying positions came her way, she rejected them all in favor of devoting her energies to the establishment of the FWA. She had demonstrated to Chávez that she could be counted on, and he benefited from her loyalty, firmness of purpose, counsel, and honesty. Their friendship and partnership forged during these early years would lead to the achievement of many historic victories for farmworkers. Their alliance and commitment made in the early 1960s would sustain them in numerous battles on behalf of farm laborers for more than thirty years.

A key to Huerta's commitment to the farmworkers' movement rested on her assessment of Chávez. Her estimation of Chávez evolved over the late 1950s and early 1960s before the union had made national headlines. Prior to their formal introduction, Huerta had repeatedly heard of his notable organizational skills from Fred Ross. When Chávez and Huerta finally met, she was disappointed. He did not match her image of a dynamic, high-powered, larger-than-life individual. Speaking to a reporter, she recalled, "I didn't get a chance to talk to him the first time I met him, and he didn't make much of an impression on me."[19] Over the years, her earlier estimation changed. What progressively impressed her was his dedication, hard work, leadership style, and philosophy.

Reflecting on her initial reaction, she later remarked, "You couldn't tell by looking at him what he could do; you had to see him in action to appreciate him."[20] In the brief period 1962 to 1964, she saw Chávez's complete dedication to the farmworker cause. His modesty and lack of ego appealed to her. She became convinced that the unionization of farmworkers, and not self-promotion, was the motivating force driving him. Huerta admired his work ethic and concentration. He threw himself fully into organizing, even depriving his family of his personal attention and time.

Huerta also came to believe that she had underestimated his aptitude for leadership. Originally perceiving him as low-key and ordinary, she increasingly appreciated his simple but compelling style, his fairness, and his steadiness. She also prized the esteem he bestowed on colleagues. He did not ask anything of anyone that he was not willing to undertake himself. In her view, he sought and was willing to listen to different points of view. Huerta experienced this quality in their relationship. He perceived her as a coequal, not as a follower. Although they often disagreed, she felt the freedom to state her opinions. She also believed that he accepted her limitations and shortcomings. She gradually determined that his unassuming manner was a strength rather than a weakness. His brand of leadership projected a model of commitment, cooperation, perseverance, and integrity.

Above all, Huerta respected Chávez's core values, beliefs, and philosophy. In the early years of their partnership, she shared his view of the dignity of the individual, regardless of one's station in life. She observed firsthand his deep outrage at the exploitation of farmworkers and their families. She witnessed his fervent conviction that farm laborers had the power to change their own lives. She discovered his ability to adopt the tactic of nonviolence from the civil rights protests and adapt it to the farmworkers movement. These principles and faith in the mission provided the guidance and direction to lead La Causa during the difficult trials of bitter strikes, long fasts, prolonged boycotts, legal hurdles, and political obstacles that would challenge the union in the years to come.

Notes

1. Jacques Levy, *César Chávez: Autobiography of La Causa*. New York: W. W. Norton, 1975), 166.

2. This set of correspondence is part of the National Farm Workers Association papers, housed at the Archives of Labor and Urban Affairs, Walter P. Reuther Library Detroit, Box 2, Correspondence Huerta to Chávez, 1962–1964 (hereafter cited ALUA). Most of these letters are undated. Unless otherwise noted, the quoted material in this essay comes from this source.

3. Peter Matthiessen, *Sal Sí Puedes: César Chávez and the New American Revolution* (New York: Random House, 1969), 45–49.

4. Margaret Eleanor Rose, "Women in the United Farm Workers: A Study of Chicana and Mexicana Participation in a Labor Union, 1950 to 1980" (Ph.D. diss., University of California, Los Angeles, 1988), 34–39.

5. Ronald B. Taylor, *Chávez and the Farm Workers* (Boston: Beacon Press, 1975), 88.

6. Dick Meister and Anne Loftis, *A Long Time Coming: The Struggle to Unionize America's Farm Workers* (New York: Macmillan, 1977), 92–96.

7. César Chávez to Fred Ross, 17 August 1962, Box 3, Series I, Folder 6, Fred Ross Collection, ALUA.

8. Margaret Rose, "Traditional and Nontraditional Patterns of Female Activism in the United Farm Workers of America, 1962 to 1980," *Frontiers* 11 (No. 1, 1990): 27–28.

9. Taylor, *Chávez and the Farm Workers*, 105.

10. Dolores Huerta, interview by author, Keene, Calif., 8 Feb. 1985.

11. Taylor, *Chávez and the Farm Workers*, 101.

12. César Chávez to Fred Ross, 14 Dec. 1962, Box 3, Series I, Folder 10, Fred Ross Collection, ALUA. 102

13. See Ernesto Galarza, *Merchants of Labor* (Charlotte, Calif.: McNally and Loftin, 1964).

14. Linda C. Majka and Theo J. Majka, *Farm Workers, Agribusiness, and the State* (Philadelphia: Temple University Press, 1982), 151–66.

15. Margaret Rose, "Dolores Huerta," in *Notable Hispanic American Women*, ed. Diane Telgen and Jim Kamp (Detroit: Gale Research, 1993), 212. Huerta would eventually bear four more children when she began a relationship with Richard Chávez in the 1970s.

16. Joan London and Henry Anderson, *So Shall Ye Reap* (New York: Thomas Y. Crowell, 1970), 149.

17. Dolores Huerta, interview by author, Keene, Calif., 4 Feb. 1985.

18. See Eugene Nelson, *Huelga: The First Hundred Days of the Great Delano Strike* (Delano, Calif.: Farm Worker Press, 1966).

19. Matthiessen, *Sal Sí Puedes*, 50.

20. Ibid.

4

Traditional and Nontraditional Patterns of Female Activism in the United Farm Workers of America, 1962–1980

Margaret Rose

One of the most inspiring social movements of the post World War II era was the historic struggle for the unionization of California farm workers that began in the early 1960s. Studies of the United Farm Workers of America, AFL-CIO (UFW), and the farm worker insurgency that developed during this period have focused on its male leadership and provided a patriarchal interpretation of its origins.[1] Perpetuating this view, a recent history textbook noted, "[A] thirty-five-year old community organizer named César Estrada Chávez set out single-handedly to organize impoverished migrant farm laborers in the California grape fields."[2] Such male-centered interpretations have distorted the history of the UFW and the role of women in its development. The following pages document the heretofore "invisible" participation of Mexicanas and Chicanas in the founding and management of the UFW and analyze the impact of gender on this union. Women's commitment to the union, however, was not uniform. To illustrate the wide range of women's contributions to the UFW this investigation contrasts the experiences of the rare women, such as Dolores Huerta, whose style of leadership fit a "male" model of labor organizing with the more common but no less vital endeavors of women, such as Helen Chávez, whose activism fit a more "female"

Originally published in *Frontiers: A Journal of Women Studies*, 11, no. 1, Las Chicanas (1990): 26–32. Reproduced by permission of the University of Nebraska Press. Copyright © 1990 by Frontiers Editorial Collective.

model of collective action—that is, work performed, often behind the scenes, in an auxiliary or supportive fashion.

During the past two decades scholarship in women's labor history has uncovered the diversity and distinctiveness of women's working-class heritage.[3] Most of this work has concentrated on Anglo or ethnically European women, and more recently on black women in the South.[4] The protests of Chicanas and Mexicanas in UFW campaigns demonstrate a continuity with women in other labor struggles in the United States. Thanks to a growing body of research that emerged during the 1980s, the experiences of women of Mexican heritage can also be considered in relationship to the past and contemporary struggles of their ethnic sisters—striking Mexicana laundresses in El Paso at the turn of the century, Mexican cannery operatives in California in the 1930s and 1940s, the wives of Mexican miners who formed women's auxiliaries in copper strikes during the 1950s, militant garment workers at Farah in the 1970s, and female employees in maquiladoras (export-oriented, in-process assembly plants operating along the U.S.-Mexican border).[5] Indeed, Chicanas and Mexicanas have a rich and detailed labor history and have frequently resorted to collective action to resist unjust working conditions. The present inquiry examines how ideologically defined gender roles have shaped such activism within the UFW.[6]

UFW women have taken two different paths to trade unionism.[7] Observers of the UFW are most familiar with the career of Dolores Huerta, the union's cofounder and first vice president. Yet Huerta's union activism is atypical. She rebelled against the conventional constraints upon women's full participation in trade union activism, competing directly with male colleagues in the UFW. Her activism resembles that of other well-known Chicana labor leaders of earlier generations, such as Emma Tenayuca and Luisa Moreno; it can only be labeled "nontraditional." A more "traditional" model is that of Helen Chávez, wife of UFW president César Chávez. Chicanas and Mexicanas adopting this approach juggle the competing demands of family life, sexual division of labor, and protest in a unique blend of union activism. But their contribution to union building is obscured because it occurs in the context of domestic responsibilities.[8] Despite her marriage to a prominent labor reformer, Chávez can be readily likened to hundreds of other Mexicanas and Chicanas who participated in strikes and picket lines but remained anonymous and forgotten.

Huerta's and Chávez's differing experiences of and attitudes toward politicization, union work, visibility, and domesticity illustrate two distinct ways in which Chicanas and Mexicanas attain and exercise power in this trade union. And their personal backgrounds indicate how class and generational distance from Mexico, in addition to gender, influence women's opportunities and social expectations for themselves.

Superficially, it would seem that these two Mexican American women share much in common. Both grew up during the Depression era; Helen Chávez, née Fabela, was born in Brawley, California, in 1928 and Dolores Huerta, née Fernández, in Dawson, New Mexico, in 1930.[9] Both women wed in the surge of marriages in the post–World War II years. Chávez married in 1948 at age twenty; Huerta married one day shy of her twentieth birthday, in Stockton, California, in 1950.[10] As practicing and devout Hispanic Catholics, both women valued large families: Helen Chávez bore eight children, Dolores Huerta eleven.[11]

Yet despite these similarities, notable differences in the two women's lifestyles and personal histories reflect the complexity and diversity of the experience of the Mexican American woman in the twentieth century. Huerta, on her mother's side of the family, was a third generation New Mexican; her maternal grandmother was born in Las Cruces, her grandfather in Carrizozo. Both her mother and her father were born in Dawson, a small mining town in the northern part of the state. Helen Chávez was a first generation Mexican American. Her mother was from Sombrerete, Mexico, her father from San Jacinto, Mexico; the two immigrated separately to the United States in the years after the Mexican Revolution and married in Los Angeles, California, in 1923. In terms of bilingualism, economic opportunity, education, and social class, Huerta's family was more assimilated than Chávez's into North American society.[12]

Chávez's parents were farm workers who lived first in the Imperial Valley in California, not far from the Mexican border, and later moved to the San Joaquin Valley in central California, eventually settling in a small rural agricultural community south of Delano. Forced to quit high school after the death of her father, Chávez worked in the fields and vineyards full time in order to help her widowed mother provide for the family of five children. Chávez's poverty and lack of education typify the experience of immigrant Mexican farm worker women, who often had even less education, spoke no English, and had to make the difficult adjustment of living and working in a foreign country and culture. Huerta, on the other hand, had a more middle-class upbringing, particularly after her mother moved to Stockton, California, where she operated a hotel with her second husband. Huerta's comfortable lifestyle and family resources enabled her to graduate from high school and community college, a rare accomplishment for Mexican-heritage women in the years just after World War II.[13]

Both class and ethnicity affected the opportunities and social outlets open to these women during the 1950s. The years after the war were a time of civic pride and growing political awareness in the Mexican American community.[14] For Helen Chávez, politicization began with her membership in the Community Service Organization (CSO), a grassroots Mexican American self-help group that established a chapter in San Jose, California, in 1952.[15] A young mother, Chávez became involved through her husband's interest in the CSO. As was customary for this generation of women, her activities were essentially auxiliary; she helped in the office, mimeographing fliers or sorting the mail, but usually she worked at home in the evenings, after her domestic chores were done and the children were asleep. "If we were going to have a meeting," she recalled, "I would address all the envelopes or address post cards, whatever had to be done."[16] The voluntarism of Helen Chávez and other women behind the scenes made the CSO one of the most successful associations for Mexican Americans in California during this time.

Huerta also began with traditional, female-defined activities in community-based philanthropy and volunteer work for Mexican American groups, but by the late 1950s she evolved into a more nontraditional activist leader. Huerta's middle-class resources, particularly her education, gave her valuable skills and confidence, aiding this transformation. Her association with the CSO began in 1955, when a chapter was established in Stockton, California. At first she performed a variety of traditionally "female" tasks—making arrangements for CSO meetings, participating in voter registration drives, and teaching citizenship classes for individuals in the community—as opposed to the "male" tasks of organizing new chapters and serving as an elected officer.[17] Soon, however, she moved into a more demanding position of responsibility and authority: that of paid legislative advocate for the CSO in Sacramento, an unusual pursuit for most women in the 1950s, and particularly so for ethnic women.[18] Through the CSO Huerta also became interested in the poverty and exploitation of farm workers, in 1958 becoming a charter member of a local group, the Agricultural Workers Association (AWA), and serving as an elected official of the AFL-CIO–sponsored Agricultural Workers Organizing Committee (AWOC), founded in Stockton in 1959.[19] Huerta's active participation in the AWA caused opposition from male colleagues:

> But Father McCullough [an AWA founder] didn't want me to be involved. He said farm labor organizing was no place for a woman. So I kind of worked under cover, doing the work through my husband [Ventura] and my brother [Marshall].[20]

This gender-based reaction indicated that Huerta was challenging the customary division that separated acceptable volunteer activity for women from the traditionally male-dominated world of highly politicized union organizing.

A similar contrast appears in the types of work the two women performed in the National Farm Workers Association (NFWA), the precursor to the UFW founded in 1962. Helen Chávez's work, like that of most Chicanas and Mexicanas in the UFW, was administrative and supportive. Yet her participation, and that of other female family members and friends, was vital in building the union and carried risks. "The registration crew will most likely be made up of women," noted César Chávez in a letter to a colleague. "I have most of mine and Helen's relatives on the hook, but they are a little afraid of getting evolved [sic] and being black-balled. Will most likely keep their names out in the beginning so as to protect them."[20] During subsequent demonstrations and strikes, Helen, along with other Chicanas and Mexicanas and their children, joined picket lines to demand union recognition in the face of taunts, intimidation, and threats of physical harm.

After the NFWA was on more solid ground, Helen was persuaded to quit her work in the fields to assume office duties. Hesitating because of her lack of training, she accepted the responsibility reluctantly. "We wanted her [Helen] to learn the credit union bookkeeping," recalled Dolores Huerta years later. "[During one of our board meetings], he [César] yelled at her [Helen] one night into the kitchen, 'You're going to be the assistant bookkeeper.' She yelled back, 'No, I won't either,' but we voted her the job. Boy was she mad! But you should see her books. We've been investigated a hundred times and they never find a mistake." For over twenty years she has managed the UFW's credit union. Since she is the only full-time staff member, without Helen Chávez this union service probably would not have survived. While this work is essential to the institutional apparatus of the UFW it has been underrated because it is an area traditionally reserved for women and one that does not attract the public attention given to strikes and organizing campaigns.[23] In her association with the union Helen Chávez did not seek a policy-making role. Although she wielded considerable informal influence over her husband, and by extension the UFW, this influence was exercised in the privacy of her home.

Huerta's service to the union, on the other hand, has clearly been nontraditional. As a cofounder of the union with César Chávez, and as first vice president, Huerta has held a decision-making post in the UFW from the outset.[24] She was also the union's first contract negotiator, founding the negotiations department and directing it in the early years. "[César] Chávez left the negotiations up to Dolores Huerta," observed one commentator.[25] Collective bargaining talks such as the mid-1960s Christian Brothers negotiations were demanding, drawn out, and tedious. "They were difficult," Huerta recalled, "and this is where persistence pays off, you just have to keep hammering away. You may have to have five meetings to change two words . . . this is where César gets uptight. He never really quite trusted what I did until he started to negotiate himself; then he found it was pretty hard to get the kind of language that I had gotten, and he started respecting what I had done."[26] As she assumed responsibilities and stances that were traditionally held by white males, Huerta encountered criticism based on both gender and ethnic stereotypes. One grower representative reacted to Huerta's forceful negotiating style and uncompromising positions, "Dolores Huerta is crazy. She is a violent woman, where women, especially Mexican women, are usually peaceful and calm."[27] Such comments indicate the depth of her challenge to the political, social, and economic power of California agribusiness, as well as to the ideology of male dominance.

Another major responsibility for Huerta was the directorship of the boycott in New York City, the largest grape distribution center in the U.S., and her service as East Coast boycott coordinator in 1968 and 1969. Her leadership there contributed to the success of the boycott in mobilizing labor unions, political activists, community organizations, religious supporters, women's clubs, peace groups, student protesters, and concerned consumers behind the union. "The whole thrust of our boycott is to get as many supporters as you can," she declared. "You have to get organizers who can go out to the unions, to the churches, to the students and get that support. You divide an area up—in New York we split it up into eight sections— and each organizer is responsible for an area. We get supporters to help us picket and leaflet; we go after one chain at a time, telling the shoppers where they can find other stores."[28] The power of this grass-roots coalition forced the Coachella and Delano grape producers to negotiate the historic table grape contracts in 1970. Huerta's executive abilities and influence were also apparent when she returned to New York to administer the lettuce, grape, and Gallo wine campaigns from 1973 to 1975.[29] The pressure of revived cross-class and cross-cultural cooperation in New York and across the nation led to the passage of the Agricultural Labor Relations Act, the first law to recognize the collective bargaining rights of farm workers in California."[30] During the late 1970s Huerta's leadership was spotlighted again; she assumed the directorship of the Citizenship Participation Day Department (CPD), the political arm of the UFW, which she administered until 1982.[31] In all these capacities, Huerta has served on the executive board of the UFW and participated in the highest levels of policy making in the union. She has proved a formidable strategist in the political contests for power within the union and has had a direct influence on guiding the UFW.

Chávez's and Huerta's differing approaches to trade union activism are also revealed in their relationship to the public world.

Helen Chávez has always preferred to remain out of the public eye—a personal choice, but also the result of a more traditional Mexican upbringing, lack of confidence due to limited education, and the fact that English is her second language, characteristics she shares with immigrant Mexicanas, many of whom speak only Spanish and have even less schooling. The most visible aspect of her life has been her four arrests, two of which were widely reported. The first occurred in the Delano area in 1966, when she was arrested with the celebrated group of "forty-four," many of whom were members of the clergy, for shouting "huelga" (the Spanish word for "strike"). "Being in jail didn't scare me," she explained, "because I know that what I'm doing is right and that I'm doing it for people who have worked and sacrificed so hard."[32] The second highly publicized incident took place in Arizona in 1978, when she was arrested with her husband for violating an all encompassing ban on picketing issued by a local magistrate. The two Chávezes underwent arrest to test the constitutionality of the ruling. "It was a disgusting, filthy jail," she recalled. "I went there and I started cleaning up the place where I had to stay. Mopping. And it was the worst jail I had been in."[33] Although her acts of civil disobedience have been few, her example has encouraged other Mexicanas and Chicanas to undergo arrest, thus expanding the social sphere for wives, grandmothers, aunts, and daughters in addition to women field workers in the UFW. Significantly, however, Helen Chávez shuns public appearances on her own and feels very uncomfortable in this role. One of her rare solo ventures occurred in Los Angeles at a fundraiser in 1976. "I will not speak [formally to the audience] because I have not spoken in front of a crowd," she told a reporter who was covering the event.[34] Instead, opting for the more traditional practice of female hospitality, Chávez chose to greet people personally in a reception line.

In contrast, Dolores Huerta's educational background and middle-class resources gave her self-confidence and made her, from her earliest association with the union, a sought-after public speaker. She has addressed countless labor, student, religious, women's, political, antiwar, environmental, and consumer groups. Through print, radio, and television, she has raised much-needed funds as well as public awareness of the UFW struggles.[35] Huerta has also been a very able lobbyist and advocate on behalf of farm workers before national, state, and local governmental committees. In frequent appearances before congressional bodies, she has forcefully argued the union's position on a wide range of issues from amending migration labor laws to the health problems of field workers to immigration policy. In 1984 she testified before a House committee:

> The Simpson-Mazzoli bill is a thinly disguised effort to stop labor organizing among farm workers. The other provisions of this bill, legalization, that would apply to so few it would be meaningless, sanctions that would be another political tool in the hands of the Immigration Service, would be used as they have always used their power: against unionization.[36]

Although an altered version of the bill eventually passed, the UFW's opposition to a guest worker provision prevailed. Probably Huerta's greatest asset has been her constant presence in the public eye as a representative of the UFW and the ease with which she has related to diverse constituencies, such as student, religious, labor, women's, and ethnic groups. A four-day trip to Michigan in 1974 typifies her total immersion in and dedication to *la causa*.

> In addition to boycott day, Dolores participated in a rally on the University of Michigan [Ann Arbor] campus, an Ecumenical Service in Detroit, a reception of trade union women, sponsored by the Coalition of Labor Union Women (CLUW) and a Mexican Independence Day Celebration in Pontiac, Michigan. Dolores appeared on two television programs, radio programs and did taped interviews. On the boycott day rally we got news coverage on 2 Detroit T.V. stations, a newspaper story, several radio stations and three feature articles were written on Dolores.[37]

Huerta, in contrast to Chávez, clearly relishes the demands of a public life.

Finally, the contrast between Chávez's traditionalism and Huerta's nontraditionalism appears in their divergent attitudes toward domesticity and home life. Chávez described her role as follows:

I felt that my job was at home taking care of my children. That was the most important thing to me and I felt, as a woman, [that] that's very important to a child. You have children and I think that your children should be raised by you, not by a babysitter.[38]

Despite the fact that Chávez went to work in the onion fields and grape vineyards to support her family during difficult economic times while her husband organized field workers, and despite her management of the UFW credit union, she still maintains that a woman's proper place is in the home. This value reflects the aspiration of many working-class Chicanas and recently immigrated Mexicanas who desired to care for their families like middle-class Anglo wives and mothers but were denied this opportunity because of economic need. Like black women, who were also forced to work, they were pushed into the labor force by the inferior wages their husbands earned in a racially segmented labor market.[39]

Huerta's perception of domesticity contrasts greatly with that of Chávez. To accommodate her hectic work and travel schedule and frequent residential changes, she made unorthodox child care arrangements, often leaving her children with nonfamily members and union supporters for extended periods of time. "You have to make a decision," she once told a reporter, "that if working with people, the people have the priority and the family must understand."[40] In another interview during a fundraising trip to Chicago, Huerta indicated her total commitment to the union. "There is so much to be done. My life is the union, every minute of it."[41] Like other prominent female labor leaders—Mother Jones, Lucy Parsons, Emma Tenayuca, and Luisa Moreno—Huerta reversed the traditional female priorities, placing personal autonomy and trade union activism before family life.[42]

Women who did not conform to the conventional model of femininity and domesticity were often subject to criticism and, at the very least, ambivalence.[43] While Chávez was praised by women in the union for keeping her family together under trying circumstances, Huerta, like her well-known predecessors, endured criticism from family, union colleagues, and the public at large for her nontraditional attitudes toward her personal and family life. "You could expect that

I would [get criticism from] farm workers themselves, but it mostly comes from middle class people," she explained in an interview. "They're more hung-up about these things than the poor people are, because the poor people have to haul their kids around from school to school, and women have to go out and work and they've got to either leave their kids or take them out to the fields with them. So they sympathize a lot more with my problems in terms of my children."[44] Huerta's distinct perceptions of wifehood and motherhood have also contributed to her two divorces. "I knew that I wasn't comfortable in a wife's role but I wasn't clearly facing the issue," she acknowledged. "I hedged, I made excuses, I didn't come out and tell my husband that I cared more about helping other people than cleaning our house and doing my hair."[45] Where many women might have resented household tasks, Huerta simply disregarded them.

One might argue that these differences with regard to politicization, work, public visibility, and domesticity merely reflect Huerta's and Chávez's differing personalities; and, indeed, personality does play a role in their choices. However, because the great majority of Chicanas and Mexicanas in the UFW follow Helen Chávez's path to union activism, a deeper process than temperament seems to be indicated here. That path is influenced by complex factors—class, cultural values, social expectations, views of motherhood, childrearing, and the sexual division of labor.[46]

Female UFW volunteers—such as María Luisa Rangel, who moved her family of nine to Detroit, Michigan, in 1968 for the grape boycott, or Juanita Valdez, who transplanted her eight children to Cincinnati, Ohio, in 1970 for the lettuce campaign, or Herminia Rodríguez, who relocated her family of six to Washington, D.C., in 1973 for the renewed grape, lettuce, and Gallo wine boycotts—have all participated as part of a family unit and juggled the competing interests of family, work, and union activism on behalf of the UFW. Chicanas and Mexicanas who manage the campesino (service) centers located primarily in rural communities throughout California continue in the Helen Chávez tradition. Female administrators of other union programs, such as Antonia González at the Agbayani Village (retirement home for farm workers), also emulate this pattern. Because their contribution to union building has blended with domestic responsibilities, it remains largely hidden from public view and goes unrecognized.

In contrast, Dolores Huerta's style of union activism attracts widespread attention and conveys the inaccurate impression that women in the UFW see in her a model for their own trade unionism. In actuality, Huerta's approach is a rare phenomenon. Women, usually U.S.-born, who rose to positions of prominence in the boycott, such as Jessica Govea, director of the Montreal operation, and Hope López, head of the Philadelphia effort, were exceptions like Dolores Huerta. In June 1969, out of forty-three boycott coordinators in major cities, thirty-nine were men and five were women. The elevation of those five to power was accomplished in spite of ambivalent and in some cases even hostile male attitudes toward women with authority. Recognizing their uncommon and tentative status, Hope López, whose ascent to the upper echelons of the union hierarchy was facilitated by the chronic shortage of male candidates and the crisis atmosphere of the union's early years, noted, "Of course, the real test for the female farmworkers will come after we win this strike. The female farmworker will either continue to help the administration of labor or she will be sent back to the labor room."[50] Chicanas and Mexicanas who aspire to nontraditional positions of power and decision making, such as women in the ranch committees (local union governance bodies), are also few in number and encounter obstacles to and gender-based criticism of their participation in this traditionally male-dominated activity. Ranch committee-women Mary Magaña, Carolina Guerrero, and Cleo Gómez demonstrated stamina and determination in resisting opposition from male family members and coworkers who did not accept women's participation at this level. Organizer Jessie de la Cruz remembered,

> It was very hard being a woman organizer. Many of our people my age and older were raised with the old customs in Mexico: where the husband rules, he is king of his house. The wife obeys, and the children, too. So when we first started it was very, very hard. Men gave us the most trouble—neighbors there in Parlier! They were for the union, but they were not taking orders from women, they said. When they formed the ranch committee at Christian Brothers—that's a big wine

company, part of it is in Parlier—the ranch committee was all men.[51]

Dolores Huerta's example encourages women struggling in such male-dominated areas of the union. But the admiration for her model also overshadows more traditional types of women's union activism, so that the essential contribution of the rank-and-file female union activists remains taken for granted.

The irony of this situation is that Huerta is an atypical, and perhaps impractical, model of female trade unionism in the UFW today. Huerta's activism most closely resembles the example of César Chávez, who

> Approached the work of helping the poor to help themselves in the only way his nature allowed with a single-mindedness that made everything else in his life—home, family, personal gain—secondary. For Chávez, nothing short of total immersion in the work of forcing change was enough. If his wife inherited virtually the entire responsibility for raising their children, Chávez remained unshaken in his belief that the promotion of the greater good made every sacrifice necessary and worthwhile.[52]

Given the existing sexual division of labor in the union and in society, few women are able or willing to relegate their personal lives or families to a secondary position in order to pursue union organizing. Thus, the more common form of female participation, a la Helen Chávez, remains "invisible"—unrecognized and unappreciated by union members as well as historians. Far from being a "single-handed" effort, the UFW was built and sustained by rank-and-file union members and supporters, including a great many Chicanas and Mexicanas. To appreciate fully the contribution of thousands of ordinary women to the process, researchers need to develop an expanded definition of union activism that takes into account the commitment of women who combine family responsibilities with labor activism.

Notes

I would like to thank Nancy Gabin, Carol Gioneman, and the anonymous readers at *Frontiers* for their thoughtful criticisms and suggestions.

1. For early popular treatments of the UFW see John Gregory Dunne, *Delano: The Story of the California Grape Strike* (New York Farrar, Straus and Giroux, 1966); Eugene Nelson, *Huelga: The First Hundred Days of the Great Delano Grape Strike* (Delano, Calif.: Farm Worker Press, 1966); Peter Matthiessen, *Sal Sí Puedes: César Chávez and the New American Revolution* (New York: Random House, 1970); Mark Day, *Forty Acres: César Chávez and the Farm Workers* (New York: Praeger Press, 1971); Joan London and Henry Anderson, *So Shall Ye Reap* (New York: Thomas Crowell Company, 1970). A second wave of literature about the UFW appeared during the mid 1970s and was written primarily by reporters who had covered the story firsthand; see, for example, Ronald B. Taylor, *Chávez and the Farm Workers* (Boston: Beacon Press, 1975); Jacques E. Levy, *César Chávez: Autobiography of La Causa* (New York: W. W. Norton, 1975); Dick Meister and Anne Loftis, *A Long Time Coming: The Struggle to Unionize America's Farm Workers* (New York: MacMillan, 1977); Sam Kushner, *Long Road to Delano* (New York: International Publishers, 1975). A quick review of the titles reveals the emphasis on César Chávez, president of the UFW. For the most scholarly work to appear on the UFW (which also includes analyses of previous farm labor insurgencies), see Linda C. Majka and Theo J. Majka, *Farm Workers, Agribusiness and the State* (Philadelphia: Temple University Press, 1982). While this monograph is the most analytical and interpretive work, it very rarely mentions the participation of Dolores Huerta, cofounder and first vice president of the union, in contrast to the earlier, firsthand, journalistic accounts. See also J. Craig Jenkins, *The Politics of Insurgency: The Farm Workers Movement in the 1960s* (New York: Columbia University Press, 1985).

2. Quoted in James Kirby Martin, et al., *America and Its People, From 1865.* Vol. 2 (Glenvine, IL.: Scott Foreman and Company, 1989), 930.

3. Alice Kessler-Harris, *Out to Work: A History of Wage-Earning Women in the United States* (Oxford University Press, 1982); Susan Levine, "Labor's True Woman: Domesticity and Equal Rights in the Knights of Labor" *Journal of American History* 70, no. 2 (September 1983): 323–39; Jacquelyn Dowd Hall, "Disorderly Women: Gender and Labor Militancy in the Appalachian South," *Journal of American History* 73, no. 2 (September 1986): 354–82; Nancy Gabin, "'They Have Placed a Penalty on Womanhood': The Protest Actions of Women Auto Workers in Detroit-Area UAW Locals, 1945, 1947," *Feminist Studies* no. 2 (Summer 1982): 373–98; Ruth Milkman, *Gender at Work: The Dynamics of Job Segregation by Sex during World War II* (Urbana: University of Illinois Press, 1987); Susan Porter Benson, *Counter Cultures: Saleswomen, Managers, and Customers in American Department Stores 1890–1940* (Urbana: University of Illinois Press, 1986); Patricia Cooper, *Once a Cigar Maker: Men, Women, and Work Culture in American Cigar Factories, 1900–1919* (Urbana: University of Illinois Press, 1987).

4. Jacqueline Jones, *Labor of Love, Labor of Sorrow: Black Women, Work, and the Family from Slavery to the Present* (New York: Basic Books, 1985); Dolores E. Jarnewski, *Sisterhood Denied: Race, Gender, and Class in a New South Community* (Philadelphia: Temple University Press, 1985); Karen Tucker Anderson, "Last Hired, First Fired: Black Women Workers during World War II," *Journal of American History* 69 (June 1982): 82–97; Lois Rita Helmbold, "Downward Occupational Mobility during the Great Depression: Urban Black and White Working Class Women," *Labor History* 29, no. 2 (Spring 1988): 135–72. Asian and Native American women have received the least historical treatment of all ethnic women. See for example Sylvia Van Kirk, *Many Tender Ties: Women in Fur-Trade Society, 1670–1870* (Norman: University of Oklahoma Press, 1980) and Evelyn Nakano Glenn, *Issei, Nisei, War Bride: Three Generations of Japanese American Women in Domestic Service* (Philadelphia: Temple University Press, 1986). For a recent historiographical article on women of color in an understudied region see Elizabeth Jameson, "Toward a Multicultural History of Women in the Western United States," *Signs* 13, no. 4 (Summer 1988): 761–91.

5. Mario T. García, "The Chicana in American History: The Mexican Women of El Paso, 1880–1920—A Case Study," *Pacific Historical Review* 49 (May 1980): 315–37; Vicki L. Ruiz, *Cannery Women, Cannery Lives: Mexican Women, Unionization, and the California Food Processing Industry, 1930–1950* (Albuquerque: University of New Mexico Press, 1987); Sarah Deutsch, *No Separate Refuge: Culture, Class, and Gender on an Anglo-Hispanic Frontier in the American Southwest, 1880–1940* (New York: Oxford University Press, 1987); Rosalinda M. Gonzáles, "Chicanas and Mexican Immigrant Families 1920–1940, Women's Subordination and Family Exploitation," in *Decades of Discontent, 1920–1940*, edited by Lois Scharf and Joan M. Jensen (Westport, Conn.: Greenwood Press, 1983), 59–84; Michael Wilson, with commentary by Deborah Silverton Rosenfelt, *Salt of the Earth* (Old Westhury, N.Y.: The Feminist Press, 1978); Laurie Coyle, Gail Hershatter, and Emily Honig, "Women at Farah: An Unfinished Story," in *Mexican Women in the United States: Struggles Past and Present*, edited by Magdalene Mora and Adelaida R. Del Castillo (Los Angeles: UCLA Chicano Studies Research Center Publications, 1980), 117–43; Patricia Zavella, *Women's Work and Chicano Families: Cannery Workers of the Santa Clara Valley* (Ithaca, N.Y.: Cornell University Press, 1987); Vicki L. Ruiz and Susan Tiano, eds., *Women on the US-Mexico Border: Responses to Change* (Boston: Allen & Unwin, 1987).

6. For a fuller explanation of this idea, see Margaret Eleanor Rose, "Women in the United Farm Workers: A Study of Chicana and Mexicans Participation in a Labor Union, 1950–1980" (Ph.D. diss., University of California, Los Angeles, 1988).

7. Although dealing with different places, times, and industries, the following articles have influenced my interpretation: Louise A. Tilly, "Paths of Proletarianization: Organization of Production, Sexual Division of Labor, and Women's Collective Action," *Signs* 7, no. 2 (Winter 1981): 400–17; Temma Kaplan, "Female Consciousness and Collective Action: The Case of Barcelona, 1910–1918," *Signs* 7, no. 3 (Spring 1982): 545–66.

8. Maxine Baca Zinn, in "Political Familism: Toward Sex Role Equality in Chicano Families," *Aztlán* 6, no. 1 (1975): 13–27, notes the phenomenon of family

participation in the struggle for Chicano civil rights. See also Kessler-Harris, *Out to Work*, passim.

9. Interview with Helen Chávez, Keene (La Paz), California, 12 July 1983, 1 (hereafter Chávez Interview). Helen Chávez was born 21 January 1928. Interview with Dolores Huerta, 2, Keene (La Paz), California, 4 February 1985, 69 (hereafter Huerta Interview 2). Huerta was born 10 April 1930.

10. For statistical data on the increased marriage rate in the postwar years, see U.S. Department of Commerce, Bureau of the Census, *A Statistical Portrait of Women in the United States* (Washington, D.C.: Government Printing Office, 1976), 15–20. For Chávez's courtship and marriage, see Levy, *Cesar Chávez*, 86–87, and Chávez Interview, 9. Huerta's first marriage was noted in the local newspaper, see *Stockton Record*, 20 April 1950.

11. Chávez Interview, 11. The following is a list of Helen Chávez's children's birth order and birth dates.

Fernando	20 February 1949
Sylvia	15 February 1950
Linda	22 January 1951
Eloise	13 May 1952
Anna	11 September 1953
Paul	23 March 1957
Elizabeth	15 February 1958
Anthony	12 August 1959

The list of Huerta's children was compiled from the following sources: Huerta Interview, 2, 80–81, 88–92; Interview with Dolores Huerta, 5, Keene (La Paz), California, 19 February 1985, 172–73 (hereafter Huerta Interview 5); Lori Head Survey (La Paz) 12 June 1984, 4; Alicia Huerta Hernández Survey (La Paz), 12 June 1984, 4. Head and Hernández are Huerta's daughters.

Celeste	1951	First Marriage
Lori	1952	
Fidel	1956	Second Marriage
Emilio	1957	
Vincent	1958	
Alicia	1959	
Angela	1963	
Juanita	1970	Third Relationship
María Elena	1972	
Ricky	1973	
Camilla	1976	

12. Richard Griswold del Castillo, *La Familia: Chicano Families in the Urban Southwest, 1848 to the Present* (Notre Dame, IN: University of Notre Dame Press, 1984), 96–106. The author discusses the variations between native-born Mexican American and immigrant Mexican families in terms of bilingualism, assimilation, employment patterns, economic conditions, and cultural values. New Mexican Hispanics have considered their history and experience distinct from that of immigrant Mexican families; for an exploration of their past, see Nancie L. Gonzáles,

The Spanish-Americans of New Mexico: A Heritage of Pride (Albuquerque: University of New Mexico Press, 1967), 1–85. For biographical data see Interview with Dolores Huerta, 1, Keene (La Paz), California, 16 March 1984, 1–8, 14, and 39 (hereafter Huerta Interview 1), and Chávez Interview, 1–3, 5–6.

13. Huerta graduated from Stockton High School in 1947 and later went onto Stockton Junior College, where she was awarded an Associate Arts degree (a two-year program); see *Who's Who in Labor* (New York: Arno Press, 1976), 283, and *Stockton Record*, 20 April 1950. See also Jean Murphy, "Unsung Heroine of La Causa," *Regeneración* 1, no. 10 (1971): 20. For statistics on college attendance for Spanish-surnamed women, see U.S. Department of Commerce, Bureau of the Census, *Population Characteristics of Selected Ethnic Groups in Five Southwestern States* (Washington, D.C.: GPO, 1960), 2. Graduation from high school and college attendance were rare accomplishments for Latinas, as revealed by this census report conducted in 1960. Even in these later years, only 14.2 percent of Spanish-surnamed women in the Southwest completed four years of high school. This number contrasted with a figure of 31.2 percent for Anglo women. Latinas who achieved between one and three years of college fell dramatically, to 3.2 percent. The corresponding figure for Anglo women was 13 percent. Huerta's family provided her with advantages and exposure not generally available to Mexican American women of her generation.

14. Rodolfo Acuña, *Occupied America. A History of Chicanos*, 2nd ed. (New York: Harper & Row, 1981), 329–30.

15. Dunne, *Delano*, 66–67. On these pages, Fred Ross, an organizer for the CSO, explained that he got the Chávezes' name as prospective recruits from a Mexican American public health nurse employed at a well-baby clinic visited by Helen Chávez. See also Matthiesen, *Sal Sí Puedes*, 43–50 and Levy, *César Chávez*, 97–99.

16. Quoted in Chávez Interview, 23. For an analysis of the CSO see Ralph Guzmán, *The Political Socialization of the Mexican American People* (New York: Arno Press, 1976), 137–43.

17. Huerta is mentioned by name as a contact person in a newspaper article describing a regional CSO meeting in Stockton; see *Stockton Record*, 25 July 1958.

18. Huerta's activity as the CSO legislative representative is noted in *CSO Reporter*, n.d. (circa 1959), Ernesto Galarza Collection, Box 13, Folder 8, p. 2, Department of Special Collections, Stanford University (hereafter Galarza Collection, Stanford).

19. London and Anderson, *So Shall Ye Reap*, 39–78 and 79–98. The authors have devoted a chapter to the Agricultural Workers Association (AWA) in which they mention the activities of Dolores Huerta. London and Anderson also discuss the AFL-CIO–sponsored Agricultural Workers Organizing Committee (AWOC), founded in 1959, in which Huerta participated. The director of AWOC notes the hiring of Dolores Huerta and her election to the office of secretary of AWOC; see correspondence from Norman Smith to Don Vial, 13 July 1959, AWOC Collection, Box 2, Folder 7, Archives of Labor and Urban Affairs, Walter P. Reuther Library Wayne State University, Detroit, Michigan (hereafter ALUA).

20. Quoted in Levy, *César Chávez*, 145.

21. Quoted in letter from César Chávez to Fred Ross, 2 May 1962, Fred Ross Collection, Box 3, Folder 6, ALUA.

22. Quoted in Barbara L. Baer and Glenna Matthews, "'You Find a Way': The Women of the Boycott," *The Nation*, 23 February 1974, 237.

23. Helen Chávez, along with her husband, was an original member of the credit union; see Articles of Incorporation of Farm Workers Credit Union, 21 July 1963, UFW Small Collection, Box 4, no folder, ALUA. (The original document is now stored in the archive's vault. Note: Most of the UFW collection is unprocessed.) Statistics collected by the National Credit Union Administration for 1985 reported a membership figure of 2,389 and listed the total number of loans issued for the year as 273; see National Credit Union Administration, Financial Statement for UFW, 1985, 3–4.

24. Huerta was the only woman elected to the National Farm Workers Association, the precursor to the UFW. She was a vice president. The other original officers were César Chávez, general director; Manuel Chávez, secretary-treasurer; Gilbert Padilla and Roger Terrones, vice presidents. See César Chávez to Fred Ross, 24 January 1963, Fred Ross Collection, Box 3, Series I, Folder 11, Correspondence, 1963, ALUA.

25. Quoted in Taylor, *Chávez*, 217. Huerta explained that she used the ILWU (Long-shoreman) pineapple-worker contracts for Hawaiian workers as her model. For an example of early UFWOC contracts, see Collective Bargaining Agreement between DiGiorgio and United Farm Workers Organizing Committee, 13 January 1966, Anne Draper Collection, Box 20, Folder 173, Department of Special Collections, Stanford University (hereafter Draper Collection, Stanford). For a winery contract, see United Farm Workers Organizing Committee (hereafter UFWOC), Box 2, Folder: Almaden Vineyards Contract, 1967, ALUA. The Almaden contract was negotiated by Huerta after a card check election held 28 June 1967. A minimum wage of $1.80 plus standard UFWOC benefits were guaranteed; see *El Malcriado*, 16 August 1967.

26. Taylor, *Chávez*, 217.

27. Quoted in Barbara L. Baer, "Stopping Traffic: One Woman's Cause," *The Progressive* 39, no. 9 (September 1975): 39–40. For an opposite opinion, see Kushner, *Long Road*, 185.

28. Taylor, *Chávez*, 229–30.

29. For Huerta's involvement in the 1968 boycott, see a sample of her correspondence with New York union leaders: letter from Dolores Huerta to Patrick Gleason (Retail Food Clerks), 18 January 1968, in UFWOC, New York Boycott, sec #376, Box 6, Folder 6, Huerta Correspondence, 1968, ALUA. Huerta generated a tremendous amount of publicity on the strike and boycott; see, for instance, [New York] *International* (official publication of the Seafarers' International Union of North America) 1, no. 2 (February 1968). Vivid accounts of Huerta's participation in the negotiations with Delano grape growers in 1970 appear in Levy, *César Chávez*,

313–25, and Day, *Forty Acres*, 161–68. Huerta again headed the New York boycott effort and coordinated the East Coast boycott operations in 1973. For a typical staff meeting and local coordinators' reports, see Minutes, Staff Meeting, 22 May 1973, UFW New York Boycott Office (acc 6125/78), Box 1, Folder: Weekly Meetings-Minutes, ALUA. For a report on success in the chain store campaign, see East Coast Boycott News, 27 July 1973, UFW Chicago Boycott Office (sec 2/3176), Box 2, Folder: Dolores Huerta File, ALUA.

30. Majka and Majka, *Farm Workers*, 233–47. See also Meister and Loftis, *A Long Time Coming*, 215–28.

31. Huerta's assumption of the directorship of the CPD is noted in an open letter to UFW supporters; see "Dear Brothers and Sisters from the Northern California Boycott Staff," n.d. (circa April 1978), Anne Loftis Collection, Box 8, Folder 2, Department of Special Collections, Stanford University (hereafter Loftis Collection). For César Chávez's congratulatory comments on Huerta's legislative achievements as director of the CPD, see *Acta de cuarta convención constitucional de la unión de campesinos de America*, AFL-CIO, 12 Agosto 1979, Salinas, California, 24–25 (Proceedings of the Fourth Constitutional Convention of the UFW).

32. Quoted in Chávez Interview, 33. For the first arrest of Helen Chávez in 1965, see *Bakersfield Californian*, 20 October 1965. See also Levy, *César Chávez*, 192–93.

33. Quoted in Chávez Interview, 33–34. Accounts of her Arizona arrest with her husband, César Chávez, were reported in several newspapers; see *Yuma Daily Sun*, 14 June 1978, and *Los Angeles Times*, 25 June 1978. See also Majka and Majka, *Farm Workers*, 253.

34. *Los Angeles Times*, 2 February 1976.

35. For example, after her address to the delegates, Huerta was presented with a $10,000 check by the Amalgamated Clothing Workers of America at their convention held in Miami in 1968; see (Washington, D.C.) *AFL-CIO News*, 8 June 1968, UFWOC Box 9, Folder: *AFL-CIO News*, 1968, ALUA. In addition, Huerta has made countless speeches and commentaries on radio and television. See, for example, Transcript, PBS, "The Advocates": 8 March 1973, "Should You Support the National Lettuce Boycott?" Dolores Huerta, discussant, Vertical Files, Chicano Studies Center Research Library, UCLA.

36. Quoted from U S. Congress, House, Subcommittee on Labor Standards of the Committee on Education and Labor, Hearings on Immigration Reform and Agricultural Guestworkers, 98th Cong., 2nd sess., 11 April and 3 May 1984, 21–27, especially 21. For earlier examples of her testimony, see U.S. Congress, Senate, Subcommittee on Migratory Labor of the Committee on Labor and Public Welfare, Amending Migratory Labor Laws: Hearings on S.1864, S.1865, S.1866, S.1866 and S1868, 89th Cong., 1st and 2nd sess., 16 March 1966, 690–95. See also U.S. Congress, House, Special Subcommittee on Labor of the Committee on Education and Labor, Extension of National Labor Relations Act to Agricultural Employees: Hearing on HR. 4769, 90th Congress, 1st sess., 1, 4, 5, 8, 9, and 12 May 1967, 81–91.

37. Report on Activities for International Boycott Day, 14 September 1974, UFW Boycott Central (sec May 1977), Box 2, Folder: Michigan, Detroit 1974, ALUA. [Detroit] *Sunday News*, 15 September 1974. [Detroit] *Solidaridad Motor-City Boycott*, November 1974, UFW Cleveland, Ohio Boycott (acc 1/17175), Box 1, Folder: Boycott Newsletters, 1973-74, ALUA.

38. Chávez Interview, 23-24.

39. Zavella, *Women's Work and Chicano Families*, 154-59. The author also notes women's ambivalence over work and family roles. For black women see Jacqueline Jones, *Labor of Love*, passim.

40. Quoted in typed transcript of interview with Dolores Huerta by Ron Taylor at the AFL-CIO convention in Miami, 1974, Ron Taylor Collection, Series 11, Box 9, Folder 21, ALUA.

41. Quoted in *Chicago Tribune*, 19 April 1975.

42. James J. Kenneally, *Women and American Trade Unions* (St. Albans, VT: Eden Press Women's Publications, Inc., 1978), 92-118; Carolyn Ashburgh, *Lucy Parsons: American Revolutionary* (Chicago: Charles Kerr Publishing Co., 1976), passim; "Living History: Emma Tenayuca Tells Her Story," *The Texas Observer*, 28 October 1983): 7-15; Ruiz, *Cannery Women*, 104-5, 107-8, 113, 116, 119.

43. Kessler-Harris, *Out to Work*, 235. Hall, "Disorderly Women," 354-82.

44. Quoted in [San Bernardino, Calif.] 82 *Chicano* 7, no. 34 (25 January 1973): 3. In addition, Huerta cites her father's opposition to her unconventional family and personal life. Huerta's second husband, Ventura Huerta, vigorously opposed her nontraditional attitudes and child-care practices. Huerta alludes to her disagreements with her husband over the care of their children in Barbara L. Baer and Glenna Matthews, "'You Find a Way,'" 234. See also Huerta Interview, 1, 43-49.

45. Quoted in Baer, "Stopping Traffic," 39.

46. Kessler-Harris, *Out to Work*, passim. Milkman, *Gender at Work*, passim.

47. Margaret Rose, "From the Fields to the Picket Line: Huelga Women and the Boycott: 1965-1975": *Labor History* (forthcoming).

48. Rose, "Women in the United Farm Workers," chapter 6.

49. Interview with Antonia Guajarda Gonzáles, Delano, California, 7 October 1983.

50. Quoted from rough draft of typed text, no title, "The female farmworker is as unique . . ." [by Hope Lopéz), 20 March 1970, UFW, Philadelphia Boycott Office, Box 5, Folder 13, ALUA.

51. For quotation from de la Cruz, see Ellen Cantarow, "Jessie López De La Cruz: The Battle for Farmworkers' Rights" in *Moving the Mountain: Women Working for Social Change*, edited by Ellen Cantarow, Susan Gushee O'Malley, and Sharon Hartman Strom (Old Westbury NY: The Feminist Press, 1980), 136-37. For ranch committee women, see Rose, "Women in the United Farm Workers," chapter 7. For the difficulties of other working women in the male-dominated world of trade

unionism, see Ruth Milkman, "Women Workers, Feminism and the Labor Movement since the 1960s" in *Women, Work, and Protest: A Century of US Women's Labor History*, edited by Ruth Milkman (Boston: Routledge & Kegan Paul, 1985), 306.

52. Quoted in Cletus E. Daniel, "César Chávez and the Unionization of California Farm Workers" in *Labor Leaders in America*, edited by Melvyn Dubofsky and Warren Van Tine (Chicago: University of Illinois Press, 1987), 360.

Dolores Huerta on Picket Line, Delano, 1966. Courtesy of John A. Kouns.

5

Unsung Heroine of La Causa

Jean Murphy

If César Chávez is the hero of the farm workers' movement, Dolores Huerta is its unheralded heroine.

As vice president and director of negotiations for the AFL-CIO United Farm Workers Organizing Committee, Mrs. Huerta plays a key role as she has since its beginning—in the union's struggle for contracts with California's growers. However, her name is almost unknown outside the movimiento. The role is not easy. Eighteen hour days of planning the lettuce boycott, of speaking at rallies, of negotiating, or traveling and of seeking public support for La Causa are more common than not.

$5 a Week

Nor is the work well paid. Like all other union officials and employees, she makes a salary of $5 a week and a subsistence largely depending upon contributions of food and clothing.

"All of us have very exotic wardrobes. We get our clothes out of donations," Mrs. Huerta said during a recent trip to Los Angeles, where the only adornment on her hand-me-downs was a new boycott button.

Clothes and comfort mean little to her. Home these days is a sofa in an organizer's house in Fresno but she sleeps wherever her work takes her. She eats, when she remembers to eat, "the groceries our supporters give us."

Down from Delano

She is divorced and her seven children are scattered from the University of Oregon to the homes of relatives and friends. She is known

Originally published in *Regeneración*, I, 1971, p. 20.

among co-workers as a dedicated, tireless leader, second only to Chávez, who is devoting her life to the movement.

The union, she said, is seeking to replace the "inhuman" piece rate system with contracts providing for minimum hourly wages, medical and death benefits and pesticide controls.

"The average life span of a farm worker is 49 years," she said. "It makes you want to cry. None of us want our food at that price."

Mrs. Huerta, 40, began as a farm worker when she was a 14-year-old Stockton girl, picking cherries and tomatoes. . . . Her mother worked in canneries but refused to work in the fields.

Real Problems

"With no toilets in the fields, even going to the bathroom was a real problem," explained Mrs. Huerta, who, even after her marriage, worked in the vineyards of Delano.

In the meantime, she had earned a provisional teaching credential by attending Stockton Junior College and taking night classes at the University of the Pacific. She taught for a year in Stockton.

"I realized one day that as a teacher I couldn't do anything for the kids who came to school barefoot and hungry," she said.

She joined Chávez in the Community Service Organization and, in 1962, they began organizing the farm workers. Today, about 30,000 farm workers are covered by union contract.

"We couldn't have a union without the women," says Mrs. Huerta, who insists that other women are the real heroines of the movement. "Their sacrifices have been unbelievable. And the participation of women has helped keep the movement nonviolent.

"They're so damn poor. It's necessary for most of the women to work in the fields. Imagine trying to keep a family together when you're migrant workers living in extreme poverty and your kids still have to work in the fields, too."

Bad Treatment

"Women in the fields get treated very badly . . . with additional humiliation and indignities. When you get propositioned by a foreman, all you can do is quit.

"I can remember picking tomatoes for 11 cents a lug—one day my husband and I together made $4—and there was just one old beer can for all of the workers to drink water out of.

"Those are some of the reasons women are so strong for the union. They want to get rid of this system."

Among women field workers who now hold positions of responsibility in the union are Mrs. Chávez, its credit union manager; Gloria Soto, in charge of services; and Ester Uranday, in charge of membership.

"Working in the fields is the only other work they've done," Mrs. Huerta said.

The only woman among five vice presidents of the union, Mrs. Huerta is also often the only woman at the negotiating table.

"César doesn't like to negotiate," she said. "And maybe the growers take scoldings from me that they wouldn't take from a man."

6

The Women of the Boycott

Barbara L. Baer and Glenna Matthews

Dolores Huerta, vice president of the United Farm Workers, was standing on a flat-bed truck beside César Chávez. She didn't show her eight-and-a-half months' pregnancy, but she looked very tired from the days and nights of organizing cross-country travel plans for the hundreds of people who were now waiting in the parking lot along-side the union headquarters at Delano, Calif. She leaned down and talked with children, her own and others. Small children held smaller ones, fathers carried babies on their shoulders.

The parking lot was filled with cars, trucks and buses, decorated with banners and signs. People sang strike songs and Chávez spoke to them about the boycott. Dolores listened intently, nodding, brushing her straight black hair away from her face from time to time and smiling softly at the children. A priest blessed the cars and buses whose destinations read like a history of the great American migrations in reverse: *"Hasta la Victoria-Miami!"; "Viva la Huelga-Cleveland!"; "Hasta La Boycott-Pittsburgh!"*

Five years ago there would have been nothing unusual about families assembling to move out with the crops, but this time the decision to pull up roots was different. The people on the dusty blacktop were UFW members and until a week earlier they had had a commitment to stay in the area. The union had made it possible for most to have a house or rent one, send their children to a school all year, get medical care. Most of these people had spent the summer on strike lines or in jails. They, within one week of César Chávez's announcement of a national boycott of grapes, had sold their houses and everything they could not carry with them to buy the cars, winter clothing, whatever

---

Originally published in *The Nation*, February 23, 1974, pp. 232–38.

else they might need for years outside the San Joaquin Valley. They were ready to leave by the last day in August.

We had come to Delano specifically to meet Dolores Huerta. As we waited for the caravan to leave, she told us to look well at the other women. These women were "nonmaterialistic." They packed up their families and pledged them to stay out on the boycott until the union got its grape and lettuce contracts back. If the woman of a family refuses, Dolores said, the family either breaks up or is lost to the union. Families are the most important part of the UFW because a family can stick it out in a strange place, on $5 a week per person, the wage everyone in the union is paid (plus expenses). Often the leaders would be women because women were strong at home and becoming stronger in the union. The women led the fate of the union, Dolores told us.

Chávez and Dolores Huerta knew the people they were talking about—and what they were asking of UFW members they asked of themselves first. All summer the union fought to win second contracts from the grape growers in southern and central California valleys who had signed with them first in 1970. But as each contract expired, the Teamsters signed up the growers immediately—thirty at once around Delano. Chávez called the contracts illegal, "sweetheart agreements," because the workers had not voted on their representatives. Chávez called for pickets on the Teamsters-contracted fields. County courts, sympathetic to the growers, enjoined the UFW strikers from active picketing. Thousands of clergy and students came to support the farm workers and some were jailed. Jailings and trials went on all summer.

Farm workers have never won a major strike in the fields because they are not protected by the National Labor Relations Act, whose provisions guarantee the right to picket, because growers and their allies have used violence and, most important, because there is an unlimited scab labor force across the Mexican border. There is no way to win a strike when men will scab at any price.

Toward the end of the summer the picket lines became violent. In separate incidents in the town of Arvin, two union men were killed. A sheriff struck Nagi Daifullah, a Yemenite, on the head with a flashlight. Juan de la Cruz was shot as he came off the picket line.

The United Farm Workers would not fight violence with violence. When the funerals were over, Chávez called for all strikers to get ready to leave on a second national boycott. The first had lasted five years. This one, though better organized, was more complicated: there were now grapes, wines, lettuce and Teamsters as well as the growers.

By noon the dust had settled in a low haze on this crossroads between vineyards—the stucco buildings the UFW calls "Forty Acres." The union offices were nearly empty, though telephones kept ringing. We went into a bare room with a long table to talk to Dolores Huerta.

Dolores was the first person Chávez called upon to work with him organizing farm workers into a union. That was more than a dozen years ago. She became the UFW's first vice president, its chief negotiator, lobbyist, boycott strategist and public spokeswoman. And in partnership, Dolores and Chávez formulated the UFW's nonviolent and democratic philosophy.

In 1955, Fred Ross brought Dolores Huerta to a meeting of the Community Service Organization in Stockton, and she has been in political action ever since. Ross, working in San Jose with Saul Alinsky, had taken César Chávez to his first CSO meeting there. Both Dolores and César say they owe their present lives to Fred Ross, and they keep drawing the thin, spare man, now 60, away from his book about the union and back into UFW struggles.

When Dolores began organizing, she already had six children and was pregnant with a seventh. Nearly twenty years later, there are ten children, and Dolores is still so slim and graceful that we find it hard to imagine her in her youth, the age of her daughter. She has not saved herself for anything, has let life draw and strain her to a fine intensity. It hasn't made her tense, harsh or dry. She shouts a lot and laughs with people. She tells us she has a sharp tongue but it seems to us she has an elusiveness of keeping her own counsel, mixed with complete directness and willingness to spend hours talking. Her long black hair is drawn back from high cheek bones, her skin is tanned reddish from the sun on the picket line, and in her deep brown eyes is a constant humor that relieves her serious manner.

Contradictions in her life must have taken, and continue to take, a toll: her many children, Catholic faith and a divorce, her high-strung nerves and the delicate health we know she disregards. It must be that her work, the amount she has accomplished and the spirit she instills in others, have healed the breaks. We talked to Dolores Huerta for several hours in the union offices when the last cars had left Delano.

"I had a lot of doubts to begin with, but I had to act in spite of my conflict between my family and my commitment. My biggest problem was not to feel guilty about it. I don't any more, but then, everybody used to lay these guilt trips on me, about what a bad mother I was, neglecting my children. My own relatives were the hardest, especially when my kids were small; I had six and one on the way when I started and I was driving around Stockton with all these little babies in the car, the different diaper changes for each one. It's always hard, not just because you're a woman but because it's hard to really make that commitment. It's in your own head. I'm sure my own life was better because of my involvement. I was able to go through a lot of very serious personal problems and survive them because I had something else to think about. Otherwise, I might have gotten engulfed in my personal difficulties and, I think, I probably would have gone under.

"If I hadn't met Fred Ross then, I don't know if I ever would have been organizing. People don't realize their own worth and I wouldn't have realized what I could do unless someone had shown faith in me. At that time we were organizing against racial discrimination— the way Chicanos were treated by police, courts, politicians. I had taken the status quo for granted, but Fred said it could change. So I started working.

"The way I first got away from feeling guilty about neglecting my family was a religious cop-out, I guess. I had serious doubts whether I was doing the right thing, giving kids a lousy supper to go to a council meeting. So I would pray and say, if what I was doing wasn't bearing fruit, then it would be a sign I shouldn't be doing it. When good things came out of my work, when it bore fruit, I took that as a sign I should continue and that the sacrifices my family and I were making were justified.

"Of course, I had no way of knowing what the effects on my kids would be. Now, ten years later, I can look back and say it's O.K. because my kids turned out fine, even though at times they had to fend for themselves, other people took care of them, and so on. I have a kind of proof: my ex-husband took one of my kids, Fidel, during the first strike. We didn't have any food or money, there was no way I could support him. He was eating all right, like all the strikers' kids, but on donations. So my ex-husband took the boy until he was 11. I got him back just last year. He had a lot of nice clothes and short hair, but he was on the verge of a nervous breakdown. When my ex-husband tried to take another boy, the judge ruled against him. You could see the difference when you compared the two kids—one was skinny and in raggedy clothes and with long hair, but real well, happy. Fidel is coming back now to the way he used to be, and he's got long hair too.

"We haven't had a stable place to live—I haven't been anywhere for more than two months, except in New York on the boycott—since 1970. But taking my kids all over the states made them lose their fear of people, of new situations. Most of us have to be mobile. But the kids are in school, they go to school and work on the boycott. Even the 10-year-olds are out on the boycott in the cities.

"My kids are totally politicized mentally and the whole idea of working without materialistic gain has made a great difference in the way they think. When one of our supporters came to take my daughter to buy new clothes in New York, she was really embarrassed. We never buy new clothes, you know, we get everything out of the donations. She said, 'Mama, the lady wanted to buy me a lot of new things, but I told her they didn't fit me.' You know, she came home with a couple of little things to please the lady, but she didn't want to be avaricious. Her values are people and not things. It has to be that way—that's why everyone who works full-time for the union gets $5 a week, plus gas money and whatever food and housing they need to live on, live on at the minimum they can."

How has it happened, we asked, that in the very culture from which the word "machismo" derives, the women have more visible, vocal and real power of decision than women elsewhere? Dolores told us that the union had made a conscious effort to involve women, given them every chance for leadership, but that the men did not always want it.

"I really believe what the feminists stand for. There is an undercurrent of discrimination against women in our own organization, even though César goes out of his way to see that women have leadership positions. César always felt strongly about women in the movement.

This time, no married man went out on the boycott unless he took his wife. We find daycare in the cities so the women can be on the picket line with the men. It's a great chance for participation. Of course we take it for granted now that women will want to be as involved as men. But in the beginning, at the first meetings, there were only men. And a certain discrimination still exists. César—and other men—treat us differently. César's stricter with the women, he demands more of us. But the more I think of it, the more I'm convinced that the women have gotten strong because he expects so much of us. You could even say it's gotten lopsided . . . women are stronger than the men.

"Women in the union are great on the picket line. More staying power, and we're nonviolent. One of reasons our union is nonviolent is that we want our women and children involved, and we stay nonviolent because of the women and children.

"One time the Teamsters were trying to provoke a fight to get our picketers arrested. Forty, fifty police were waiting with paddy wagons. We had about 300 people. The Teamsters attacked the line with 2 X 4 boards. I was in charge of the line. We made the men go to the back and placed the women out in front. The Teamsters beat our arms but they couldn't provoke the riot they wanted and we didn't give in. The police stood there, watch us get beaten; the D.A. wouldn't even let us sign a complaint. But we had gained a lot of respect from our men. Excluding women, protecting them, keeping women at home, that's the middle-class way. Poor people's movements have always had whole families on the line, ready to move at a moment's notice, with more courage because that's all we had. It's a class not an ethnic thing."

We knew that the women of the UFW found themselves in a unique situation. Unlike the sex-determined employment of the urban poor, the jobs of farm worker women and men had always been the same. They had to work, but it wasn't housework or even factory work separating them from men. Women had picked, pruned and packed in fields, canneries and sheds side by side with men. But would the women decide to let the men organize the union? Dolores Huerta had spoken for herself alone; the resolution of conflicts between family, political, union action, would come to each UFW women in her own terms.

Lupe Ortíz has been an organizer in a union field office since she left school. She is about 25, a natural leader, with a quality of making people laugh to get work done. Yet for all her big voice and humor, she didn't know how women could assert themselves at home as they did at work. What she told us seemed the reverse of our more familiar, middle-class feminism; here, by contrast, a woman insisted on work equality, and in large part received it, but she wouldn't challenge the traditional order of the family.

As Lupe directed her male co-workers in Spanish, she expounded to us in English the differences between Anglo and Chicano women. "You Anglo women, you do it your way, but I don't ever want to be equal to my husband."

"You get the same salary; don't you want the same voice at home?"

"In work, but not at home. No, at home you have to know when to open your mouth and when not to. You have to learn you can't go places men go, like bars."

"Don't you want it to change? For men to act as though you're equal?"

"It's not exactly equality. It's our culture. I don't want our Chicano culture to change. Let men have the say-so." Lupe laughed, this time openly, as she looked at the men in the office. "I bet you split up with your husbands more often than we do because you make head-on conflicts."

Ester Yurande, a generation older than Lupe, showed a generation difference in her appearance: she was as carefully, femininely dressed, with lovely long hair and glittering earrings, as Lupe had been rugged in jeans, sweatshirt and close-cropped curls. Ester had worked in the fields until she became the bookkeeper for the Medical Clinic at Forty Acres. She had been a UFW member from the start, been jailed in the early 1960s. How, we asked her, had the union changed the lives of the women who came to the clinic?

"A doctor treats us with dignity now. We don't get charity when we're having a baby, we get care. It's to do with pride. Mexican women around here used to do what the men said, but Dolores Huerta was our example of something different. We could see one of our leaders was a woman, and she was always out in front, and she would talk back. She wasn't scared of anything."

Dolores herself had told us that she didn't hesitate to argue. "You know, César has fired me fifteen times, and I must have quit about ten. Then, we'll call each other up and get back to work. There have been times when I should have fought harder. When he tells me now, 'you're getting really impossible, arguing all the time,' I say, 'you haven't seen anything yet. I'm going to get worse.' Because from now on, I'm going to fight really, really hard when I believe something. There have been times I haven't. I can be wrong too, but at least it will be on the record how I felt."

When we asked Ester how she felt about fighting back herself, she didn't want to answer. We had become outsiders once more, women who didn't comprehend her way. Men have accepted strong women in the union, but there remains deeply engrained in these women a respect for their men's *machismo*.

There is a religious fervor about the union, which has made its members call it La Causa. Perhaps the closeness of the Catholic Church to the movement is one more reason women have been able to identify with its goals. The UFW women have brought their personal strength and their faith to the union; the union in turn has reinforced and completed their lives by giving them a direct form of action and an ideal.

Dolores, very religious herself, told us that women were most important to the union because a woman determined the fate of a whole family. If a wife was for the union, Dolores said, then the husband would be, too. If she was not, if she was afraid or too attached to her home and possessions, then the family usually stayed out of the union, or it broke up. There had been a number of broken marriages that had cost the union the strength of a united family.

María-Luisa Rangel did not want to go out on the first boycott. At that time—in 1968—many women were staying in California while the men lived together in boycott houses in Eastern cities. The Rangels, parents of eight children, had saved enough money to own part of a family store, and they owned their home in the small town of Dinuba, near Fresno. They would have to part with both if they went to Detroit for two years. Hijino Rangel was determined to go. So María-Luisa went. Looking at her unsoftened features, her inaccessible but not unfriendly black eyes, we sensed the strength that had enabled her then to wrench herself away from everything she owned and keep her family together. She had a hard time in Detroit; she didn't know much English, the climate was completely strange; and she had two operations in the city. But when they returned to the valley in 1970, the Rangels knew that they had helped win the boycott that secured the 180 union contracts with grape growers of the Coachella and San Joaquin Valleys. And the experience had worked on María-Luisa. She spoke out as a representative of the union about the present boycott. "It's just like it was then. The struggle is for the people to win, not the growers but the people. I know it, and they—the growers—know it."

Women have paid different prices for making the union part of their lives. The 100 women who spent many weeks in Fresno jails last summer (for violating anti-picket injunctions) ranged from minors to great-grandmothers. There were field workers and nuns, lay religious women and union officials. For some of the Chicano women, it was a reminder of previous jailings when no nuns had been present and the guards had beaten "the Mexicans." For others, it was the first time, and almost a vacation from their daily lives. Work-hardened baked hands became almost soft. All the women shared their experiences—the farm workers told city women like Dorothy Day, editor of the *Catholic Worker*, about their struggle, and learned from her about women's movements in the cities and in the Church.

Maximina de la Cruz and her husband, Juan, were born around 1910 in Mexico. Juan entered America on the bracero program, picked crops in Texas and then in New Mexico, where Maximina worked in a clothing factory. They married, moved with their son to the San Joaquin Valley in 1960, and joined the union during the first strikes in 1965. Juan de la Cruz was killed last summer by a man who fired his .22-caliber rifle into the picket line from a truck. Maximina told us she remembers that many times the growers or the Teamsters put on deputy badges, joined in beating the farm workers, and then arrested them on grounds of self-defense. The man who shot de la Cruz has entered a plea in valley courts that he shot defending himself from the picket line.

Maximina was observing the thirty-day mourning period when we came to her home in Arvin. Hearing us arrive, she and her mother, Porfiria Coronado, met us at their gate, and without a word, in the dark, she took us, with hands that felt like warm, worked clay, into her living room. Candles beneath pictures of saints and near a wedding photograph were the only light. As the night went on, she told us of her early life of hardship, the many moves, purchase of their small house, and the changes the UFW had made in their lives.

"We *know* the growers. They want to go back to the old days, the way it was before we had a union, when we got a dollar an hour, no toilets or water in the fields, no rest periods, and they could kick you out without any pay for not picking fast enough. A whole family earned less than one union man today. They fought us hard and dirty each time, but we didn't give in. We won't. This time we're out in the cities again to tell the good people what it is like to work here. I'm staying on here, and I'll be back at work in the fields, but not until the union gets its contracts back. I might have to wait a while but I know people will understand and help us win back our union. I'm proud to be a woman here. Juan was proud of the union. You know, on the picket lines, we were so gay, peaceful and *attrativas*, even the grandmothers. Until *they* shot their gun."

Except for the Catholic Church, the powerful and wealthy institutions of California have opposed the UFW at one time or another. Grower-biased central valley law enforcement and the courts have made a mockery of legal institutions; agri-business has never given up trying to break the union through legislation; Gov. Ronald Reagan has been photographed eating scab grapes; even the U.S. Government helped the growers by buying non-union lettuce in great quantity to ship to troops in Vietnam. Yet the greater the odds, the more the union has come to represent poor people against the rich and mighty. Dolores Huerta fights best when the situation looks bleakest. She attributes her refusal to give up to her mother's influence.

"My mother was one of those women who do a lot. She was divorced, so I never really understood what it meant for a woman to take a back seat to a man. My brothers would say, 'Mama spoiled you,' because she pushed me to the front. When I was first involved in organizing, my mom would watch the kids for me, but then she got involved herself and she couldn't baby-sit anymore. She won the first prize in Stockton for registering voters and increasing membership.

"To tell the truth, I was prejudiced against women for a long time and I didn't realize it. I always liked to be with men because I thought they were more interesting and the women only talked of kids. But I was afraid of women, too. It was in the union that I lost my fear of being around women. Or put it this way, I learned to respect women. César's wife, Helen Chávez, helped me more than anyone else. She was really committed to home. Actually, César's toughest organizing jobs were Helen, his wife, and Richard, his brother. They wanted to lead their own lives. Helen kept saying she wouldn't do anything, and she's so strong and stubborn that he couldn't convince her to change her mind. She took care of the food and the kids, and while César was organizing she was supporting them too, working in the fields. César, keeping his *machismo* intact in those days, would make her come home and cook dinner.

"We wanted her to learn the credit union bookkeeping. We yelled at her one night into the kitchen, 'You're going to be the assistant bookkeeper.' She yelled back, 'No, I won't either,' but we voted her the job. Boy was she mad! But you should see her books. We've been investigated a hundred times and they never find a mistake."

The union had to teach its members—farm workers with almost no education or training—the professional skills it required. Marie Sabadado, who directs the R. F. Kennedy Medical Plan, Helen Chávez, head of the credit union, and Dolores, chief negotiator and writer of labor contacts, taught themselves. Dolores made it sound almost easy to learn very specialized skills in a week's time.

"When César put me in charge of negotiations in our first contract, I had never seen a contract before. I talked to labor people, I got copies of contracts and studied them for a week and a half, so I knew something when I came to the workers. César almost fell over because I had my first contract all written and all the workers had voted on the proposals. He thought we ought to have an attorney, but really it was better to put the contracts in a simple language. I did all the negotiations myself for about five years. Women should remember this: be resourceful, you can do anything, whether you have experience or not. César always says that the first education of people is how to be people, and then the other things fall into place.

"I think women are particularly good negotiators because we have a lot of patience, and no big ego trips to overcome. Women are more tenacious and that helps a great deal. It unnerves the growers to negotiate with us. César always wanted to have an *all-woman* negotiating team. Growers can't swear back at us or at each other. And then we bring in the ethical questions, like how our kids live. How can the growers really argue against what should be done for human beings just to save money?

"We knew everyone was immensely proud of the union services. We also knew that the legal staff (as well as the doctors and nurses at the clinic) were volunteer lawyers from the outside. In the past, the growers got rid of nascent farm-worker organizations by breaking them in the courts. The UFW has an excellent, tough legal staff. But to stay permanently with the union doctors and lawyers need to come from the farm workers themselves. The union will have to send its men and women out of the community for training. There has never been the luxury of a few years in which to do so, and there is a certain fear of becoming 'corrupted' by the universities."

The United Farm Workers headquarters are located in Delano, between Bakersfield and Fresno, and also at La Paz, a town no larger than a half-block of post office, store and gas station, east of Bakersfield in the Tehachapi range. Union field offices lie in small towns in the central valleys. From anywhere in these valleys it is about three hours, north to San Francisco, or south to Los Angeles on any of the state's three parallel freeways. Meeting only union people, in their austere but clean and bright offices, we hadn't seen what local fieldworker conditions were like. We took a look at some company towns by leaving the freeways and taking side roads at random into the fields.

Company towns are wholly dependent for their income on the prosperity and good will of the growers. Since the big growers are the last employers in America to escape collective bargaining, one can judge their civic responsibility by the looks of the town: boarded-up or gutted buildings, cracked sidewalks, decaying stores—they all show that the growers spend their profits on themselves. Only the bars, preserves of the men, where the wine is sold, do business.

Livingston is a company town of Gallo Wines near Merced on Highway 99. Outside the town, the Gallo brothers haven't hidden their wealth. They have splendid houses, isolated even from one another, surrounded by velvety slopes leading to pools, tennis courts and greenhouses. Not far away, but well hidden, the Gallo workers live in company camps lost at dusty terminals of country roads in the shadow of enormous vats guarded by armed men. When we were there, a determined nucleus of UFW strikers who had refused to work under Gallo's new Teamster contract had also refused to obey the grower's eviction notices. For that, they had been deprived of garbage collection and water.

Downtown Livingston seemed only slightly less bleak than the camps. Fifty people had gathered in front of the local courthouse for a silent protest against the imprisonment of fellow strikers. Aggie Rose, a former elementary schoolteacher of Portuguese ancestry, was head of the union office. As she spoke to the men and women forming the procession, encouraging and exhorting them in Spanish and Portuguese to keep their spirits up, the intensity of her light eyes, her constantly moving thin figure, momentarily brought life back into the town. The line of marchers circled the courthouse for a while. Police in squad cars hovered along dark streets. There was nothing to do but disperse.

Dolores would soon be back in New York directing the East Coast boycott. She was determined that we understand, before we left, why the union would not be defeated, not even in Livingston.

"One of the reasons the growers are fighting us so hard is that they realize we're changing people, not just getting a paycheck for them. Without our militancy we wouldn't have a union. So we keep pushing our people, getting them out on other issues, like the tuition rise in California colleges, or the Presidential campaign. We had farm workers out door to door for McGovern. And when our people come back from the boycott, they will be stronger than ever."

We asked Dolores whether she had ever been scared or lacked confidence in her ability to organize people.

"Of course. I've been afraid about everything until I did it. I started out every time not knowing what I was to do and scared to death. When César first sent me to New York on the boycott it was the first time we'd done anything like that. There were no ground rules. I thought, 11 million people in New York, and I have to persuade them to stop buying grapes. Well, I didn't do it alone. When you need people, they come to you. You find a way . . . it gets easier all the time."

Dolores Huerta, circa 1965 or 1966.
Photo by George Ballis. Courtesy of
Take Stock.

7

Sorrow in the Orchards

Her Life for Years

Eileen Foley

On a typical early morning in New York Dolores Huerta, 44, gets up, changes and bottles the baby, makes breakfast for her husband, takes two older children to nursery school, and concludes her traditional housewifery for the day.

Then she may fly to Washington for a meeting of the Democratic Party National Committee, or to Detroit, as she did this weekend, to lead a boycott march and rally for the United Farm Workers.

Or, she may stay in New York and set up meetings, go on speaking engagements, picket a supermarket that sells head lettuce, table grapes or Gallo wines, or appear on television to explain her cause, the plight of American farm workers.

Dolores Huerta's name itself is symbolic of what the woman is about. She translates it from the Spanish as "sorrow in the orchard." And after she divorced her first husband in 1965 and remarried in 1968, she kept her first husband's name because it has been the sorrow of the orchards, vineyards and agricultural fields of America, which have busied this mother of 10 for almost half her life.

In the early '60s she worked in the fields of California with César Chávez as they organized farm workers. In 1967 she helped negotiate and service the first contracts between the United Farm Workers Union (UFW) and the growers. In 1968 she married Chávez's brother Richard.

Originally published in *Detroit Free Press*, 1C–2C, September 16, 1974. Reprinted by permission of the *Detroit Free Press*.

Then, last year, a union whose members are often steeped in the machismo tradition, elected her overwhelmingly and unanimously its first vice president.

"People respond to those who are willing to help and to work with them," she said. "It over-rides any machismo."

"The union has brought a lot of women into leadership positions," she added.

"People are poor so the whole family works together and whole family strikes together and pickets together . . . We are non-violent and the women bring a lot of dignity to our movement."

Ms. Huerta was in Detroit on the weekend to help local UFW supporters celebrate Saturday's International Boycott Day on grapes, lettuce and Gallo wine. People in Canada, Denmark, Sweden, Norway and England also participated, she said, since 18 percent of California grapes are exported to Europe.

The purpose of the day, Ms. Huerta said, was to win enough support for the UFW boycott to hurt the growers who have made back-door deals with the Teamsters Union in California and force these growers to permit elections so farm workers can vote on the union they want to represent themselves.

The UFW is confident of winning such an election, she said.

The farm workers need popular support for the boycott because, unlike industrial workers, they are exempt from the National Labor Relations Act. Therefore, they can be fired for union activity. Their right to organize is not protected by law, and growers cannot be forced to bargain with their representatives.

The lack of legal status has hurt the fledgling union. While it has 125,000 signed cards from farm workers requesting representation, and while in its peak years it represented 70,000 farm workers in contracts, the number of dues-paying UFW members has been reduced to 12,000.

The UFW with the help of people represented by such Michigan groups as the UAW, the AFL-CIO, the National and Michigan Councils of Churches, the U.S. Catholic Bishops, the Coalition of Labor Union Women, and other labor and religious groups, hopes to turn things around with the boycott, its only real weapon.

For Dolores Huerta and her family there has been no dividing line between her private and political lives since she took up the cause of the farm worker. She brought her baby with her to celebrations in Detroit.

Back in New York, her three-year old, Juanita, has told all the nursery school kids in her class about the boycott and has appeared on television asking people not to buy Gallo wine.

The cause, while inspiring and invigorating, as fights for justice generally are, is not a comfortable nor an easy life-style.

Dolores Huerta came to Detroit to walk in several marches in her only pair of shoes, and they weren't walking shoes, just blue, leather and suede, semi-dressy slipons.

Most of her clothes come from donations, she says, and while the dresses usually end up very nice, she finds it hard to find donated shoes in her size. She believes in the cause, however, so she makes do.

A supporter knit her a red vest with the UFW thunderbird emblazoned on the front in black on a white oval. She wears it to speak and for pictures because the emblem shows up so well.

Her family subsists. Their rent is paid. They also earn $5 a week from the UFW for each worker and dependent in the family. That's supposed to cover food and other expenses. Beyond that, everything is donated.

When her older children were young, they never had whole milk, just the powdered kind the government provided.

And three of her teenage children, who had been living with her in New York, recently returned to live with relatives. A friend of theirs was killed on their door stoop and when one of the children went to testify about the incident, he was attacked in the subway.

"They have marched and picketed and been to jail, but they were not used to that rough city life," she said with a smile, "and they left me.

"My life has been very difficult and very hard and I wouldn't give any of it or trade it for a nice secure house in the suburbs," she added.

She thinks the cause of farm workers is a natural to excite women, especially mothers, just as it has spurred women in the fields to fight for their men and their children.

The farm women, she said, are a vital force in policing contracts. They insist on clean toilets, and cool drinking water, and they enforce pesticide prohibitions in the contract and child labor laws.

They also help their men, whose life expectancy is 49, to live longer, she said.

"There's a tendency on the part of the employer to speed workers up, to work brutally," she explained. "One worker will pick six tons of grapes a day, which is, you know, beyond human endurance.

"The women make fun of the men if they try to be super-macho. Men alone try to outwork each other. The women keep the work at a good, normal pace, but not to the point where people brutalize themselves."

Non-farm worker mothers can be equally involved in the farm worker movement, Ms. Huerta said, and she thinks that involvement would be good for them and their families.

"Involvement gives women a whole different feeling about themselves," she said, "and it makes kids really tough and political minded."

A housewife, she believes, doesn't want to feed her family the products of exploitation, or food picked by children like her own who should be in school.

To involve their children in the farm workers' struggle by fasting from lettuce and grapes, for instance, and explaining to the children why this is done, would teach them to do something for someone else, give them a chance to contribute to social change, and to do both in a non-violent way, Ms. Huerta believes.

"It is a very beautiful contribution to social justice," she said.

8

Stopping Traffic

One Woman's Cause

Barbara L. Baer

"Don't be a marshmallow," she will yell. "Walk the street with us into history."

"How do I stop eleven million people from buying the grapes?" Dolores Huerta asked herself when she arrived, for the first time, in New York in 1968 to head the United Farm Workers' table-grape boycott. Huerta, like boycott leaders all over the country, had no experience outside the picket lines of rural California. The first boycott took hold slowly and grew into a national crusade. By 1970, consumer pressure hit grape sales so hard that the United Farm Workers signed more than 200 three-year contracts in a single year. By 1973, when those first contracts were about to expire, the International Brotherhood of Teamsters moved into the same territory. The Teamsters stole all but twelve of the UFW's contracts, and captured 150 new ones, without a single vote ever having been cast by the workers. Workers were simply shunted from one union contract to another.

Dolores Huerta, by then vice president of the UFW and the mother of three new children, returned to New York last year to build up the second boycott. This time the boycott was directed against table and wine grapes and lettuce. Huerta set up the boycott houses for volunteers, and within them, her own household—five of her ten children.

Only during a two-year breathing period, from 1970 to 1972, have UFW officers and staff ever taken any time off from work. César Chávez took a brief trip to Mexico. Dolores Huerta had more babies.

Originally published in *The Progressive*, September, 1975, pp. 38–40.
Reprinted by permission from *The Progressive*, 409 East Main Street, Madison, WI 53703. www.progressive.org.

Since 1973, there has been no time for anything but day-to-day strategy. As a result of losing almost all their contracts to the Teamsters, the UFW has cut back almost all its innovative services to its members. Membership dropped from the peak figure of 55,000 workers to 10,000; cash available for strike funds and running the union dropped to $259,000 last year, compared with $1.1 million in 1973. Chávez was patient as always; since the UFW represented the workers, they would win in the end. The UFW president was placing his faith in the new California state government of Governor Edmund Brown Jr., a long-time UFW supporter, and in legislation requiring a secret ballot among workers in the fields to determine their choice of union. In fact, Brown's first appointments this year of pro-UFW people gave the UFW cause for greater optimism than anyone has felt in the past eighteen months. The return to its pre-1973 strength is still an uphill battle, whose determining factor is once more the consumer boycott.

Huerta, in addition to coordinating the New York boycott, travels about the country on speaking engagements. She is an effective speaker, whether at union meetings or on campuses, because she seems to relive the history of her cause each time she begins talking of it. She speaks rapidly, in a constantly hoarse voice, using her hands and her eyes to create images of men and women bent double in burning fields in California. Finely built and thin, with an intense yet serene round face that is framed by straight black hair falling from a widow's peak to her shoulders, she makes you think of all the people she speaks for, the physically powerless but mystically driven, the strike-hardened and suntired men and women in the fields. Huerta herself has worked as a field laborer, first as a child and then when she joined Chávez in the early 1960s to organize the UFW. She has worked at every kind of militant organizing, and has suffered beatings and jailings for it. And because she is a woman, each step in her political life was made at the cost of severe personal trauma.

Dolores Fernández Huerta was born in Dawson, New Mexico, in 1930. Her mother dominated the family, leading her husband and four young children up and down the Pacific Coast as migrant farm workers during the Depression. In 1935 the family settled in Stockton, California, where Alicia Fernández, Dolores's mother, divorced her husband and bought a small hotel to which she added a restaurant.

As soon as she began making money, she provided free housing for unemployed farm workers. Having made unconventional choices herself—as a Chicana and a Catholic, she married three times against church and social prohibitions—she encouraged her children to do the same.

Dolores herself married for the first time in 1948; two daughters and a son were born before she separated from her husband and brought the children home to her mother. While her mother cared for the children, Dolores, now divorced, enrolled in college, dreaming of changing poor people's lives through education. "I knew there was something I was meant to do," Dolores recalls. "I had sense of a mission." By 1955, with her teaching credentials from the College of the Pacific in Stockton, she knew it was not education that would change things. But what was an intelligent, resourceful, emotionally high-pitched young Chicano woman to do in the mid-1950s? She married again. She and her second husband, Victor Huerta, had four more children—two boys and two girls. Children complicated, but finally did not change, the course of Dolores Huerta's life. Dolores attributes the most important change in her life to Fred Ross.

Fred Ross, a tall and pale man, was tapping sources of future organizing power in the barrios of California cities with their large, unpoliticized Chicano populations. Speaking perfect Spanish, he turned both César Chávez and Dolores Huerta into political militants by putting them to work on voter registration drives for the Community Services Organization (CSO) for which he worked. Ross took Huerta away from the charity work she had been doing and made her aware of needs in the Chicano community. Dolores campaigned to have a Spanish-speaking staff in Stockton city hospitals, to have the ghettos policed by Chicanos, to have sidewalks built. Today, choosing political action over housekeeping does not seem nearly the rebellious act it was for Dolores in 1960.

"I knew I wasn't comfortable in a wife's role," Huerta says, "but I wasn't clearly facing the issue. I hedged, I made excuses, I didn't come out and tell my husband that I cared more about helping other people than cleaning our house and doing my hair."

Her second marriage ended in 1961. Dolores threw herself into work as a kind of salvation. She would have "gone under" she believes, overcome by guilt over her divorce and by fears for the security of her seven young children, if she had not worked day and night.

"I took the family to Sacramento in 1961 to lobby the legislators into passing laws for poor people. I knew nothing about lobbying before the day I began it. CSO just sent me, paying us through contributors' nickels and dimes, and said, 'You can do it.' I had to do it, but at the same time I was too distracted to work. My husband was trying to take the kids away from me in court. I couldn't lose my children, but I couldn't quit working for people who counted on me. I went into church and prayed. I took confession for the first time in years. When I left the church, I felt my way was clear to work to pass those bills. God would take care of the rest."

Dolores has often made what she calls a "religious cop-out": she says to herself that if her work bears results—a sort of bargaining with God—then she is justified in leaving her children to be taken care of by others or to fend for themselves. In 1961 alone, fifteen important bills she lobbied for were passed. Among them were social security measures to protect aliens; pension and unemployment compensation for aliens; and tests for drivers' licenses to be given in Spanish as well as English. And Dolores won custody of all but one child, Fidel, who lived with his father for a while but eventually returned to her.

When César Chávez asked Dolores, whom he had known in CSO since 1955, to join him in Delano in 1962, it was the work she had been waiting for. The Chávez family, with eight kids, and Dolores with her children, picked grapes to support organization of the first strikes in 1965. Dolores was on the strike lines and in the fields organizing the workers from then on. "Dolores Huerta is physically and spiritually fearless," Chávez has said of her. She was particularly intuitive about organizing women. She led lines of women and children between the UFW men and goons hired by the growers—later by the Teamsters. The women have often taken the first blows, praying on their knees. Dolores knew how to touch the emotional core of others at times of crisis.

From organizing, Dolores Huerta became a contract negotiator, without any legal training. She was the first Chicano, and the first woman, to negotiate a farm labor contract. Not only did the growers have to sit at the same table with a Chicano and bargain with her as an equal, they had to listen to her impassioned condemnation of decades of repression. In the hundreds of negotiating sessions she led between 1966 and 1971, Huerta's emotional involvement was her strength and her weakness. She shouted and cried easily. She fought with insults, tears, and individuals' testimony, believing so strongly in winning everything the workers told her they needed that she would not compromise. She accused her opponents, instead of bargaining with them.

"They aren't giving you toilets in the fields because they say Mexicans don't know how to use them," she relayed in Spanish to the workers she had brought into negotiating sessions. She encouraged spontaneous political demonstrations during negotiations as the grievances were shouted out. A bargaining room was filled with chanting and waving UFW banners. Huerta's direct political tactics angered some growers to the point that she was boycotted. One public relations man representing the Delano grape growers insists she is a demonically driven woman: "Dolores Huerta is crazy," he says. "She's a violent woman, where women, especially Mexican women, are usually peaceful and pleasant. You can't live wrought up like she does and not be crazy."

David Burciaga, a Chicano and a pacifist from World War II, became the UFW negotiator in 1973. His tactics are quite different: "If I'd been on the growers' side, I might have walked out on Dolores, too. Don't misunderstand me; she's a real fighter. But she's left me in a difficult situation. The workers got used to having a free-for-all during negotiations. Today, when we're not on the winning side of the table—when the growers have the Teamsters already waiting to step in if we make a false move—we have to compromise. Dolores got some of our best results, but today we have to convince, not insult, the growers."

"She's too quick to attack, too reluctant to listen," charges John Vasconcellos, California Democratic assemblyman and a UFW supporter. But Nicholas Petris, chairman of housing and urban affairs in the California legislature, sees her belligerence in another light: "Huerta is a brave woman. She's a believer, not a broker, for her cause."

No one knows her weaknesses better than Dolores Huerta herself. She is afraid of her own temper, and checks her daily horoscope—she's an Aries—to be forewarned of a particularly dangerous situation. However, she usually disregards the astrological advice, often to her regret.

"I know I have a terrible temper. It might be that I'm still suffering from guilt about my divorce, and from the feeling that I shouldn't really be the leader people see in me. . . . I guess I just haven't forgiven myself the divorce, and if you haven't forgiven yourself something, how can you forgive others?" Dolores asks, taking a quick look at herself in a pocket mirror and adding another layer of pink lipstick.

It is not such a trivial detail that reminds you Dolores Huerta is self-conscious about her looks, about how she should appear, or what she should be like as vice president of the United Farm Workers, a title that makes her one of the top women in American trade unionism. "My personal life is a mess," she once said to me after a television news interviewer had asked her the routine question: "Are you married, Mrs. Huerta?" She had replied yes, though in fact she divorced. Two marriages, two divorces—events that have resulted from the conflict of her drive for a personal life and her compelling need to work for her people—reflect on her like a bad record. She advised her eldest daughter not to marry in the Church until she had been married a while with a civil ceremony. She is even more vulnerable—and more open—on the subject of her three youngest children, whose father, Richard Chávez, César's brother, she lives and works with but cannot marry.

Her eldest, a girl, lives in the boycott house with Dolores in New York. The two youngest, a girl of three and a boy a year younger, are kept by a foster mother in Bakersfield. Dolores is on the road too much to be able to have them with her. She had to leave the last child a few weeks after he was born. I visited the children at their foster mother's at Dolores's request, which showed me how unprotective she was about an unusual situation, especially in the still-traditional Catholic, Chicano culture to which she belongs.

Dolores Huerta, I came to believe, belongs to the older generation of Chicanas in her thinking, if not her actual age. She is open and frank except on the subject of birth control. She knows that outsiders like myself and even the younger generation of Chicanas cannot or will not understand why she keeps having children. She sees in my continual questions that I am critical of the way she risks her health to give her man as many children as he wants. She assures me she feels in the best of health, has the most energy when she is pregnant. Without saying it in so many words, she tries to assure me that her political energy and having children are not in conflict. They may well go together.

Dolores Huerta is an unusually strong and resourceful woman. She has always been exceptionally pretty. But she lacks confidence in herself. It may be that having so many children helps her retain a sense of feminine power in her own culture that she feels she loses with the real power and responsibilities she has in political life.

Many times over the last two years the press and old supporters—seemingly everyone but the men and women of the UFW themselves—have mourned the death of La Causa. Chávez and Huerta denounced the prophets of doom: the UFW would win in the end because they, not the Teamsters, were part of the people's struggle. Right, not might, would win in the long run. "We have more time than money," Chávez is fond of saying with his illuminated smile. Dolores Huerta, no less certain of the outcome of the struggle in the worst of times, becomes angry at pessimism: "Don't be a marshmallow," she will yell. "Walk the street with us into history. Get off the sidewalk. Stop being vegetables. Work for justice. Viva the boycott!"

Faith can keep Huerta, Chávez, and most of the men and women of the UFW going for a long time. And how do you begin to untangle faith and power in a movement like the United Farm Workers, and in a woman like Dolores Huerta?

Dolores Huerta, circa 1965 or 1966.
Photo by George Ballis. Courtesy of
Take Stock.

9

Dolores Huerta

La Pasionaria of the Farmworkers

Judith Coburn

Since this report was written in September, 1975, the status of union representation elections for California farmworkers has taken some dramatic turns. By early 1976, 382 elections had been held throughout California, 329 of them decisive. The United Farm Workers won 205 (representing 68.8 percent of the workers involved), with the remainder of the ranches voting for the Teamsters or no union. While UFW victories continued to pile up, grower and Teamster lobbyists in Sacramento succeeded in cutting off funds to continue the elections. As a result, the Agricultural Labor Relations Board (ALRB), which had been set up in 1975 to oversee and monitor the elections, in effect went out of business last spring. Less than a third of California's 250,000 farmworkers had had the opportunity to vote.

The UFW responded with a drive to get a proposition on the November ballot in order to permanently guarantee farmworkers' rights to free elections. In a record 29 days, they had 719,598 signatures, more than twice the necessary number. Once Proposition 14 was officially on the ballot, the Teamsters and growers dropped their opposition to continued funding and the legislature appropriated money for the ALRB to start operations again. (Elections are expected to begin again in late 1976 or early 1977). If passed, the Proposition mandates the holding of elections, increases the penalties for violations, and morally obligates the legislature to allocate funds. However, it does not bind growers to sign contracts with the unions that have won elections.

Originally published in *MS Magazine*, November 1976, pp. 11–15.

At this writing the UFW has nearly 50 contracts representing more than 18,000 workers, but this is only a small percentage of the elections they have won. Their long-standing boycott of Gallo Wine and most California table grapes continues. An additional current target for boycotts is Dole Company fresh fruits.

Sacramento, Sunday afternoon

Dolores Huerta, vice president of the UFW, is holed up in the deserted state Capitol in the office of one of the Chicano Assemblymen. Into the first statewide elections giving farmworkers the right to choose a union, the UFW needs all the help it can get. Dolores has been in Sacramento since September's bitter election at the Gallo Ranch, lobbying Governor Brown and the legislature to strengthen enforcement of the election law. Today she has been working the phones for hours, pulling together last minute details for a mass UFW picket on the ALRB headquarters. "Who's doing the tortillas?" she yells at me distractedly. "Juana! The tortillas!" she shouts after the volunteer she has just dispatched to a meeting to recruit support. What looks like chaos turns out to be the organizer's genius for handling a million things at once. A phone blinks on hold. It's César Chávez. "I'm telling the buses [of demonstrators] to come to the Capitol," she explains to him. "We'll reroute 'em there, confuse 'em [the cops] a little."

She dials long distance to her teenage son Fidel, the only of her 10 children living with his father. "Hi, you comin' to the march tomorrow? Why not? Ahhh, come on." She listens for a long moment, tries to interrupt, frowns, gives up. "Well, I'm sorry if I'm bothering you."

Hours later, Dolores and two volunteers lead me off to a barrio café. She apologizes for the catch-as-catch can interview. "I don't live *anywhere*, you know, haven't for years." UFW organizers live on five dollars a week, with bare room and board provided wherever they are assigned. Dolores Huerta has been living this way since 1962.

Dolores's chiseled, burnt-sienna face suggests more her father's Indian/Mexican heritage than her mother's Spanish blood. She was born Dolores Fernández, in Dawson, New Mexico, in 1930. Her father was a mine worker who did farmwork during slack periods. Devout but independent, her mother divorced twice. When her parents' marriage broke up, Dolores went with her mother to Stockton, California.

She describes her mother as a "Mexican-American Horatio Alger type," who saved enough as a cannery worker and waitress to buy a small hotel and restaurant, and installed the family in an integrated neighborhood. She often put up destitute farmworker families in her hotel at no cost.

Dolores went to an integrated high school where she had a few white friends, but also experienced racism. She dreamed of being a dancer, but in 1948 married her high school sweetheart, an Irishman, instead. The marriage broke up after a son and two daughters were born. While her mother took care of the kids, Dolores studied for a teaching degree.

In 1955, Dolores began working with Fred Ross, an organizer for Saul Alinsky's Industrial Areas Foundation, who was trying to catalyze political power in the Mexican-American communities of California. Ross started the Community Service Organization (CSO), which led voter registration drives, pushed for more Chicanos on the police forces, for Spanish-speaking staff at hospitals and government offices, and campaigned for sewers and community centers in the barrios. The message was power, not charity; and the way to get reform was to grab it. Because of her devotion to the work of CSO, Dolores' second marriage, to Ventura Huerta, didn't work out either.

In 1962, César Chávez, one of Ross's earliest converts, wanted to focus the efforts of the CSO on farmworkers. Dolores was one of the few to support Chávez, and left CSO with him to organize farmworkers. Since then, she has been a central figure in every UFW venture, and the union has been her life. Years of her lobbying in Sacramento and Washington resulted in migrant workers being granted certain benefits (including disability insurance, old-age pensions, and unemployment insurance) previously denied them. Although Huerta had never even read a union contract before, Chávez assigned her to negotiate the UFW's first contracts. She has organized in the fields, in boycott offices, and for the elections. She has been arrested 18 times.

We end our meal talking about the UFW's current struggle—against the Teamsters. I ask about anti-UFW feelings among some farmworkers. "At the beginning we didn't have the organization to administer the contracts efficiently, and the Teamsters have a lot of resources," says Huerta. "True, the Teamsters are getting people higher wages too, just like the UFW. But we want to change people's lives. Farmworkers kill themselves working, living nowhere, traveling all the time, putting up with the pesticides because the growers want it that way. It's a feudal system which higher wages won't change. *We* know the work can be organized so people settle down in one place with their families, and control their lives through political power and their own union—which they run themselves."

Sacramento, Monday morning

Dolores has been up most of the night in the Capitol composing a press release on the union's allegations of election violations that César will read at the demonstration. She seems beyond exhaustion, as if years ago she spent her final reserves, her intensity constant, no longer fluctuating with external events.

When we arrive at the spanking new, corporate-style ALRB offices, hundreds of farmworkers—men, women, children—are packed into one of the courtyards, shouting UFW slogans and waving picket signs. César draws Huerta aside and begins to bawl her out.

A book could be written on their complex relationship. Both are stubborn and opinionated. She is notorious in the union for combativeness. (Stories are told of growers begging to face anyone at the negotiating table except Huerta.) Chávez jokes of "unleashing Dolores"; but he respects her opinions and they generally agree on larger issues. Dolores says they fight a lot because "he knows I'll never quit, so he uses me to let off steam; he knows I'll fight back anyway." Chávez, a traditionalist in his own home life is said to privately disapprove of Dolores's divorces, her living now with his brother Richard, and her chaotic way of raising her kids. But he knows that the union is the center of her life, just as it is with his. "Dolores is absolutely fearless, physically and emotionally," he says.

Both Chávez and Huerta believe that unless an organizer can organize the woman of a family, the family will be lost to the union. Chávez himself has also spoken scornfully of certain aspects of *machismo*, especially the notion of defending one's honor with violence. With the exception of Dolores, there are no other women in the small, influential circle around Chávez; but nearly half of the union's organizers are women, and many of the UFW's important programs, like the credit union and clinics, are run by women. Huerta herself claims, "Women have one advantage over men—their egos aren't so involved. They can compromise to get what they want instead of forcing a showdown all the time."

The press conference begins. "There is nothing wrong with the new law. It is just not being enforced," Chávez says. At best, farmworker sympathizers say, the board and its employees are overwhelmed, overworked, and under experienced. At worst, they haven't the power or the inclination to oppose the combined power of the growers and the Teamsters.

While Chávez speaks, Dolores grabs an armful of picket signs and passes them out. Two older Chicana women shyly ask if they can take her picture, and she perches on a stone wall with her arm around them while a friend snaps a picture. She looks after them, then sinks down on the sidewalk wearily. "Ninety-nine percent of these workers come from Mexico where there's never been a fair election. We tried to overcome their cynicism and fear and convince them the elections would be fair. That it was worth a risk to their jobs and family. But these elections are a fraud." She stares off into the middle distance.

César beckons to her. He appoints her to go to a meeting with Brown's aides about the charges of election abuse. A delegation of farmworkers elected by the demonstrators go with her.

After the two-hour meeting, Dolores reports back to the crowd of farmworkers. Brown, who dropped into the meeting, has promised to investigate the conduct of the elections, and other UFW charges. The demonstrators begin to drift away to their buses.

After the buses leave, Dolores is at loose ends. We prowl the neighborhoods near the Capitol in my car. Suddenly Dolores spots a UFW volunteer's car parked outside a *Maríachi* bar, and we stop. On the way in, she buys us meat pies for dinner from a street vendor.

Inside the music starts, and Dolores is dancing in her seat. "Ohh, I missed the cha-cha, I was having too many babies, but now I'm getting the hang of it." Later when she shepherds us into the bathroom, she looks at herself critically in the mirror. "Haven't changed clothes in three days." Dolores combs her hair, slicks on bright-pink lipstick. "There, I feel terrific, even if *you* don't think I look any different!

"I could never go to a bar in Delano, without a man, and carry on like this." Dolores confides. "The farmworkers wouldn't like it." I ask her if the more traditional people accept her living with Richard and not being married. "They seem to," she says, "but then we've been together a long time and I don't fool around with other men."

I ask her how the clash of cultures affects her responses to feminism. "I consider myself a feminist, and the Women's Movement has done a lot toward helping me not feel guilty about my divorces. But among poor people, there's not any question about the women being strong—even stronger than men—they work in the fields right along with the men. When your survival is at stake, you don't have these questions about yourself like middle-class women do. And in our culture, raising kids is the most important thing you can do, not like among whites.

"But Mexican women can be terribly exploited, too. In Mexico women are virtual slaves to their husbands, and the men often have several wives. So when they come here the Women's Movement has an effect. You'd be surprised. In 1972, I remember seeing all these grandmothers, of ten to twelve kids, just up from Mexico, who were arrested in Delano. Two years later, you'd see them in a demonstration and they'd be in pants suits!"

It's 2:30 A.M. I'm collapsing and get up to leave. But Dolores is still going strong and decides to stay. "We'll have to do this again tomorrow—it's Mexican Independence Day!"

Sacramento, Tuesday morning

We are at a hearing at the ALRB this morning about Teamster/grower efforts to have a series of elections on various ranches around Salinas determined as one unit, with the representation at all the ranches going to the union with the highest number of votes. The UFW wants each ranch counted separately. The technical argument loops back and forth. Dolores looks alternately angry and bored.

During a break Dolores acts as an interpreter between the UFW lawyer and two farmworkers from Salinas who are going to testify about alleged grower/Teamster collusion. The farmworkers seem nervous and deferential. Afterward, Dolores greets two legislative aides sitting on the curb, waiting for her. Their boss, a state senator, has promised to hold hearings on how badly the elections are being run. Her brown eyes snapping, she recites some of the abuses. The young men are outraged, but explain that the hearings haven't been okayed because the boss has gone backpacking. Suddenly Dolores is transformed from a smooth operator to La Pasionaria. "Call him! Call him!" The aides say he's unreachable, to wait a week. But Dolores, the experienced lobbyist, knows that to get Brown to act, she needs pressure on him from the legislature now, not a week from now.

"Send him a telegram! Tell him someone died!" the aides avert their eyes, miserable. She sees they won't budge, so she dismisses them. When they're out of earshot, she says, "Those guys! All they want to do is *act* outraged, not *do* something, and it all comes down to protecting a politician. Well, I told you last night we wouldn't get anything out of them anyway."

Back in the hearing room, the two farmworkers testify about the UFW allegations of intimidation in the Salinas elections. They begin shyly, but soon speak up firmly, staring directly at the board members. One man says he was told he must sign a Teamster representation card or he couldn't work anywhere in the Salinas area. The UFW lawyer argues that the Teamsters didn't adequately represent workers at the ranches where they had already had contracts. One grower lawyer responds indignantly, "But there's nothing in the law— nothing *illegal*—about having a *non* representative union." Dolores giggles delightedly.

Late that night she gives into impulse; we'll drive to Delano where she can check in with César and attend to domestic details. The kids need clothes, and one child must be enrolled in school somewhere.

We head south, the car is now jammed with leaflets, Richard's laundry, and a 50-pound bag of chili beans donated by a UFW supporter. At 3 A.M. we pull into Livingston to a rundown wooden house where three of Dolores's kids are staying with union people. Dolores wakes them up and asks if they want to come to Delano. The two teenagers grumpily decline, but Juanita, five, is overjoyed. Juanita is soon settled in Dolores's arms chewing sleepily on a jelly doughnut. Dolores is quiet for a stretch.

"My life is a mess," she says cheerfully after a while. (This is a common refrain.) She recites the diaspora of her children: two in their twenties from her first husband, five Huerta teenagers, and three

Chávez children. "It's true, the kids resent it when the union takes time away from them," she says. Other times the kids come first; Dolores stayed home from the union's 1,000 mile march before the elections to be with the five kids who had chicken pox. "All the Huerta kids were born during big CSO fights. I was always pregnant. I don't remember anything about Elisa's childhood except nursing her in the ladies' room during breaks in city council meetings, or dropping her off at a friend's house." Dolores's kids lead a round-robin existence, staying sometimes with her, sometimes with friends—all except Fidel—working or living within the union community.

She admits that the way she's raised the kids worries many people; for a long time her family believed she neglected them, and she had bitter custody fights with her second husband. "But now that I've seen how good they turned out, I don't feel so guilty.

"Women are getting afraid to have kids. I still believe you are supposed to conceive children. Don't you want to leave something of yourself, belong to something, do that for your man?" She speaks out publicly and passionately against abortion and contraceptives. And when I tell her that some younger women in the union think she might have such a large family because it helps her retain her feminine identity in her culture while her union and organizing roles divorce her from those roots, she rewards me with a withering glance. "Poor people think big families are strong families, and I love my kids," she says firmly.

Sacramento, Friday afternoon

Dolores has just had a depressing morning: being rebuffed by a committee head over hearings. The meeting had started awkwardly. Finally Dolores broke in, "Listen, the Governor has to do something! The ALRB says it's neutral. But this is a war and staying out of it helps the Teamster/grower machine run all over everyone." Brown's aide agrees that a real problem is the lack of ALRB "police" enforcement, but that bypassing local law enforcement simply isn't legally or politically feasible. But leaving resolution of any unfair results to the courts isn't enough, argues Dolores.

She begins to push. "Before the election, one grower laid off any of the crews that were sympathetic to us, spread rumors that anyone who voted for us would be fired. A foreman passed around Teamster petitions and told workers to sign. Two days before the election, U.S. Immigration came and rounded up sixteen people, and the supervisors told workers that Immigration would be there on election day. The Teamsters broke up one rally César was at—beat up a lot of people—and the cops broke up another. We couldn't get on the property to talk to workers—I got arrested—and everyone who talked to us in town was photographed. Teamster campaign signs were all over the property and the equipment in the fields. We tried to get the ALRB to hold the election in town and to talk directly to the workers about their rights and how they couldn't be fired, but they wouldn't. On election day the growers' security guards—armed!—were allowed to vote, and at the same time as the workers. One man told me he was so scared he couldn't write. Some strikers weren't allowed to vote. The board agent gave a press conference saying the Teamsters won [223 to 131] and wouldn't count how many challenged votes there were [about 130], which everyone agrees will give the election to us."

She pauses for breath. "Everyone calls these 'technical violations,' as if they don't add up to an unbelievable climate of fear! One of our people is going to have to get killed before anyone thinks something's wrong." The meeting ends inconclusively.

At lunch, Dolores seems less depressed than I am. She says most of the union people were pessimistic about the elections underneath: "We thought Brown was more sympathetic than any other governor we'd get, so we had the best chance under him for fair elections, but you can't count on things like that."

She tells me that the night before she had a dream of millions of farmworkers carrying silver crosses marching to mark their ballots with a cross. When she gets depressed, she says, she thinks about the time 10 years ago when the union was down to fewer than 20 members and how they lost their first strike when the workers voted to go back without a contract. "That's why César always reminds us of that *dicho: Hay mas tiempo que vida.*" (There is more time than life.)

10

Dolores Huerta Mothers Eleven Kids, One Labor Union

Nelda Clemmons

She's the mother of 11 children and one labor union, this small, unassuming, dark-haired person with the warm brown eyes.

And Dolores Huerta is still the long distance manager of both—roaming the country as the vice president of the United Farm Workers (UFW); crossing paths with the three children she already has following her union footsteps; keeping tabs of the other offspring who range in age from 1 to 27.

"I'm trying to get all my kids to stay in the union," asserts the gentle but sturdy woman.

That's been the family's lifestyle for 15 years. And they've all shared the same "bounty"—the $10-a-week salary paid to Huerta and other full-time organizers plus a $5-per-person weekly food allotment. Clothes and other such frivolities have come primarily from donations.

"They've survived," Huerta said of her brood. "I guess they're pretty tough. They're very knowledgeable and organizational-minded. They've always had to do without, so they can survive. When you talk about living on $5 a week and you think about kids growing up that way—no new clothes, no new shoes . . ."

But that lifestyle has left her in tune with the farm workers she represents. And in touch with her own past. Born in New Mexico, Huerta's father was a laborer, and her mother's family came from the coal mine lines.

Originally published in the *Tampa Times*, February 1, 1978.

"My father was a farmworker, and when I was very small we used to migrate to different states—Nebraska, Wyoming—and live in little tarpaper shacks. My mother didn't let me go out to the fields," she said, after she became a teenager. The conditions there were too severe.

"After I became an adult I went back out and saw how really sordid conditions were. They're still the same. No toilets. Always subjected (to sexual harassment). Without exception, the labor contractor or foreman will try to pressure you. That's why men go with their women and take their families out together," Huerta said.

Eventually based in California, Huerta joined César Chávez, his wife Helen, and Manuel Chávez in establishing the National Farm Worker Associates in 1962, developing a grassroots, house meeting attempt to approach the problems of farmworkers in the realm of civic action. Clinics, health services, pensions, voting rights were some of their concerns.

"We passed a lot of laws like the right to register door-to-door, old age pensions, disability for farmworkers," she said of the group's early lobbying efforts in the state legislature. They became familiar and accepted figures there until the movement transformed into a labor union in 1965. That change brought down charges of "communists" on the early organizers, she remembers.

When the UFW reached official status, Huerta's energies followed the boycotts and picket lines, which surrounded the push for unionization among workers in California's fields. She directed the first grape boycott in New York City in the late '60s and the San Francisco Bay Area boycott in the early '70s.

"New York of course is just a marvelous city," she remarked, "because they're so educated laborwise. Ed Koch (now the New York mayor) was always on our picket line. Gloria Steinem and the *Ms.* women at lunch time would come down and picket," she recalled.

The work wasn't all glamorous. The picket lines in California grew violent at times, and at those times Huerta said the importance of the women in the union movement was felt in a significant way.

"Women provided an awful lot of leadership in keeping the strikes non-violent. Where you have women you also have children, and children bring out a different type of feeling," said the mother.

Both within the union's leadership structure and in organizing in the fields, Huerta felt the participation of women in the UFW has been large because of the union's "young" status.

"With poor people—all poor people, not just Mexicans—because people are still in the survival stage, women take a much more active part in that. I've thought about that a lot. Like in mineworkers' unions: most workers are men, but women have always had an active role."

Huerta has been arrested more than 20 times for activities, although never convicted of any charges. "The arrests have always been mostly for trespassing, attempting to talk to workers," she explained. The effect of arrest has carried its potence, however. "They do everything they can to degrade people," she said of her jail experiences, "like stripping the people naked. Mothers and grandmothers. That's what jail is—a humiliating experience for anybody to go through."

Her activities for the union fall into more "ladylike" positions these days, since California's action to insure workers the right to vote on unionization.

"I'm negotiating the contracts right now," she said of her current duties. "You have to get with the workers, get proposals, then get with the growers." The negotiables are as basic as health and safety, "so people won't get sprayed with pesticides," she said. Medical and retirement plans and social services are the extras.

And as a woman, Huerta is beginning to experience another advantage in her union work. She was recently invited to speak to a group of California growers' wives who wanted a minority woman represented on their program.

"I think it's a very profitable thing," she said of such opportunities, "because women talk in terms of children. I can't think of any woman who is married to a farm owner who would want to see women suffer. There is a very strong link between the woman who picks and the woman who cooks the food."

Dolores Huerta and Robert
Kennedy, Delano, 1966.
Courtesy of John A. Kouns.

11

UFW Official Operated on After S.F. Beating

Scott Forter

San Francisco officials Thursday launched two investigations into an alleged police beating that left United Farm Workers union co-founder Dolores Huerta with broken ribs and forced doctors to remove her spleen.

Huerta, 58, was listed in fair condition Thursday at San Francisco General Hospital following an incident that occurred Wednesday night when 1,000 people protested a campaign visit by Vice President George Bush, the GOP presidential nominee.

"They (police) came on viciously, without warning, and flailed at us with their clubs," UFW official Howard Wallace said Thursday in a telephone interview from San Francisco.

Outside the hospital, banner-waving friends and union leaders Thursday criticized the city and its police force for the alleged attack.

"I want to condemn the city of San Francisco and the Police Department for allowing this type of activity to go on," Huerta's son, Emilio Huerta, said at a news conference.

Dolores Huerta, who is 5 feet, 2 inches tall and 110 pounds, did not provoke the attack and tried to defend herself with her arms, UFW official Daniel Martin said Thursday at the union's national headquarters in Keene, which is about 20 miles east of Bakersfield.

There were no other reports of injuries at the demonstration.

Dr. Marion Moses, a family friend and an adviser to the UFW, said Thursday in a telephone interview from Huerta's hospital room that the labor leader could have died if she had not been rushed by ambulance to the hospital Wednesday night.

"She was hit hard enough to break her spleen," the physician said. "If she hadn't been operated on, she would have bled to death."

Huerta remained under sedation for pain Thursday, but was alert, Moses said. The physician said Huerta probably will remain hospitalized for at least a week.

"She seems to be out of danger," she said.

Several members of Huerta's family rushed from Bakersfield and Keene to be with her. Among those that gathered at her bedside Thursday were her husband, Richard Chávez, the brother of UFW President César Chávez; daughter Lori Ybarra and son Dr. Fidel Huerta.

San Francisco Mayor Art Agnos, a Democrat who has known Huerta for 20 years, visited her at her sickbed Thursday.

"I am deeply concerned and disturbed about this incident," Agnos said in a statement released Thursday. "And it is not just because a nationally respected labor leader has been hospitalized. I want to know the exact cause of any police incident that results in someone being injured, whether or not that person is well-known."

He ordered Police Chief Frank Jordan and Michael Langer, director of the Office of Citizen Complaints, to investigate claims that some officers acted improperly at the protest.

The mayor also telephoned César Chávez, who is recovering from his 36-day fast in protest of pesticides, and told him about the investigations that are under way.

Huerta, the union's first vice president, and Wallace, who is head of the UFW boycott office in San Francisco, headed for the rally at Union Square in downtown San Francisco on Wednesday so she could talk to reporters covering Bush's speech at the posh St. Francis Hotel.

Earlier in the day, at a rally in the Fresno County farming community of Kingsburg, Bush had said he opposed the UFW boycott against California table grapes. Huerta planned to hand out copies of a news release she prepared Wednesday rebutting Bush's opposition to the boycott.

The 1,000 demonstrators crossed police barricades and began heading across Powell Street, said San Francisco Police Officer David

Ambrose by telephone Thursday. He said the 100 riot police officers who were equipped with batons then tried to herd the crowd
backward.

"We do not hit them over the head, but we do strike in the midsec-
tion, on the arms," he said. "And that's an accepted police practice."

The police moved in after the protesters ignored warnings for 20
minutes, he said.

However, Wallace said the police did not tell the demonstrators to
return to the other side of the street.

"They basically corralled us like animals and began jabbing at us,"
he said. "It was simply an unwarranted, vicious assault."

The alleged beating of Huerta prompted a flurry of public statements Thursday by UFW allies.

U.S. Reps. Ron Dellums, D-Oakland, and Nancy Pelosi, D-San
Francisco, criticized the police. Jack Henning, executive secretary of
the California Labor Federation, AFL-CIO, called for a federal investigation of the incident.

Democratic state Sen. Bill Greene of Los Angeles, chairman of the
Industrial Relations Committee, urged Agnos and Gov. Deukmejian to
offer a reward to anyone who provides information that leads to the
conviction of the officer or officers who injured Huerta.

A Roman Catholic, Huerta was resting Thursday on a Catholic
feast day that has special significance for her—the Feast Day of
Dolores Our Lady of Sorrows.

Father Ken Irrgang, a Catholic priest who works at the UFW headquarters, said Thursday that Huerta has suffered a great deal during
the 30 years she has worked on behalf of farm workers.

"It's a nice little reminder to us," he said of the coincidence. "We
don't think it's divine intervention or anything."

12

From the Fields Into the History Books

Ruth Carranza

What do Hispanic professional and farmworker women have in common? "A lot," says Dolores Huerta, Vice President of the United Farmworkers Union (UFW) and mother of eleven children. "In terms of women's issues, the problems are the same; workplace discrimination, sexual harassment, childcare needs, overwork, shouldering housework and homelife demands with those of the work place, to name a few. All working women face these problems," she asserts.

"Women farmworkers, however, do not have the financial independence of professional women—farmworkers live on the edge. Like pioneer women, their energies are focused on getting food on the table and holding the family together: Finding enough work to keep the family fed, enough money for clothes and shelter, and, if you're lucky, keeping your children in school and not having to pull them out to work alongside you are the main differences. It's hard for professional women to realize that, for many Hispanics, life is just trying to eat each day and maintain a roof over one's head," says Huerta.

In an incident that shocked the country, news broadcasts last October showed Huerta being beaten by San Francisco police at a rally for then presidential candidate George Bush. Huerta was passing out press statements condemning Bush's attack of Democratic Presidential candidate Dukakis' endorsement of the grape boycott. As the crowd grew increasingly vocal, the police pushed and clubbed people. "I was hit in the back with a police stick which ruptured three ribs. They hit me so hard my spleen was totally mashed and had to be

Originally published in *Intercambios Femeniles* (Winter 1989): 11–12.

surgically removed. I've never had anything like that happen to me before," she says.

Now that Mr. Bush has been elected, Huerta and the UFW are strategizing for the next four years. "When we first organized the union, Reagan was governor and Nixon was president. We are used to organizing under adverse political circumstances. But, if people stop buying grapes there's nothing that Bush or Governor Deukmejian can do. We (the UFW) don't really need the government, although it would be nice to have their support. Politicians talk about solidarity in Poland, but they don't support farmworkers or the labor movement in their own country. We will continue to appeal to the public," says Huerta resolutely.

Formed in 1960 [*sic*], the United Farmworkers called its first strike in 1965. Bringing in people from out of state and Mexico, growers broke the strike and obtained court injunctions preventing the UFW from picketing. The UFW appealed to the public, calling for a boycott of California table grapes. Within a few years, the growers were at the bargaining table negotiating a contract with the workers.

When the contracts expired in 1973, the growers sidestepped elections and signed a contract with the Teamsters' Union. "About 10,000 workers went out on strike," says Huerta. "Many were jailed and beaten. Two were killed. So, we called a second grape boycott," she recalls. That boycott was again a success.

But the scenario changed with the election of George Deukmejian in 1980. "His refusal to enforce collective bargaining laws granting California farmworkers the right to organize has given growers the leeway to avoid bargaining. They are walking away from contracts and intimidating organizers," she says. Huerta fears that conditions have started to regress to pre-union days.

"One of the worst situations, of course, is the use of pesticides," says Huerta. "In our agreement contracts, employers had to notify us before they used any kind of pesticide. Without a contract, they do whatever they want. As a result, hundreds of thousands of farmworkers have been poisoned. Children are born deformed—without arms and legs—and we have seen an increase in cancer cases in agricultural areas like McFarland and Delano," she says.

Misuse of pesticides was the reason for "Grape Boycott III." On

July 16, a frustrated César Chávez, President of the UFW, began a thirty-six day fast which resulted in a national fast among celebrities and public supporters, among them Jesse Jackson, Martin Sheen, Whoopi Goldberg, Robert Blake, some of the Kennedys and hundreds of other individuals and organizations.

"A union is an organization for workers," explains Huerta. "There will always be a need for working people to belong to an organization. This is their club, their association." She notes that corporations or employers, like the growers, belong to a large number of organizations: the Farm Bureau Federation, the Western Grower's Alliance, the California Tree Fruit League, the Western Grower's Association, the Associated Farmers, to name a few. "They have their marketing associations, for grapes and oranges, for example. Each employer/grower probably pays dues to a dozen organizations. How can they justify their membership in all these organizations and yet deny the farmworkers their right," asks Huerta.

"It's really dangerous to eliminate labor unions," warns Huerta, noting that in countries where workers' organizations are eliminated, fascism or some form of dictatorship quickly ensues. It happened in Chile and in Germany under Hitler. Labor organizations were destroyed first. It's happening right now in Central America. They're going after the labor leaders, she adds. In this country, laborers are called 'temporary workers.' Once you start eliminating middle class organizations, the situation gets very scary. Then, I think, a totalitarian government is right around the corner," she concludes.

Huerta's egalitarian family background has contributed to her leadership style. She attributes this to the lack of sexual discrimination in her home. "My mother raised me and was a dominant figure in my early years. At home, we all shared equally in the household tasks. I never had to cook for my brothers or do their clothes like many traditional Mexican families," she explains.

In 1962, when César Chávez started the United Farmworkers' Union, he asked Huerta, an experienced organizer, to assume a leadership position and later run for the vice presidency. She won the election and continues to work in that capacity.

But not all women have been so successful in unions, a traditional male bastion. "Many women union executives have gotten married and chosen to stay home with the children, or have gone on to school, or other endeavors. Leaders like Diana Lyons, a former farmworker who now heads up the union's appellate division, for instance, left the union for a career in law. But others remain. Rebecca Harrington, for instance, won unemployment insurance and workmen's compensation for Texas farmworkers. "She won those two laws and has done great work," says Huerta. "I hope that more women will decide to compete and go for the executive board."

As a woman, and a union leader, Huerta has become one of the more influential, visible Hispanas. She has been the subject of plays and *corridos* are sung chronicling her efforts. To which she humbly responds, "I like to organize and help people. I like social change. I feel humble because I've been very fortunate. God has put me in this position and provided the opportunities to get things done," she says. And then, as an afterthought, she complains, "I should be doing more than I am."

Dolores Huerta, Rodolfo "Corky"
Gonzáles, and César Chávez, 1970.
Courtesy of John A. Kouns.

13

UFW Co-Founder Comes out of Labor Shadow

Lisa Genasci

In history, women's accomplishments are often forgotten or tucked behind those of their male colleagues.

That's how it has been for Dolores Huerta, co-founder with the late César Chávez of the United Farm Workers of America.

Chávez, the union's charismatic president until his death in 1993, has been credited with organizing the union and its nationwide grape boycotts to win better pay and conditions for farm workers. But her admirers believe the credit should be shared with Huerta, the union's first vice president since its founding in 1962.

A small Mexican American woman with soft eyes but steely determination, Huerta at 65 still spends much of her time traveling, organizing migrant workers, negotiating contracts with growers and giving speeches. She averages about four hours of sleep a night and is often away from her Bakersfield home.

In her spare time, she has raised 11 children.

Before he died in 1993, Chávez described Huerta, the grandmother of 15, as "totally fearless, both mentally and physically."

One example of that courage: In 1988 Huerta was in San Francisco, handing out news releases on the UFW's longstanding grape boycott outside a hotel where President Bush was speaking. She was beaten by police and suffered a ruptured spleen and three broken ribs. The run-in with police and injuries didn't stop Huerta from fighting for her cause.

Associated Press article published in *Los Angeles Times*, May 11, 1995, p. 8. Courtesy of YGS Group and used with permission of The Associated Press.

Eleanor Smeal, president of the advocacy group The Feminist Majority Foundation and a longtime admirer of Huerta, described her as a "dedicated, inspired leader."

"She is the hardest working, most determined yet optimistic crusader for people I have met," Smeal said. "She thinks nothing of taking a red-eye flight from California to New York or elsewhere and then a red-eye on to somewhere else. She is tireless."

Said Karen Nussbaum, director of the Labor Department's Women's Bureau: "She was the most important woman labor leader in the 1970s. She led the picket lines, stared down the bosses, negotiated the contracts, sustained the beatings and carried on."

Former California Gov. Jerry Brown described her as "a fighter, dynamic, creative."

But he also described her as "embodying the spirit of César Chávez," and there lies the rub.

"That's the history of the world. His story is told, hers isn't," Huerta said in a recent interview. "I feel that has to change and women are going to have to change it."

So Huerta in recent years has added to her union work an advocacy for women, with a focus on getting women elected to public office in California.

"At some point in my career in the union I realized that women were not being valued for what they were doing," Huerta said.

"Women have the ideas and men take the credit for them. It happens all the time."

Huerta was born in 1930 in Dawson, N.M., a small mining town. Her father was a miner and union activist. He was, she said, charismatic, intelligent, handsome and a chauvinist. Her mother was a cannery worker and cook, quiet, genteel and a hard worker.

When Huerta was 6 her parents divorced and her mother moved the children to Stockton, Calif., where she raised them alone, eventually saving enough money to buy a simple 70-room hotel.

Huerta and her siblings did much of the work. At the same time, however, her mother believed strongly in culture, buying the children symphony tickets and encouraging them to play musical instruments.

As a teen-ager, Huerta took dance lessons offered free under the

Works Progress Administration—tap, ballet, flamenco and regional Mexican dances. She believed for a long time she would dance professionally.

But reality set in, and at 20 she married Ralph Head, a manual laborer, had two children and held an array of clerical jobs. The marriage ended about the time she started work on a teaching degree, taking night courses at what was then Stockton College.

She then married Ventura Huerta, with whom she had five children and whose name she took for her own. In Spanish, Dolores means "sorrow" and Huerta "orchard"—appropriate names for a union organizer, she and Chávez later thought.

After completing her degree, Huerta took a job at a local grammar school, but said she soon realized teaching was not for her.

"I couldn't stand seeing kids come to class hungry and needing shoes," Huerta said. "I thought I could do more by organizing farm workers than by trying to teach their hungry children."

Partly, that realization came after meeting a community organizer, Fred Ross, who taught Huerta what he knew about union organizing.

She was deeply moved by the living conditions of the farm workers, who she said were treated almost as indentured servants by some growers.

"We would see their dirt floors, the wooden boxes for furniture," Huerta said. "They had no money for food and worked so hard."

Ross introduced Chávez to Huerta and after several attempts to organize the mostly Mexican farm workers for other unions, the two formed their own, the United Farm Workers.

Huerta and Chávez used community and public support to pressure growers to negotiate. Strikes and three nationwide grape boycotts eventually forced growers to sign contracts with the United Farm Workers.

In her division of labor with Chávez, Huerta did much of the negotiating, the legislative work, and organized the 1970 and 1975 grape boycotts. Chávez spent more time in the fields with workers.

Huerta successfully lobbied for state bills that removed citizenship requirements for public assistance and legislation that created disability and unemployment insurance for farm workers and aid for dependent children. Republican administrations in the

1980s, however, eroded some of the gains made the previous decade, she said.

Also in the 1980s, the union began fighting the increasing use of pesticides, after finding high rates of cancer and birth defects in migrant workers.

Meanwhile, Huerta raised her children, including four more with her current companion, Richard Chávez, César's brother.

Between organizing meetings, Huerta changed diapers and nursed babies. The older children sometimes stayed with friends and supporters; they often ate donated food and coped with frequent moves.

"Although we weren't a traditional farm worker family whose livelihood depended on harvesting crops, we felt that way," said Emilio Huerta, 37, an attorney for the union. "As a labor organizer, my mother had to follow workers in their seasonal patterns, and we traveled around with her . . . Sometimes we attended as many as three or four different schools in a year."

Emilio Huerta said that on the last day of fourth grade his mother picked him up from school and they moved to another town for the summer without taking anything, depending on donations of clothing once there.

"At certain times it was hard having a mom who always worked and wasn't your typical mother," said María Elena Chávez, a daughter and a performance artist who also works with the union. "As I get older it becomes easier to understand why those sacrifices were made."

The way the children were raised made them resourceful, and at the same time exposed them to a life most people won't experience, Chávez said.

"We have always known that we can overcome any obstacles with a lot of determination, time and sacrifice," she said.

And why did Huerta choose to bear 11 children?

"She wants to pass on life, have her children carry out what she stands for," Chávez said. "She's always reminding us what she stands for."

14

Woman of the Year

Dolores Huerta, For a Lifetime of Labor
Championing the Rights of Farmworkers

Julie Felner

"Why is it that farmworkers feed the nation but they can't get food stamps?" Dolores Huerta, co-founder and secretary-treasurer of the United Farm Workers (UFW), asks an adoring crowd. Huerta has a gift for crafting sound bites of substance, and tonight, like most nights, she is reeling them off, this time before a group celebrating the 20th anniversary of the Chicana/Latina Foundation, a San Francisco-based leadership organization. As Huerta [goes] from topic to topic—from promoting women's studies to preventing domestic violence to preserving affirmative action—the women feed off her enthusiasm. What started out as a stately affair has become relaxed and interactive, with the well-heeled guests chiming in throughout Huerta's speech. When she says, "I have a T-shirt that says, 'Behind every successful woman is herself,'" California assemblywoman Liz Figueroa, the first Latina in northern California elected by a non-Latino district, shouts out, "Or other Latina women!"

The evening theme's is "Las Generaciones: Our Past, Present, and Future," and perhaps no one embodies the spirit of that theme better than Huerta, the link between the past, present, and future of both the UFW and the Chicano civil rights movement. Thirty-five years ago, Huerta and César Chávez brought the union to life, and quickly transformed it from a hand-to-mouth organization with a staff of five to a powerhouse boasting more than 400 staffers and 70,000 members.

Throughout the union's heyday in the late 1960s and 1970s, Huerta was on the front lines and in the back rooms. She wrote up the UFW's first contract and became its foremost and fiercest negotiator. She directed the grape boycott of 1968–70, one of the largest and most successful boycotts in U.S. history, which resulted in the first collective bargaining agreements for California farmworkers. She stayed with the union through a slump in the 1980s when membership fell to about 20,000 and the UFW faced long and expensive legal battles to enforce its contracts. And now, four years after Chávez's death, Huerta is helping to bring the UFW into the 21st century as it mounts its most ambitious campaign in years—organizing the 20,000 workers in California's strawberry industry, many of whom lack the basic rights that Huerta and Chávez first fought for—a living wage, clean drinking water and toilets in the fields, decent housing, health benefits, and the freedom to work without sexual harassments and assault.

As Huerta's speech comes to a close, she leads the crowd in a rousing round of vivas (long live . . .) and abajos (down with . . .). "Viva la Latina/Chicana Foundation! Viva the UFW! Abajo Sexism! Racism! Homophobia! Abajo Newt [Gingrich] and [Pete] Wilson!" And then with hands clapping, voices chanting, energy racing, the crowd breaks into a chorus of Sí se puede, the UFW's enduring motto: Yes, it can be done. Sí-se-pue-de.

This isn't the first time Dolores Huerta has turned a posh affair into a political rally. For Huerta, every moment is an organizing opportunity, every person a potential activist, every minute a chance to change the world. And her schedule reflects this single-minded devotion to social change. During any given week, you'll find the peripatetic 67-year-old flying from Washington State to Washington, D.C., with three or four stops along the way, attending union conferences or political rallies, giving lectures on college campuses or testimony before Senate subcommittees.

Huerta never slows down, never really stops moving. "She's indefatigable," says Eleanor Smeal, president of the Feminist Majority Foundation, where Huerta has served as a board member for ten years. "I don't know of any other leader who has the schedule she has . . . She'll fly in from South America on the red-eye for a board meeting and she'll stay and participate the whole time. If you say, 'Can you stay another day?' she will." Huerta spends most of her "downtime" up in the air, reading newspapers and a book or two as she flies to her next destination. "She's like a character on Star Trek. She doesn't really need sleep or food," says her daughter Juanita Chávez, the eighth of Huerta's 11 children.

Huerta's almost superhuman stamina is legendary. This is, after all, a woman who gave birth to her first child at age 20 and her eleventh at 46. And who, ten years later, in 1988, survived a brutal beating at a San Francisco rally, when a six-foot-seven police officer clubbed the five-foot-one Huerta in the back, sending her to the hospital, where she had emergency surgery to remove a ruptured spleen and repair three broken ribs. Huerta, who had been demonstrating against then-presidential candidate George Bush over his position on pesticides, lost so much blood she should have died. Instead she recovered fully and successfully sued the city's police department to change its crowd-control procedures during protests.

"I imagine that if I had known Emma Goldman, she would have been something like Dolores," says Gloria Steinam [sic], who has known Huerta for three decades. "She's not a person whose life is divided into public and private, work and play—it's all of a piece." Huerta's approach to mothering was equally undivided. Rather than choose between being with her children and going to work, she brought her children to work (and, as they became adults, put them to work). In the early days of the union, Huerta, then a twice-divorced single mother raising seven children, would nurse the youngest between meetings, pack them all in the car at night and on weekends as she drove around the state visiting migrant labor camps, move them from Chicago to New York to Los Angeles as she led the grape boycotts in those cities. Her children grew up on the picket lines, and they have inherited Huerta's sense of civic duty (among them are a doctor, a lawyer, a massage therapist, a teacher, a budding public health specialist, an aspiring film maker, a poet).

But both Huerta and her children admit that there were a lot of sacrifices along the way. There were her long absences when the children would stay with family members or union supporters, countless missed birthdays and school events. Huerta was earning between $5 and $35 a week, whatever money the union had left after paying all the bills, and the family often lived on donated food and clothing. "Like most working women, you have these guilt complexes, especially in my case because we lived in poverty and my kids didn't have the proper care they needed," she says. "But when people ask, 'How could you do it?' Well, you do it without thinking about it, because if you think about it, you can't do it."

The union always came first, says Huerta's 45-year-old daughter Lori de Leon—before the children and before her long-distance companion of more than 25 years, Richard Chávez, César's brother and the father of Huerta's four youngest children. "I remember, as a child, one time talking to her about my sadness that she wasn't going to be with me on my birthday," recalls Lori. "And she said that the sacrifices we as her children make would help hundreds of other children in the future. How can you argue with something like that?"

But Lori also emphasizes that her mother has always managed to let her children know how important they are to her: "It never fails to amaze me that each time I was in the hospital having a baby . . . and I was there lying on the table and my mom's supposed to be 2,000 or 3,000 miles away, she shows up at the foot of the bed saying, 'O.K., push.'"

Twenty-six year-old Juanita says that her mother is without question her hero. "But what I love about my hero is that she doesn't try to be perfect. She will be the first to admit her faults." Indeed, Huerta readily fesses up that the woman responsible for winning some of the labor movement's most decisive battles is equally good at losing things—wallets, papers, keys, clothing, a computer. Once she even managed to misplace a piano. Lori affectionately calls her mother "the disorganized organizer." Friends and family members note that Huerta often shows up at the airport without ID, without luggage, without a plane ticket even, but she always manages to get where she needs to be.

Huerta's assistant has taken to buying replacement reading glasses by the cartonful. Thankfully, Huerta, who manages to go through two pairs of glasses a week, has never lost her true vision. It is a vision of social change she's had since she was a teenager growing up in Stockton, a port town at the tip of the San Joaquin Valley, California's agricultural center.

Huerta was born in 1930 in Dawson, New Mexico. Her parents divorced when she was five, and her mother, Alicia, moved Dolores and her siblings to Stockton, where Alicia worked as a waitress and cook and eventually opened a hotel in a neighborhood of Latino, black, Italian, Japanese, and Native American families. Dolores inherited a passion for justice (and a commitment to farmworkers' rights) from her mother, who would often let indigent farmworkers stay for free at the hotel. "She absolutely got her feminism from our mother," says Alicia Arong, Dolores' younger sister. "Mom was a women's libber before her time. She felt very strongly that women should get out and work and participate in the community."

So it is no surprise that in 1955, when a young Anglo organizer named Fred Ross wanted to form a Stockton chapter of the Community Service Organization, a Mexican American rights group he had started a few years earlier in the barrios of L.A., both mother and daughter signed on. Huerta was working as an elementary school teacher at the time, but something clicked when she met Ross. "When I saw all these things they were able to do—bring in health clinics, fight the police—it was like a revelation," she says. Soon Huerta was working as a full-time activist, leading voter registration drives and storming the welfare department to demand public assistance for farmworkers.

She had an innate political savvy, and politicians began to take notice. One was Phil Burton, then an unabashedly liberal state assemblyman, who encouraged Huerta to begin lobbying for farmworkers' rights in Sacramento, the state capital. From 1960 to 1962, Huerta successfully lobbied for 15 bills, including landmark legislation that allowed farmworkers to receive public assistance, retirement benefits, and disability and unemployment insurance, regardless of whether they were U.S. citizens.

It was through the CSO that Huerta first met another of Ross's star recruits, César Chávez. Though the shy and unassuming Chávez didn't make much of an impression on her at first, they were both drawn to the plight of the farmworkers and began to work closely together. Huerta and Chávez became like brother and sister—throughout their lives, they would fight bitterly over strategy but always remained fiercely loyal to one another.

Farmworkers have historically been excluded from federal labor laws that guarantee the right to picket and form unions. Back then, a combination of racism and apathy had led the largely white leadership of mainstream unions to dismiss the idea of organizing farmworkers—a migrant workforce mostly made up of Filipinos and Latinos, many of whom were undocumented. In 1962, Chávez said to Huerta, "You know, there's never going to be a farmworkers' union unless we start it."

And so they formed the National Farm Workers Association, the precursor to the UFW, with Chávez as president and Huerta as second in command. The first few years were frustrating; Huerta was daunted by the slow and arduous task of building a membership. But things picked up in 1965, when the NFWA joined up with the Agricultural Workers Organizing Committee, a small group of striking Filipino grape workers. Years before, Huerta had also helped start the AWOC; now the two groups came together to organize the Delano Grape Strike, an event that catapulted them into the national spotlight. After their victory in Delano, the NFWA and AWOC merged to become the United Farm Workers Organizing Committee, which later became the United Farm Workers of America, AFL-CIO.

And the rest is history. Or at least it should be. Perhaps the greatest irony of Huerta's career is that you're more likely to find a detailed report of her activities in FBI files and police records (she's been arrested more than 20 times) than in the pages of history books. At the height of the Delano strike, an FBI report called Huerta "the driving force on the picket lines of Delano and Tulare County," but in John Gregory Dunne's popular chronicle of the events, *Delano: The Story of the California Grape Strike*, Huerta gets merely one passing mention. While volumes have been devoted to Chávez's life, a search through the library for articles about Huerta yields little more than a smattering in progressive magazines.

Much of why Huerta was never given her proper due is pure and simple sexism. She went up against growers who had never before dealt directly with a Chicano, much less a Chicana. Though some refused at first to work with her, growers eventually came to begrudgingly respect this forthright woman who, in one grower's words, "had balls." But Huerta also had to confront sexism within the union's own ranks. Though the UFW had always made a point of aiming for gender equity and supporting woman's rights, the culture inside the union was still rife with sexism. "For a long time I was the only woman on the executive board," she remembers. "And the men would come out and say their stupid little jokes about women. So I started keeping a record. At the end of the meeting, I'd say, 'During the course of this meeting you men have made 58 sexist remarks.' Pretty soon I got them down to 25, then ten, and then five."

Huerta acknowledges that when the union first started, she wasn't really thinking about the rights of women. "In the sixties and seventies, many of us were working hard to get justice for la raza, not for women. We should have been doing more for women at the same time. We've had to do a lot of catching up," she says.

These days Huerta is making up for lost time. She has made sexual harassment a centerpiece of the strawberry workers' campaign. She has fought vigorously against state and federal legislation that takes away women's rights—from the Welfare Reform Act to California's anti-affirmative action Proposition 209. And she has pushed to get women into leadership positions inside and outside the union. From 1991 until Chávez's death in 1993, Huerta took a leave from the UFW to work on the Feminist Majority's Feminization of Power campaign, traveling around the U.S. encouraging Latinas to run for office. Friends and family believe that one of her dreams for the future is to create a grassroots Latina leadership organization.

As the Chicana/Latina Foundation banquet winds to a close, a small group is out on the dance floor. It is midnight and in a few hours' time Huerta will arrive at her daughter Camila's place in Oakland, catch some sleep, and leave at the crack of dawn (without her wallet) to join Jesse Jackson for an anti-209 rally in Sacramento. But right now all Huerta wants to do is dance. She has always loved dancing—everything from ballroom to the Macarena. As Huerta joins friends on the dance floor, the bands starts to play an unintentional, though fitting tribute: Gloria Gaynor's classic feminist anthem "I Will Survive."

Dolores Huerta and Joan Baez, 1973.
Courtesy of John A. Kouns.

15

The Eternal Soldadera

James Rainey

In a nondescript Santa Rosa hotel conference room, another day of tortuous negotiations with the world's largest winemaker has sputtered to a close.

Half a dozen farm workers slump around a long table as the sun sets. In their jeans, T-shirts and cowboy boots, the men listen glumly as their leader—a tiny, 69-year-old grandmother with a community college education—assures them that they are making progress against the bevy of lawyers and consultants from Gallo of Sonoma Vineyards.

Dolores Huerta, co-founder of the United Farm Workers of America, is certain: "Something happened today. It's another step forward."

For the tired workers, it hardly seems that way. Gallo has fended off the farm workers and Huerta for a quarter century. This round of contract talks has dragged on for two years. And today the men have lowered their wage demand, again, only to receive no response.

The leather-skinned workers can only joke about their counterparts from Gallo, who huddle in a neighboring conference room in their crisp suits and white shirts. The winery's top lawyer must have made another $1,000 today, the farmhands guess. Ruefully, they smile.

Then, incongruously, one of the men spreads his arms wide, throws back his head and laughs. It is the laugh, not of a vassal, but of a king.

"When we finally win, this is how I will laugh," Carmelo Salas, a broad-faced father of three, tells Huerta and his fellow campesinos in

---

Rainey, James. "The Eternal Soldadera." *Los Angeles Times*, August 15, 1999. Copyright, 1999, *Los Angeles Times*. Reprinted with permission.

Spanish. "Because all the foremen said we would never win. And he who laughs last, laughs best."

For nearly four decades, thousands of field hands like Salas have put their lives and livelihoods in the hands of Dolores Huerta and the United Farm Workers of America, the nation's most mythologized and misunderstood union. They have thrown their bodies alongside Huerta's to block loads of nonunion grapes, locked arms with her against the blows of 2-by-4-wielding thugs, and, raging to go on strike, stayed in the fields at the insistence of this mercurial little woman.

Fabled union founder César Chávez has been dead more than six years. Current UFW President Arturo Rodríguez struggles with the daily task of winning new members for a rebuilding union. That leaves Huerta as the union's emotional compass and its most potent symbol.

The longtime secretary-treasurer has pushed relentlessly toward the goal of building a national farm workers union—even as agribusinessmen have dug in their heels, even as new immigrants have continued to accept low wages, even as old liberals have forgotten the field hands and moved on to new causes.

Small victories sustain Huerta. For her followers, there is nostalgia and, especially, faith.

"With César [Chávez] in heaven looking down and Dolores at the table negotiating for us," Salas promises, "1999 is the year that the growers really have to worry."

❖ ❖ ❖

It has been this way since 1961, when César Chávez called Huerta to his home in East Los Angeles and told her: "We have got to start the union. If we don't do it, nobody else will."

What followed has become legend from the barrios of East L.A. to the liberal salons of SoHo and Santa Monica: the strikes, long marches and grape boycotts that blossomed in the fertile political soil of the 1960s. The contracts and substantial wage increases for transient farmhands, who some thought could never be organized.

And the weeks-long fasts for nonviolence that landed shy, little César Chávez on a saintly perch from which, for some, he has never descended.

Today, the Left heralds Huerta as a hero. Mexican Americans consider her a seminal figure in the Chicano power movement. Labor leaders and feminists have installed her in their Halls of Fame.

The faithful strum their guitars and sing new corridos for the "Madonna of the Fields." At marches, brown-skinned parents push their small children forward to ask for autographs. Huerta, whose name, fittingly, means "Sorrowful Orchard," scrawls boldly across vintage UFW flags, the blood-red field emblazoned with a defiant black Aztec eagle. "Sí, se puede," she writes. "Yes, it can be done."

But the audience for such ethnic populism has its limits. Most Americans probably would be surprised to learn the farm workers union still lives; and that it still wants them to boycott grapes.

A quarter century after the plight of farm workers captured the national conscience, the UFW is battling to recapture its past glory. Membership has finally pushed back over 25,000, but it's still less than one-third of its peak and not even 10% of California's semipermanent farm workers. An estimated three-quarters of all field workers earn less than California's minimum wage, $5.75 an hour. Fewer than one-third receive health insurance. Ephemeral labor middlemen have proved too evasive for most union organizing drives. And when farm workers have gone to the state Agricultural Labor Relations Board for relief, they have seldom found it.

The UFW also has suffered at its own hand, stumbling through in-house purges and straying from the face-to-face organizing that was its strength. During the 1980s, Huerta and union leaders obsessed over internal conspiracies, while membership withered.

Ironically, it took Chávez's death in 1993 to revive the union. Now it has entered a new era under the leadership of Chávez's son-in-law, Arturo Rodríguez. During the past five years, the UFW has won 18 union elections and signed 23 new contracts. But the gains have been mostly in small crops such as mushrooms and roses. The union's biggest push—to represent notoriously low-paid strawberry workers—has stalled, despite a three-year campaign and heavy financial support from the AFL-CIO.

Never mind that, says Huerta. "I feel that, as long as we keep fighting, we can't lose."

◆ ◆ ◆

Like some presidential contender, Huerta whips across the landscape today, as if her next speech might be the one that finally enlightens a slumbering nation. During a typical five-day swing, she rushes from a meeting at a Florida ranch, where UFW workers would soon sign a contract; to a student rally in Georgia; to an appearance with California Assembly Speaker Antonio Villaraigosa in Los Angeles; then on to marches in East Los Angeles and Salinas; before speeding north to San Francisco, where rock legend Carlos Santana played a concert in her honor.

Her name still opens doors in Sacramento and Washington, D.C. This year, she helped push through federal and state relief for farm workers who lost their jobs in the citrus freeze, then got the state to raise the amount the distressed workers could earn and still receive unemployment benefits.

At an age when she might be doting on her 11 grown children, 14 grandchildren and four great-grandchildren, Huerta alights at her two-story stucco home in Bakersfield only long enough to repack and hit the road again.

At most of her stops, she listens as others paint her as an icon. Then Huerta takes center stage—often wearing a rakish red beret atop long hair, rinsed black—and tells a story about "César."

The final flourishes have become a mantra. Huerta calls out the names of the movement's heroes—Chávez, the campesinos, the "martyrs" killed during the union's heyday. The crowd responds to each with shouts of "Viva!" She then recites targets of union antipathy— pesticides, Proposition 187, the once-Republican-dominated state farm board. The crowd answers with "Abajo!" ("Down with.") Then rhythmic clapping and chants of "Sí, se puede! Sí, se puede!"

To some, the routine might seem tired or anachronistic. But Huerta seems ever-inspired. She will not leave a room until she has talked to every well-wisher. Richard Chávez, César's younger brother and father of Huerta's four youngest children, once joked that she seemed to suck energy out of the crowds like some powerful extraterrestrial.

Thirty years ago, Huerta remained sharp during all-night contract negotiations while others faded. Today, she stays up salsa dancing and partying until 3 A.M. with her youngest daughter, Camila, and her 20-something friends; then it's up early to march through a rainy San Francisco morning, paying homage to Chávez.

In San Antonio this spring, she stayed at seven homes in seven nights. Someone from a network of union members and admirers— veterans of decades of labor conflict—always seems to turn up at the right time to offer a ride or a change of clothes.

Gone are the days when she and other UFW leaders paid themselves just $5 a week. But Huerta draws a salary of just $10,000 a year and still relies heavily on friends and union supporters.

In 40 years, this doyenne of American labor recalls only one true vacation—a week she spent in Puerto Vallarta with a son. Other respites came only when she was hospitalized for exhaustion.

"There is just so much work to be done, and someone has to do it," Huerta says. "In organizing, you are not going to reach every person, but you just have to keep pushing for the next one."

◆ ◆ ◆

Throwing herself in front of brawling men, giving birth to four children out of wedlock, working rather than staying home to rear her children, Huerta shattered the mold for a Catholic Latina of her generation. Contemporaries sometimes clucked about her absentee parenting and vagabond lifestyle. Traditionalists found it distasteful that a woman was so outspoken, so radical.

But others found in the beautiful young provocateur the logical extension of a cultural tradition. During the Mexican Revolution, a handful of women followed Emiliano Zapata, Pancho Villa and others into battle. The people called them *Soldaderas*, women warriors. The most revered member of the fighting sorority was named Adelita.

When Huerta railed against greedy landowners at a rally in San Francisco, an old lettuce picker in the audience applauded. "Nuestra Adelita," the man murmured, smiling. "Our Adelita."

Like the soldaderas, Huerta, then union vice president, would be dispatched everywhere to do anything to keep the fledgling organization afloat. In 1963 in the UFW's home base of Delano, the young mother would show up at all hours at pool halls and on front stoops, recruiting workers. When the great grape strike of 1965 began, it was Huerta who marched up and down the picket lines, rallying the men and keeping them out of the fields. When the growers formed a bloody, anti-UFW alliance with the Teamsters union, it was Huerta who flew to Miami Beach and camped for a week outside Jimmy Hoffa's suite, pleading—futilely, as it turned out—with the Teamsters boss to back down.

Before the union's first walkout—at the Mount Arbor Rose Co. in McFarland—she led a final unity meeting for nearly 100 workers. Huerta held out a cross and had the mostly Catholic workers place their hands on it. They had to swear they would stick together.

Not trusting providence alone, she was up before dawn the next day, patrolling in front of the workers' homes. When one group of men appeared as if it might break ranks, Huerta rolled her car in front of their driveway. She hid the keys and would not move. (The strike eventually led to a pay raise, although not a permanent contract.)

When the first proud grape grower finally buckled in 1966, Huerta negotiated the contract—the first in the state's history between a corporation and a union led by nonwhite workers. Then she went to San Francisco and learned from longshoremen how to run her union's first hiring hall.

Huerta framed every fight as part of a larger class struggle. Some of the growers seemed as pained at being depicted as greedy oppressors as they did at granting wage increases. They called Huerta "the dragon lady."

Three decades have not softened the view of one old foe, a Central Valley farmer, who said: "You don't get anything from Dolores Huerta unless you fight for it and you earn it. . . . She is vindictive and carries a certain amount of resentment. I wouldn't ever expect anything to be relented by her."

The same persistence is viewed by the UFW stalwarts as the union's greatest strength.

"She went about this stuff with an amazing confidence," says Marshall Ganz, a former UFW executive and now an instructor at

Harvard's John F. Kennedy School of Government. "She went in face to face with these lawyers or professional management people and she was just very impressive. She more than held her own."

Huerta felt union leaders could only be limited by their own imagination and resolve. She once drove a 19-year-old grape picker to the Port of Los Angeles, handed him a picket sign and told him to stop longshoremen from loading nonunion grapes. Huerta then sped off to a meeting. Fourteen hours later, young Eliseo Medina was still sitting on the dock. He never saw a single grape that day. But if he had, "Dolores just thought I would figure it out and stop those grapes all by myself," recalls Medina, later a UFW vice president and now the western chief of the Service Employees International Union, which has 1.3 million nurses, doctors, janitors, clerks and other members.

"Dolores had a gift for making you believe in yourself," Medina says. "She has an ability to inspire you and urge you to do things you could not think were possible. She is one of those life-changers."

History also had a way of freezing Huerta in its bright strobe.

On the night in 1968 that Bobby Kennedy won the California presidential primary, among his last utterances was a thanks to Chávez, Huerta and the UFW, whose precinct walkers inspired a 90%-plus vote for Kennedy in some East Los Angeles neighborhoods. Moments later, Huerta followed Kennedy off the podium at the Ambassador Hotel, ready to direct him to a room where Maríachis would serenade the presumptive Democratic nominee. Instead, Kennedy walked into the hotel's kitchen, where Sirhan Sirhan shot him dead.

Two decades later, in 1988, Huerta suddenly found herself at the end of a San Francisco policeman's nightstick as she and others peacefully picketed an appearance by Vice President George Bush. A television camera captured the assault, which ruptured Huerta's spleen and nearly killed her.

The incident led to a rewriting of the San Francisco Police Department's policies on crowd control and discipline. The city also awarded Huerta $825,000, a legal settlement that pays her $2,000 a month to this day.

Chávez once summed up his right hand quite simply: "Totally fearless, both mentally and physically."

◆ ◆ ◆

Not long ago, Huerta's daughter Juanita was writing for a San Francisco State University publication. Her elegant essay begins with a recollection of the day she waited in a junior high school parking lot for her mother to drive her home.

The minutes pass and Dolores fails to appear. The 12-year-old's emotions vault from anger to sadness to despair. A train rushes past the lonely parking lot, and the girl begins to cry. The locomotive evokes in Juanita an image of her mother "... rattling all the windows behind me, blaring out its horn, announcing its simultaneous arrival and departure with an incredible clamor, but rushing constantly forward. . . ."

Dolores Huerta did not make life easy for those around her, whether in her blood family or her union one. The fire and quixotic nature that moved the faithful often left those close to her scrambling for solid ground.

Chávez had his wife, Helen, to raise their eight children. But Huerta was often on her own, having split with her two husbands. The second, Ventura Huerta, had been alienated by Dolores' refusal to stay home and be a traditional wife and mother.

So when Dolores drove up and down Route 99 to her latest meeting or negotiation, she would likely be nursing another new baby. (She once said she had so many children because they were lucky, like angels.) Her older children sometimes had to forage among friends and neighbors for dinner and a place to stay.

She would miss birthdays, communions and school open houses. The children could not help but feel jealous of their mother's first love, the union. But they basked in a feeling that they were a part of history. "We understood very quickly she wasn't ours to have," says Emilio, now 42 and a lawyer for the National Farm Worker Service Center in Bakersfield. "She sort of belonged to the farm worker movement. And it was our job to support her."

Her crusade only gave her pause, Huerta says, when it put her children in danger.

When Emilio was 9, he slipped fliers to workers on a giant produce ranch, sprinting to safety just ahead of a pickup truck driven by an angry ranch supervisor.

One night in Delano, two anti-union agitators came to the door at 4 A.M. and tried to force their way in. When they couldn't, they smashed a picture window, sending shards of glass just past Emilio. Huerta and her children huddled in terror in a bathroom, shaking uncontrollably until the men went away.

"It was our families who sacrificed," she conceded to friends and family at her 69th birthday last April. She then told a story about limping to school one day, with a carload of children, on a slashed tire. "That was kind of how we made it through life," she said.

Now Huerta's children seem largely to be flourishing. They devote at least some of their time to the movement. Fidel, 43, is a doctor at a public health clinic, 47-year-old Lori is acting director at the César Chávez Foundation and Juanita, 28, teaches fifth-graders in Los Angeles. Among Huerta's other children are a chef, a nurse, a film student, a public health outreach worker. Her greatest heartache has come from her eldest, 49-year-old Celeste, who has schizophrenia and has sometimes wandered the streets but now lives in an L.A. nursing home.

Her union family and allies also found Huerta to be an unpredictable partner.

Chávez appreciated that Huerta would speak her mind, but the two clashed so routinely that others tended to shrink from the room in anticipation of their encounters. Huerta quit or was fired by Chávez more times than anyone can remember. Within a day or two, she would be on the phone or back in the office, talking strategy as if nothing had happened.

Some of her co-workers were rankled by Huerta's inability to follow a schedule. Others complained that, for all her negotiating and motivational skills, she could not execute an organizational plan. And she has a reputation for never forgiving a slight.

Art Torres, chairman of the state Democratic Party, suffered Huerta's fury when he was a state assemblyman. Although he once worked as a UFW lobbyist, the union attacked him with a vengeance when he failed to support the UFW choice for Assembly speaker. The union gave generously to Torres' opponent, and Huerta would not even speak to her old ally.

Torres won despite the union opposition, but he and Huerta

"didn't speak for years and years and years," he recalls.

By some accounts, such stridency exacerbated the union's long slide, which began in the mid-1970s when Chávez became preoccupied with "malignant forces" he insisted were trying to topple the union. Some core staff members were deemed too preoccupied with leftist politics and pressured to leave. Others were ostracized because—no longer content to work for little more than room and board—they asked for salaries.

When a group of dissident field representatives in Salinas attempted to elect their own candidates for the UFW's executive board in 1981, Huerta was dispatched to fire the 10 leaders of the rebellion. She insists that they were not responding to worker grievances. To this day she claims the real culprit was Marshall Ganz, the former UFW executive who gave 15 years of his life to the union with virtually no pay.

Critics say that the dark side of Huerta's zealotry came out during those low years for the union. "All through that period, Dolores played a negative role," says Ganz. "I think she exacerbated César's difficulties and acted as an amplifier of the union's paranoia."

Those who knew her as a child could not have predicted what a force Dolores would become. She was skinny and prone to illness. She relished the middle-class life her mother built for her in Stockton. Dolores took violin lessons, joined the Girl Scouts, loved to tap dance. She even became a majorette.

But she also learned from her single mother, a hotel manager, the importance of community service. Alicia St. John Chávez made sure even her poorest tenants had something to eat. And Huerta's father, Juan Fernandez, was a fiery union leader who had served in the New Mexico Legislature. According to family lore, he identified one fellow legislator as "a dirty scab" and punched him out on the floor of the House.

Dolores began to flower as an activist in the mid-1940s. As a high school student, she organized a teen center, where kids gathered to listen to a jukebox, dance and play games. She was popular and excelled in school.

But the sharpest memories of those years were of rewards denied, opportunities missed. She won a Girl Scout essay contest, but high school administrators would not let her miss two weeks of classes to accept the trip that was her prize. She sold the most war bonds, but the promised award was never presented. School officials would not accept a Mexican American as a winner, she says.

Then police ordered the teen center shut down, apparently because they did not like whites socializing with Mexican, black and Filipino kids. Huerta said those setbacks so alienated her that she cannot remember a single detail from her senior prom or graduation. "It was terrible," she recalls. "I just blacked the whole thing out."

In the years that followed, that sting would never leave her. After attending Stockton College, Huerta became a teacher. But she left about a year later because, as she once told an interviewer, "I couldn't stand seeing kids come to class hungry and needing shoes. I thought I could do more by organizing farm workers than by trying to teach their hungry children."

In 1955, at age 25, Huerta found the perfect outlet for her restless energies when she met Fred Ross Sr., a liberal activist who helped teach working-class people how to register voters, fight police brutality and demand government services. Huerta helped found the Stockton chapter of Ross' Community Service Organization. A few years earlier, a former farm worker named César Chávez had taken the same path in a San Jose barrio named Sal Sí Puedes (literally, "Get out, if you can").

The CSO would help win many new rights for its poor, mostly Mexican American, constituents, including state pensions for immigrant noncitizens. As a CSO leader in Stockton, Huerta began to organize farm workers. Chávez was doing the same in Oxnard. They shared a frustration: After a few victories, they would turn over the workers to larger unions, who ignored the poor, Spanish-speaking migrants.

Even when Chávez rose to the CSO's top job in California, the organization's convention voted against organizing farm workers. A distraught Chávez bolted [from] the group in 1962 and Huerta soon followed.

Chávez moved his family to Delano, a modest Central Valley town surrounded by rows of Emperor grapes and groves of fine almond trees. There he started his union with the help of his friend Dolores Huerta and, later, a child of the migrant camps, Gilbert Padilla.

"I thought, 'Wow, we are finally going to do it!'" Huerta recalls. "We are finally going to make it happen."

The old soldadera speaks much the same way about the union today. So closely does she relate to la causa that questions about her personal life inevitably turn back to the union. She seldom allows herself to express regret or loss. She answers questions about setbacks with reports on the latest union victories. Rarely by herself, she seems the fanatical embodiment of the old 1960s axiom—the personal is political.

Huerta is familiar with many people but gives the impression that she is intimate with very few. If this is sad to anyone else, it is not so to Huerta, who considers her life's work totally energizing.

"You could just feel this power you could generate from people working together," she says. "It was just very awesome. We were doing what we loved and so we didn't really sacrifice anything."

◆ ◆ ◆

At a bucolic hideaway in the mountains above Bakersfield, Richard Chávez waits.

He has retired from most of his union responsibilities, except for an occasional march or a tribute to his late brother. Soon he plans to move out of Nuestra Señora de La Paz, Our Lady of Peace, the 200-acre retreat in the Tehachapi Mountains where many of the union's leaders live and work.

Richard Chávez spends most of his days at the base of a boulder-strewn hill, about a half mile from La Paz, where César Chávez is buried in a simple grave beside a gravel road.

He is toiling away on a retirement cottage. Here Richard will be close enough to his union family and friends, but distant enough to avoid being dragged into every union intrigue. He and Huerta have mostly lived apart in recent times, although she recently took him into her home when he was ill.

Chávez hopes the two will be reunited in the small hillside cottage, living out their days together. He concedes, though, that his sometime-partner has not shown much interest in this plan. "She wants to build this national union," says Chávez, a kind and quiet man of 69. "And she feels she is running out of time."

The old carpenter keeps at it—installing the dry wall in the cottage and raising rough wood beams. He adds a picture window and other touches he thinks Dolores will like. But he laughs a little at his efforts, realizing the woman warrior is not yet prepared to strip off her armor.

"I hope to spend a few hours with her before I fall over," he says, still smiling. "I've been waiting and waiting and waiting. I guess I will just keep on waiting."

16

Labor Leader Dolores Huerta Credits Family and Faith

María Luisa Torres

"My message to [you] as college graduates, as future professionals, is that [your] main responsibility is to working people, to poor people, to those who don't get the chance to go to college, to those who don't have a voice in society.

"I encourage [you] to serve [your] communities—to serve the working poor—through the work [you] choose to do, to help make the world a better place."

Such was the message relayed by legendary labor leader and civil rights activist Dolores Huerta during a May 29 commencement ceremony at California State University, Northridge (CSUN), where she was presented with an honorary degree, a Doctor of Humane Letters.

"It's very good being recognized, not only as a woman, but as someone who represents the struggles of working people," Huerta, a parishioner at St. Francis Church in Bakersfield, told *The Tidings*. "It's that recognition—that respect—that makes it good."

Huerta played key roles in the founding and evolution of the United Farm Workers of America (UFW) since the union's inception in the early 1960s. Along with co-founder César Chávez (who just passed away in 1993) and other union supporters, Huerta organized on behalf of farm workers to support just wages and benefits by various means, from negotiating the UFW's first collective bargaining agreement to directing its political and lobbying efforts to heading its national grape boycott campaign.

As first vice president emeritus of the UFW, Huerta has officially resigned from the day-to-day responsibilities of her former position,

---

Originally published in *The Tidings*, May 31, 2002.

though she remains active by regularly speaking at select lectures and special events, continuing to support the union's efforts through her voice and unbreakable spirit.

Huerta's life-long devotion to standing in solidarity with the voiceless has its roots in both her faith and family. Her work as a labor leader and civil rights activist has "been a continuation of the type of beliefs we had in our family," she explained.

One of five children, Huerta was born in New Mexico in 1930. She and her siblings later moved to the agricultural community of Stockton, Calif., where her mother owned a restaurant and a 70-room hotel, which often provided free room and board for local farm workers and their families.

"My mother was my greatest influence," said Huerta, 72, herself a mother of 11 children, with 14 grandchildren and four great-grandchildren. "Ever since I was a little girl, my mother would tell me, 'If you see something that needs to be done, you have to do it.'"

Years later, those childhood lessons endured. After going to college and earning a teaching degree, Huerta became a grammar school teacher, but later decided she could "do more by organizing the farm workers than by teaching their hungry children."

In 1955, she became a founding member of the Stockton chapter of the Community Service Organization (CSO), which led voter registration drives, pushed for improved public services, battled segregation and police brutality, and fought to enact new legislation. Through her work with CSO, Huerta met César Chávez.

In an effort to directly address the needs of farm workers, Chávez and Huerta jointly launched the National Farm Workers Association (the predecessor to the UFW) in 1962 and went on to organize farm workers—and make history.

"It was always a challenge and a fight, but the workers themselves were always very supportive," said Huerta. "I think organized labor is a necessary part of democracy. Organized labor is the only way to have a fair distribution of the wealth; it helps create a middle class. Without a middle class, there would be no democracy."

When Huerta first left her job as a teacher in 1955, she knew it was a risky endeavor, financially, emotionally and spiritually. At the time, Huerta already had seven children and was going through a divorce.

Without a steady source of income from teaching, she and her children faced an uncertain future.

Yet, at once, Huerta said she felt called to help support and serve the labor community. Seeking solace, Huerta said she turned to her faith, asking God "to give me a sign, to show me if I was doing the right thing." And then the sign came—the form of many little signs—beginning the following day.

"When I made the decision to quit teaching, it took a lot of faith," recalled Huerta. "After I had made that decision—the very next morning—I woke up to find that someone had left a box of groceries on my porch."

In another instance, Huerta didn't have a coat for the coming winter season, but over the next several weeks—before the cool winter weather arrived—she received four coats from friends and relatives.

"I saw all of these as little signs, and over the years, my decision has been affirmed many, many times in so many little ways," she said. It was further affirmed by the support of her family and others. For example, Huerta's sisters helped care for her children, and Huerta's older children helped care for their younger siblings.

In addition, Huerta routinely took her children along with her to out-of-town gatherings, where fellow union workers and local supporters lent a helping hand by baby-sitting her children.

"It wasn't perfect; there were difficult times, but there was always food and the kids were always cared for," Huerta said of her children. "And as Hillary Clinton says, 'It takes a village to raise a child.'"

Today, those 11 now-grown children, ranging from 26 to 50 years of age, have gone on to establish diverse careers: there is a teacher, an attorney, a doctor, a nurse, a filmmaker, and a musician, among others.

"I feel I've been very blessed; I have been so richly rewarded in my personal life, with my children, family and friends," said Huerta. "And it really has been a blessing to have had the opportunity to do the type of work that I've done—and continue to do."

Dolores Huerta, circa 1980s.
Courtesy of Jon Lewis.

17

Campus Workers Urged to Unite

Ryan Floersheim

"Unionizing is the key to success," was the message from one of the country's most noted political activists and labor organizers when she spoke at UNM Wednesday.

Dolores Huerta, a native New Mexican who worked with such revolutionaries as César Chávez, spoke to a crowd of more than 100 at the SUB about the importance of protecting workers' rights and securing a level of treatment in all organizations, including the University.

"There has been such a strong anti-union climate in New Mexico for years, and we need to change that," said Huerta, whose visit at UNM was part of a weeklong effort to train union organizers throughout the state. "The roots of unionization began in New Mexico. We need to bring those ideals back."

A union, as Huerta described it, is "just an organization of workers coming together to fight for their basic rights and to feed and clothe their children."

Huerta said she started a career as a teacher more than 40 years ago but couldn't stand the economic disparity she witnessed in the school system. Since then, she said she decided to spend her life dedicated to human equality.

She said the basic organization of the country's corporations has gotten "screwed up," in recent years, with company CEOs having job security by placing the organizations in larger conglomerations of businesses.

"These people don't need job security or someone looking out for their rights as employees," Huerta said. "The worker who is living

Originally published in the *Daily Lobo*, October 30, 2003. University of New Mexico.

paycheck to paycheck needs that protection. The average worker is getting shafted by their own government in this country."

Charlotte Walters, a United Staff-UNM member, said Huerta's speech was part of a larger statewide celebration of Gov. Bill Richardson recently enacting the New Mexico Public Employee Bargaining Act.

The act allows workers at public institutions and businesses to organize unions.

"Public employees . . . may form, join or assist a labor organization for the purposes of collective bargaining . . . without interference, restraint, or coercion," according to section five of the act.

"Unionizing is the only way for workers to have any real rights on the job," Walters said, adding that one of the biggest issues US-UNM has faced since its inception is pay equity. "I hope Dolores (Huerta) serves as a catalyst to encourage all employees at UNM to unionize."

Lucille Farrington, president of US-UNM, said she respects Huerta just as much as she respects other labor activists such as Martin Luther King.

"Until her last day I know she will be organizing and supporting unions in the best interests of workers everywhere," Farrington said.

Huerta said she has spent a lot of time meeting with the heads of major U.S. corporations, trying to convince them that allowing their workers to form unions will benefit their business.

She said they are afraid of giving workers too much power.

"Workers who are unionized tend to work harder because they are content that their best interests are being looked out for," Huerta said. "Their profits will increase as a result."

Part Two

DOLORES HUERTA SPEAKS

18

Dolores Huerta Talks about Republicans, César Chávez, Children, and Her Home Town

The name César Chávez and the struggle to unionize farm labor have become virtually synonymous. People associate few other names with the United Farm Workers Union. But Dolores Huerta, the union's fiery Vice President, doesn't seem to mind being overshadowed by Chávez the Personality. She thinks of herself as a "common soldier" in the union's army of workers and volunteers, and shies away from publicity whenever possible.

But her leadership ability is undeniable. Huerta went to the 1972 Democratic Convention as a delegate from California and turned this meeting of a political party into what seemed to be a gathering of lettuce boycotters. As one of the union's chief negotiators, she matches the opposition's highly trained highly paid lawyers with her own self-taught negotiating skills fortified with a strong-minded inborn stubbornness.

Taking time out last month from the successful battle against Proposition 27 which brought her to the Bay Area, she revealed to *La Voz del Pueblo*, in an unusually candid conversation, little-known facts about her life and her work. Her story follows.

My family goes way back to the 1600's in New Mexico. My father was a migrant worker who used to travel from New Mexico to Wyoming, following the work, living in little shacks. My mother was a very ambitious woman. She got a little lunch counter together, then she got a bigger restaurant, and when the war came she got a hotel. That's how

---

Originally published in *La Voz del Pueblo*, January 25, 1973, pp. 3–4.

I was able to go to school and how I got a more affluent background than the other kids.

When my dad and my mom divorced, he stayed in New Mexico and she came to California. I would beg my mother to let me go to the fields when I was little, but she would not let me. My brothers used to go pick tomatoes in Stockton, but my mother wasn't going to let *her* daughter go work in any field. So when I was 14, I went to work in the packing sheds instead, which were just as bad.

I was a little bit luckier than most Chicanos because I was raised in an integrated neighborhood. All the Chicanos who went to school where I did are all making it. We grew up in Stockton but we weren't in a ghetto. In our school, there was Mexican, Black, White, Indian, Italian; we were all thrown in together. We had all of the old guard teachers who treated everybody very mean. But they didn't discriminate against one or the other. They treated us all equally mean. So we all hated the teachers, but we didn't hate each other. We didn't have a whole bunch of hang-ups, like hating Anglos, or hating Blacks.

When I got into High School, then it was really segregated. There was the real rich and the real poor. We were poor too, and I got hit with a lot of racial discrimination. My four years in high school hit me very hard and it took me a long time to get over it.

When I was in High School I got straight A's in all of my compositions. I can't write any more, but I used to be able to write really nice, poetry and everything. But the teacher told me at the end of the year that she couldn't give me an A because she knew that somebody was writing my papers for me. That really discouraged me, because I used to stay up all night and think, and try to make every paper different, and try to put words in there that I thought were nice. Well, it just kind of crushed me.

I couldn't be active in College though, because it was just too early. I was the only Chicano at Stockton Junior College. At that time, there was just a handful of us that you might call liberals.

I was frustrated. I had a fantastic complex because I seemed to be out of step with everybody and everything. You're trying to go to school and yet you see all of these injustices. It was just such a complex!

Then my mother took me to Mexico City when I was about 17. She had never been there either. It was our first trip. But that opened my eyes to the fact that there was nothing wrong with Chicanos. I felt inside that everybody was wrong and I was right. They were wrong in beating the people up in the streets and all of the things they did to people. I felt I had all of these frustrations inside of me, so I started joining Chicano organizations—El Comité Honorífico, Women's Club, all of these organizations that didn't do anything but give dances and celebrate the Fiestas Patrias.

By the time I was 25 years old, I had been married and gotten a divorce. I was still living in Stockton when Fred Ross came into town and he started telling us about forming this organization, the Community Service Organization (CSO). And he told us about how in Los Angeles they had sent these policemen to San Quentin for beating up a Mexican. At that time, I didn't even talk about things like that publicly. Everybody knew that the cops did it, but you just accepted it. Now these two cops were sent to San Quentin and Fred had organized it.

When Fred started telling us that if we got together we could register voters, elect Spanish-speaking representatives, and turn everything around, I just didn't believe it. He showed us how they had gotten these clinics in San Jose and he told us about César Chávez. He showed me all those pictures of big meetings with 100 to 200 people together. Well, I thought he was telling me a fairy tale.

I thought he was a communist, so I went to the FBI and had him checked out. I really did that. I used to work for the Sheriff's Department. See how middle class I was. In fact, I was a registered Republican at the time. I don't think I was ever a real cop-out, though, because I had always been real close to a lot of the people. My mother even used to tell me all the time that all my friends were either ex-cons or pachucos.

But I always thank the day that I met Fred. I always hated injustice and I always wanted to do something to change things. Fred opened a door for me. He changed my whole life. If it weren't for Fred, I'd probably just be in some stupid suburb somewhere.

Anyway, I started my first job getting people to register to vote. Eventually, some of the people started paying attention to us. So then we started fighting the Police Department and we got them to stop searching and harassing people arbitrarily. Then we had a big fight with the County Hospital and we turned that around. But it was just like magic. You start registering people to vote and all of these things start happening.

I was actually in the organization for two years before I got to talk to César (Chávez). I met him once, but he was very shy. He wouldn't talk to anybody except the people he was organizing. But I heard him speak one time at a board meeting and I was really impressed. Well, after a big voter registration drive in 1960 where we registered 150,000 people, César got this bright idea to send me to Sacramento.

So I went to Sacramento and we got all these bills passed. I headed up the legislative program in 1961 when we fought for the old-age pension for the non-citizens, for *los viejitos*. I lobbied the welfare bill through so that the parents could stay in the home. César and I and the rest of us worked to get the right to register voters door to door, and the right for people to take their driver's license exams in Spanish, and disability insurance for farm workers, and the right for people to get surplus commodities. And, of course, we were the ones that ended the Bracero Program. I have a lot of experience in legislation, and I guess I've become sort of a trouble-shooter in the union.

I guess because I'm articulate, I came to the forefront. A lot of people who do a lot of hard work in the union are not mentioned anywhere. *Son los soldados razos del movimiento.* And that's what I consider myself—just a person working at what I'm supposed to be doing. The fact that I get publicity is sort of a by-product of the union. But there's an awful lot of people who have worked continuously since the union started, a lot of women, for example, who nobody even knows.

There's been no reaction from the farm workers to my role as a woman within the union. They will appreciate anybody who will come in to help them. In terms of the leadership itself I get very little friction from anybody, really. Any one who can do the job is welcome to come in and share the suffering.

There are a lot of other women in the union besides me and they share some of my problems. But I think it's mostly a personal conflict and it depends how much you let it hang you up in terms of what you're doing. If you let it bug you when people say that you're not being a good mother because you're not with your kids 24 hours a day, well then of course it will deter you from what you're doing. In the union, you know, everybody cooperates to take care of your kids.

The idea of the communal family is not new and progressive. It's really kind of old fashioned. Remember when you were little you always had your uncles, your aunts, your grandmother and your comadres around. As a child in the Mexican culture you identified with a lot of people, not just your mother and father like they do in the middle class homes. When people are poor their main interest is family relationships. A baptism or a wedding are a big thing. In middle class homes you start getting away from that and people become more materialistic. When you have relatives come to visit it's a nuisance instead of a great big occasion.

While I was in jail some of my kids came down to Delano to see me, but my little girl, Angela, didn't come. She wrote me a little note which said, "Dear Mom. I love you very much, but I can't come because the people need me. I've got to go door-knocking this weekend and I can't leave my job." I think that's really great because she puts her priorities on the work she has to do instead of coming down to see me.

The time I spend with my kids is very limited. This year I was in Washington, D.C., for almost two months, then I was in Arizona for another week, then I was in Los Angeles working on the McGovern campaign for another two weeks. So this year I've spent very little time with my children. Since August the 27th I've seen them twice for visits for about an hour.

Sure, it's a hardship for me, but I know that my kids are all working in the union itself. They have to grow up with the responsibility of their work, but they have fun too. Probably the problems they have are like the kind of schools that they go to which are very reactionary.

I think it's important for the children to be fed and clothed, which they are. When I first started working with César I had this problem worrying about whether my kids were going to eat or not, because at the time I started working for the union I was making pretty good money, and I knew I was going to start working without *any* money, and I wondered how I could do it. But the kids have never gone hungry. We've had some rough times, particularly in Delano during the strike because my kids went without fresh milk for two years. They just had powdered milk we got through donations. It's made them understand what hardship is, and this is good because you can't really relate to suffering unless you've had a little bit of it yourself.

But the main thing is that they have their dignity and identity.

My family used to criticize me a lot. They thought that I was a traitor to my Raza, to my family and to everybody else. But I think they finally realized that what I'm doing is important and they're starting to appreciate it now. They thought that I was just neglecting my children and that what I was doing was just for selfish reasons.

The criticism came mostly from my dad and other relatives, but my brothers are very understanding. My mother was a very active woman, and I just followed her. She's dead now, but she always got the prizes for registering the most voters, and she raised us without any hang-ups about things like that. You could expect that I would get a lot of criticisms from the farm workers themselves, but it mostly came from middle class people. They're more hung-up about these things than the poor people are, because the poor people have to haul their kids around from school to school, and the women have to go out and work and they've got to either leave their kids or take them out to the fields with them. So they sympathize a lot more with my problem in terms of my children. Sometimes I think it's bad for people to shelter their kids too much. Giving kids clothes and food is one thing, you know, but it's much more important to teach them that other people besides themselves are important, and that the best thing they can do with their lives is to use it in the service of other people. So my kids know that the way that we live is poor, materially speaking, but it's rich in a lot of other ways. They get to meet a lot of people and their experiences are varied.

I know people who work like fools just to give their kids more material goods. They're depriving their family of themselves, for what? At least my kids know why I'm not home. They know that I'm doing this for something in which we're all working—it makes a whole different thing. My children don't have a lot of material things but they work hard for what they do get, just like everybody else, and that makes them really self-sufficient. They make their own arrangements when they go places. They all have a lot of friends and they don't get all hung-up about having a lot of goodies. I think my kids are very healthy both mentally and physically. All the women in the union have similar problems. They don't have to leave their families for as long as I do. But everybody shares everything, we share the work.

The way we do the work is we do whatever is needed regardless of what we'd really like to do. You have a problem when you develop into a kind of personality like César because that really takes you away from the work that has to be done with the farm workers in education and development of leadership. That's what I'd really like to do. I'd just like to keep working down there with the ranch committees and the farm workers themselves because they have to take over the union. I can put my experience there. César would much rather be organizing than anything. He loves to organize because it's really creative. But he can't do it because right now he has to go around speaking, as I am doing also. I'd rather be working on the strike.

It's hard when you learn how to do something but you have to do something else. But they've kept us on the run. We had been successful in organizing farm workers so in order to try to stop the union they introduced this bill, AB 964. This bill was just exactly like Proposition 22 [to outlaw consumer boycotts] and they thought they could get it through the legislature. Well, we mobilized and were able to stop it. Thousands of farm workers' supporters went to Sacramento to stop it. That was 1971. They tried it again in 1972 but the bill didn't really go very far. We had been involved with the lettuce negotiation all of last year, after we stopped the boycott. Then they got the bright idea in the Nixon administration to try to take the boycott away from us in the federal courts. What they were using as an argument was that we were covered by the National Labor Relations Law (NLRB) so that we couldn't boycott. They took us to federal court in Fresno saying we were part of the NLRB. Well, this is ridiculous because we've never been part of it. So what this means is that it's strictly a political issue and logic and justice, none of these factors have anything to do with it.

We went to Washington and started putting heat on the Republican Party all over the country. We picketed people like Banuelos (U.S. Treasurer Ramona Banuelos) and Senators Tower, Percy and Hatfield. I was in Washington talking to the Republicans and the Democrats trying to stop this thing, kind of coordinating it.

In a way they might win by keeping us on the run but in a way they lose. Arizona is a good example, I was there for about two months before César went out there. They passed a proposition in the legislature similar to Proposition 22 here. So I called César up to ask him to come to a rally. I said "The Governor's going to sign the bill but maybe if you come we can at least make a good protest." So we called the Governor's office to tell him that César would be coming, and would he please give us the courtesy of meeting with us before he signed it. We thought we still might have a chance to stop it. Well, the Governor knew that we were having this noon-time rally so he signed the bill at 9 o'clock in the morning without even meeting with us. So what's happening now is we're getting everybody registered to vote, we're going to recall the Governor and turn the state upside-down. We organized the whole state just because the Governor signed the stupid bill. So you might say that they win because they make us come out to the cities, but maybe while we're here, we're organizing too. Every time they try to do something against the union it works in our favor.

The main thing they keep us from doing is working with the farm workers. We'd be going after other growers and going to other states but we can't do that right now. But maybe that's the way it's supposed to happen. It's like this letter that this farm worker wrote me. *Dice que parece que estamos siguiendo un mandamiento de Dios.* We see these things as bad things that are happening to us right now but maybe they're good things and we can't see them that way because God wants us to do them. Every time we had some problem that kept us from ending the grape strike, I'd always tell César it's because God wants us to organize something else before the grape strike is over.

We've been working more and more with the Democratic Party, because it's been the most liberal of the two parties. We depended on the Democrats to pass all those bills I told you about. You hardly ever get Republicans to vote for you. We live in a practical world, in a world of survival. And when the Democrats do us dirt, *tambien los ataquamos a ellos*, although on an individual basis. So we maintain a certain amount of independence because our first responsibility is to the farm workers.

It's not true that both parties are just as bad for Chicanos, because the few benefits that we have gotten have come through the Democratic Party. The only thing I have to say to people who attack the Democrats, is that they should attack the Republicans. They should be going after Nixon, after Secretary of Agriculture Butz, after

Reagan and all of these Republicans in the valley who vote against us every time. That's who they should be going after, not after the guys who are trying to help us.

On the other hand, if anybody needs straightening up in the Democratic Party, they straighten them up. We went after certain guys, like Alex García who's a Mexican, and we almost got him defeated. He won by 200 votes and if it wouldn't have been for the fast in Arizona and our work on the McGovern campaign, we would have beaten Alex García, and Alex knows it.

I think that if people are dissatisfied with the Democratic Party they should get involved and take it over. I've told Assemblyman Moretti that he can make a decision either for or against the poor people, and that if he's against us we're going to fight him. But you can't go saying this to Reagan. He won't even meet with us.

There were some problems at the Democratic Convention. It was really unfortunate because there was a little clique that was trying to put down McGovern. The rumor was going around that McGovern wouldn't talk to Chicanos. Well, this was ridiculous because in East Los Angeles McGovern would go to every little place Chicanos wanted him to go, and speak to them. But there were people who were spreading this rumor around. I think they were part of the Nixon sabotage squad. (Laughter.)

I know that the farm worker issue is not the only Chicano issue. But in terms of the visibility of the Chicano issues, I think first of all there wasn't an agreement among the Chicanos themselves on what the issues were. Some people talked about bilingual education, other people talked about something else. I don't know, there just wasn't that much of a consensus on what we wanted to make public. So I talked to Senator McGovern's staff, Frank Mankiewicz, and some other people, and I told them that Chicanos wanted more visibility there. Naturally, they turned to me and said they wanted me to make a seconding speech for Senator Eagleton or somebody. And I told them that I didn't want to be in the limelight, that other Chicanos wanted the focus. So that's when they had Mondragon make the speech he made.

I would say the Chicanos were disorganized. They had a platform with a lot of Chicano issues which they wanted to submit. But it was put together kind of fast, I think. You didn't have a kind of cohesiveness. But that's not unusual, you see, because in the black caucus you had the same kind of divisions.

Understanding that Chicanos have to come from all walks of life from different experiences and different communities, you're not always going to get everybody to think the same. I think the Chicano Caucus they had in San Jose is a good idea, where you can get Chicanos to decide the two or three priorities we want for California and get everybody to push together on them. But again, you got too many factions going. Everybody wants their own thing.

We're just now reaching a level where we can get mature political participation. We're going to get it as people get more interested in politics and make it a life long thing, like Art Flores who ran against Alex García in East Los Angeles. Art really likes politics and he wants to do the right thing and he's not afraid to tell a guy he's an S.O.B. Then there's Peter Chacon, who's an Assemblyman, *pero es muy cobarde*. When people are doing something against Chicanos he's afraid to tell them so, because he says he has to rely on a lot of white votes. So he lets them tell *him* what to do. But if we would have had 15 Chicanos in California who were really involved in politics, *pero que no fueran miedosos*, the whole McGovern campaign would have been run by Chicanos. But we didn't have enough guys who had the political savvy.

But that's all going to change. If you ever get a chance, go down to Parlier. Chicanos turned around the whole City Council there. So when the farm workers set up a picket line in Parlier, the cops wouldn't even come near us. There's a whole change in the picture because those people exercised their political power, they participated in democracy.

The worst thing that I see is guys who say, "Man, they don't have no Chicanos up there and they're not doing this or that for Chicanos." But the "vatos" are just criticizing and they're not in there working to make sure that it happens. We criticize and separate ourselves from the process. We've got to jump right in there with both feet.

Most of the people doing the work for us are "gabachillos." When we get Chicano volunteers it's really great. But the Chicanos that come down to work with the farm workers have some hang-ups, especially the guys that come out of college. *En primer lugar, le tienen miedo a la gente.* Unless they come out of the farm worker communities themselves, they get down there and they're afraid of the people. I don't know why it happens, but they're afraid to deal with them. But you have to deal with them like people, not like they were saints. The Chicano guys who come down here have a very tough time adjusting. They don't want to relate to the poor farmworkers. They tried so hard to get away from that scene and they don't want to go back to it.

We have a lot of wonderful people working with us. But we need a lot more because we have a whole country to organize. If the people can learn to organize within the union, they can go back to their own communities and organize. We have to organize La Raza in East Los Angeles. We have to do it. We have 1,000 farm workers in there right now organizing for the boycott. In the future, we would very much like to organize around an issue that isn't a farm worker issue. But we just can't because we just don't have the time.

Maybe someday we can finish organizing the farm workers, but it's going so slow because of all the fights we have to get into. We'll have a better idea of where we're at once the lettuce boycott is won. See, there's about 200 to 300 growers involved in the lettuce boycott. The same growers that grow lettuce grow vegetables like artichokes and broccoli. So if we get that out of the way we'll have about one-third of the State of California organized. That's a big chunk. From there, hopefully, we can move on to the citrus and get that out of the way. We have to move into other states, like we did into Arizona.

It would seem that with the Republicans in for another four years, though, we'll leave a lot of obstacles. Their strategy was to get Chicanos into the Republican Party. But we refuse to meet with, for example, Henry Ramírez (Chairman of the Cabinet Committee on Opportunities for the Spanish Speaking). He went around said a lot of terrible things about us at the campuses back East. He thought that we didn't have any friends back there. But we do, and they wrote us back and told us that he was saying that the farm workers didn't want the union, that César was a Communist, and just a lot of stupid things. This is supposed to be a responsible man.

Then there is Philip Sánchez (National Director of the Office of Economic Opportunity). I went to his home in Fresno once when a labor contractor shot this farm worker. I was trying to get the D.A.'s office to file a complaint against the labor contractor. So I went to see Philip Sánchez to see if he could help me. But the guy wouldn't help me. Later when the growers got this group of labor contractors together to form a company union against us, Sánchez went and spoke to their meeting. It came out in the paper that he was supporting their organization. As far as I'm concerned, Philip Sánchez has already come out against the farm workers.

It's really funny. Some of the Puerto Riquenos who are in the President's Committee for the Spanish-Speaking, man, they *tell* the Administration what the Puerto Ricans need. *Se pelean con ellos.* But the Chicanos don't. They're caught. They just become captives.

I spoke to a lot of the guys in Washington who were in these different poverty programs. Some of the Chicanos had been dropped in their positions of leadership. They put these guys over them and they put watch-dogs on them to make sure that they don't do anything that really helps the farm workers. The guys are really afraid because there's just a few jobs and they can be easily replaced. They're worse off than the farm workers, you see. The farm workers at least have the will to fight. They're not afraid to go out on strike and lose their jobs. But the guy who has a nice fat job and is afraid to go out and fight, well, they've made him a worse slave than the farm workers.

An ex-priest told me one time that César should really be afraid somebody might write a book to expose him. I said, "Don't even kid yourself that César is afraid of anybody because he's not. The only ones that might scare him are God and his wife, Helen. But besides that he's not afraid of anyone."

He's got so much damn courage, *y asi come es el*, that's the way the farm workers are. They have this incredible strength. I feel like a big phony because I'm over here talking and they're out there in the streets right now, walking around in the rain getting people to vote. *Son tan dispuestos a sufrir*, and they take whatever they have to take because they have no escape hatch.

Being poor and not having anything just gives an incredible strength to people. The farm workers seem to be able to see around the corner, and César has that quality because he comes out of that environment. César's family were migrant workers. It was kind of the reverse of mine because they started with a farm in Yuma but lost it during the depression. They had to migrate all over the state to earn a living, and they had some really horrible times, worse than anything we ever suffered. So there was a lot more hardships in his background. But his family had a lot of luck. His mom and dad were really together all the time.

César always teases me. He says I'm a liberal. When he wants to get me mad he says, "You're not a Mexican," because he says I have a lot of liberal hang-ups in my head. And I know it's true. I am a logical person. I went to school and you learn that you have to weigh both sides and look at things objectively. But the farm workers know that wrong is wrong. They know that there's evil in the world and that you have to fight evil. They call it like it is.

When I first went to work in the fields after I had met Fred Ross, the first thing that happened was that I was propositioned by a farmer. People who work in the fields have to take this every day of their lives, but I didn't know how to handle it. So I wondered if I should be there at all, because I had gone to college. I had gone to college to get out of hard labor. Then all of a sudden there I was doing it again.

I feel glad now that I was able to do it. It's good my kids have done field work now, too, because they understand what it all means. I feel very humble with the farm workers. I think I've learned more from them than they would ever learn from me.

Dolores Huerta and Gloria Steinem,
circa 1990. © Victor Alemán/2 Mun-Dos.
Com.

19

Interview with Dolores Huerta

Early Family Influences

Vincent Harding

The Veterans of Hope Project

Vincent Harding: I wonder if you could remember out loud some of the people, some of the situations, some of the institutions that you feel had an important influence on you and who you were becoming and who you would become.

Dolores Huerta: Well, I believe that part of who I am began where I was born which was in the state of New Mexico, which is a bilingual state. That was important, because as a young child I grew up speaking both English and Spanish as did my grandparents who were both born, on my mother's side of the family, born in the state of New Mexico. In our classes, although I left when I was only seven, but going to kindergarten and to first grade, our teachers spoke to us both in Spanish and in English. So it was a very natural type of way of communicating in both languages, and, of course, that really enriches one's life.

My father was very intelligent, very intelligent, he had a very strong personality, a very handsome man. He looked very Indian, in fact I look like my father, but he had green eyes. So he had a very striking appearance and he had a very good way with words and I can see my father as an organizer. In fact, my Dad, wherever he went he was a very strong union man. He organized the government employees union at the government facility where he was working. He was very strongly devoted to the cause of unionism. He felt very strongly about that. I would hear stories about them organizing the union when I was small, around my dad.

Reprinted with permission from The Veterans of Hope Project.
http://www.veteransofhope.org/show.php?vid=51&tid=46&sid=77.

My grandfather was very . . . he said you should never lie, never tell lies. He always used to say that the English language was the language of liars. He wouldn't let us speak English in his presence. We had to speak Spanish although he could speak English as well as I can. I caught him once speaking English. He said that the Anglo culture demanded you put everything in writing because they didn't have— their word wasn't any good.

My mother, also, she didn't believe in profanity. Especially if you swore at another person. Even to call—there's a common word in Spanish that they use which is *pendejo*, which means, kind of dumb. But my mother had a totally different translation for that. When you called somebody a *pendejo* that meant that person did not have God's grace. So you always wanted to be in God's grace, right? And the way that you did that is to help people, to help other people out. Never expect any type of remuneration for that help. If you saw someone that needed help, your obligation was to help that individual. If you had the ability to help them you needed to help them.

California Childhood

The neighborhood that we lived in was very diverse. We had on the left hand side there was an Italian family. They were recent Italian immigrants. Across the street there were Italians. Our neighbors on the right hand side were an African-American family, the Smiths. We had around the corner Filipinos. These were all new immigrants, right? A Filipino family. There were Chinese and Japanese, Native Americans, Greeks. People that had come in from Oklahoma, the Okies as they were called.

V. Harding: What town was this where you had this diverse group?

Huerta: Stockton, California. So it was just this very poor neighborhood, but it was so wonderful because we had all of these—all of our friends were from all these different ethnic groups. That made it so, to me, that was a preparation. A universal preparation for the world.

In our grammar school and junior high school we had the last of the old guard teachers. You know the single, the old maids. They were very strict. They were very hard, but they were hard on everybody, equally. You didn't ever feel that you were being discriminated against. The White kids got the rough treatment just like we did and everybody had to learn to read and write. But then when we went to high school it was a whole different scene. The racism was severe, just severe, in our high school.

V. Harding: How was it expressed?

Huerta: Oh, in many ways. I used to love to write—and I say used to because it's very difficult for me to write. I had pen pals. I wrote poetry and I spent a lot of time on all my essays to make sure they were perfect, my term papers. In my senior year my teacher, whom I liked a lot—she was my favorite, her name was Miss Lovejoy. I liked this teacher a lot. She gave me a C for my grade, when I had gotten A's on every one of my papers. And so I asked her why did I get a C. She said, it's obvious that somebody else has been writing your papers. She just devastated me. They were always punishing the Latino kids and the African-American kids so by the time I reached my senior year most of the Latino kids had dropped out. We had a very clean group of kids that we hung out with. We didn't do dope. We didn't drink, you know, but they were just always investigating us. One of the things, I think, looking back now, in fact I know this now—is because we were integrated. Because we had an integrated group of kids that hung together. We had these White girls that hung out with us. In fact, when I was sixteen I started a teenage center.

V. Harding: You started a teenage center?

Huerta: I started a teen center because we needed a place to hang out. This friend of my mother's, who was a business person, had a storefront. So I asked him if he would let us have this storefront to do a teen center. He said, fine. So we brought in a juke box. We brought in table tennis tables. We had jitterbug contests. All the kids would come over there and hang out. And the cops closed us down. They closed us down. They closed us down because they didn't want to see these White girls hanging around with Filipinos, and Mexicans, and Black kids.

My mother, was, of course, very supportive of me as a young woman and always pushed me to be out in front, to speak my mind, to get involved, to be active. My mother was a very quiet, a calm kind of a personality but she had a lot of quiet energy and did a lot of things.

My mother was a fabulous cook. She was a wonderful cook. She was a person who could do everything. She sewed. She cooked. She could plaster. She could wallpaper. I mean she was like a renaissance type of a person. She really believed in culture. She bought us season tickets to the symphonies. I also took dancing lessons. My ambition as a youngster was to be a dancer. From the time I was very little, I was about five or six, I always wanted to be a flamenco dancer. Of course, growing up in the forties it was a very exciting time especially in terms of music. Our big entertainment was dancing. We'd dance, and dance, and dance forever.

I would get tickets to the Jazz at the Philharmonic. All my friends would caravan up to San Francisco to hear Charlie Parker and Dizzy and the rest of the great musicians up there. So that just became— our whole life was kind of centered around music. I would work all week just so that we could have the money then to go to the Bay Area to hear the great musicians. We kind of lived for music. The reason I guess that was important, too, was because I had to give that up when we started the union. I remember my last music act was going to the Monterey Jazz Festival before I went to Delano and how painful that was for me because I had to give up music. Number one not being able to afford it any more and being down in the Delano area where all you get is country-western, right?

"You Just Have to Do It"

At the time that we started the union, I was going through a divorce. I had seven children. So can you imagine? What man would ask a woman with seven kids to help start a union with no money? Talk about faith! Naturally when I went to Delano also, I had been—I had a job as a school teacher. There were only three bilingual teachers in the whole county, and I was one of three. So you can imagine we were very popular. I always had a lot of work to do. But I quit my teaching job and, again, you know you get these little signs. I remember thinking, "Well, I'm going to go. I'm not going to have any money." Because I was supporting my children. I had seven kids, right? The day after I made my decision somebody left a big box of groceries on my porch.

I remember feeling really badly because one of my daughters was going to make her confirmation and I didn't have money to buy her shoes. And I was kind of embarrassed about that. My daughter was coming down the aisle with her tennis shoes with holes in them and I was wincing. And then just behind her there were other farmworker children coming down the aisle with tennis shoes with holes in them. So these are the kind of signs that you get that you're doing the right thing. To me they are very, very strong signs.

We'd go to city council meetings, or we were fighting this, or the county supervisors—fighting this particular fight that we were having at that particular time. Often I'd walk in with a safety pin on my blouse. I remember once I went to a city council meeting, and one of the city council members said, "Excuse me, but weren't you pregnant last year when you were here? Is this a different pregnancy?" I said, "Yes it is." But you know, you had to do it and I did a lot of the work out of my home, out of the house. You just do it. You don't think about how to do it. I always say that if you start to think about all of the things that you have to do to prepare to do, it's not going to happen. You just have to get out there and do it and then play catch up afterward.

Organizing Strategies

V. Harding: How did you go about building up a new group of organizers?

Huerta: Through house meetings. He [Fred Ross] kind of stumbled upon this whole method of using house meetings as a basic step of organizing, which is something that the farmworkers had actually, he says, taught him. Because they said, come over to my house, I'll invite some of my friends over and you can tell them what we're trying to do.

V. Harding: That's what a house meeting is, huh?

Huerta: Fred says a big light went off—*Ding, ding, ding.* This is it. This is it. From that meeting then they would get another meeting where a person at the first meeting would invite someone else and then they would have a few friends come over. And then a whole chain of these house meetings would be held. After you had a whole series of house meetings then you had a general meeting where you called all the people who had been involved in the house meetings to a big meeting. At that meeting then, we set up the organization, electing officers, and setting the program.

In the house meeting approach you never got more than—you didn't try to get more than say, six to eight people at a meeting. And you always tried to have the family involved. You tried to make sure that the wife or the husband was also in that meeting. The meetings were short, they shouldn't be over an hour, hour and a half. You tried to have the host have refreshments. The whole trick of those meetings was to make the host of that meeting invite his or her friends because it's very hard to refuse a friend when they invite you to come over to their home and hear any kind of presentation. Something like the Tupperware party approach.

The Grape Boycott

V. Harding: One of the things that the United Farm Workers is perhaps best known for in mainstream American society is the grape boycott. Could you talk a little bit about how that was organized and what influence it had on your work?

Huerta: We had been on strike for a few months and the growers were bringing in strike-breakers from Mexico. They went and got court injunctions limiting us to five people per field. Can you imagine five pickets on a big thousand acre field? So we were kind of stymied in terms of trying to keep the people from breaking the strike. In fact, at that time I even went to Juárez, Mexico. That's where I met the poet Lalo Delgado, where he did a leaflet for me to keep the people from Juárez from breaking the strike in Delano.

So we were talking about it and there was this Jewish attorney that was volunteering to help us out, named Stu Weinberg. So, he said, "Have you thought of doing a boycott? The civil rights movement is doing a boycott. Have you thought of doing a boycott?" So we said, "Hey, well let's try it." So we had these young volunteers that had come to work with us together with farmworkers, and we had no money. So these volunteers hitch-hiked out to the east coast. They hitch-hiked to St. Louis. They hitch-hiked to New York, they hitch-hiked to Chicago. Then we picked as our boycott target, because they say that liquor is easy to boycott, so we picked the Schenley company who had a wine grape operation which hired about 400 workers. We picked them as our first target.

The strike broke out in September of 1965. Then the march to

Sacramento was decided on which was done in the Lenten period of 1966. People were marching to Sacramento, the farmworkers were marching to Sacramento, carrying signs that said "Boycott Schenley." So before the march got to Sacramento, the Schenley company decided to recognize the union.

So the strike lasted five years. It was a five year strike and we had a lot of the young people who came to join the strike from Berkeley. Then the doors were wide open. I mean, everybody came in and then we were out there on the road raising money for the strike. We invited Luis Valdez to come down and start the *Teatro Campesino*. Which I did, I invited him to come down and he did a *teatro* which César saw and César liked it. So then he became a permanent fixture in the strike and that was the beginning of the *Teatro Campesino*.

The whole boycott is a nonviolent tool. It's an economic sanction, so to speak, but it's a way that people can participate. One thing about nonviolence is that it opens the doors for everyone to participate, the children, the women. And women being involved on the picket lines made it easier for the men then to accept nonviolence. They would always say if they didn't have a woman, "We need some women on our picket line. We need some women here." It makes it a lot easier for them. Then they can justify not being macho tough, or macho revenge, you know. Just having the women there made it possible, I think, for the organization to practice its nonviolence.

Nonviolence

I consider nonviolence to be a very strong spiritual force because it's almost like an energy that goes out and it touches people.

In the first strike there was a lot of violence by the growers. So we had to have this big meeting because people said, "It's one thing to be nonviolent against the growers or the labor contractors. But here the Teamsters are coming in and they are beating up our organizers and beating up the farmworkers. So why do we have to use nonviolence against them?" So we had to have this major meeting. We had to have this big discussion with the strikers and César made everybody take a standing vow for nonviolence. And then some of the organizers and young people were arguing against him. He said, "Well if one of you wants to take over this union, you can, but I will not be the leader of this union if you're going to use violence." And he said, "If you start using violence against the Teamsters, you're going to use it against each other." So everybody had to take a standing vow for nonviolence and to practice it.

Most of them were either first generation Mexican-Americans or recent immigrants. To get them to accept the whole philosophy that you can create a movement with nonviolence was not easy. It was not easy. To get them to understand that—and this you could see happening in people, that they would become transformed. They would actually become stronger through practicing nonviolence. They became much stronger people and had to use strategies and tactics instead of violence to be able to win.

Then César started doing something. He would always do things that would make people uncomfortable and I think that's what you have to do when you're fighting for justice. You have to kind of, as they use the words now—push the envelope, right? You know what I mean? Always doing things to make people uncomfortable. He always believed in fasting, again getting that from Gandhi. He would do these seven-day fasts and everybody would do like little fasts when we were going to do something really important. He would ask everybody to please fast and to pray before we embarked on some strike or something. But, then he started doing those twenty-five day fasts for nonviolence. So we'd have these press conferences to let people know that César was fasting. Well you can imagine what these tough, burly labor leaders from New York thought when we told them our leader, our president, was fasting. "What's wrong with him? Is he crazy?" I mean they were just—they went ballistic. Because in New York, especially during that time, they'd go into a place and wreck it up. They would wreck it all up to get a contract and here we had our leader who was *not eating*. All he would do was take Holy Communion every day.

Every night while César was fasting they would have a big Mass and then farmworkers brought their tents there to our headquarters, the Forty Acres in Delano. People put up their tents there so they could be with César while he was fasting. It was kind of interesting, too, the reactions of people. They didn't understand it. They couldn't comprehend it. Just like some religious people didn't like—the more traditional—they didn't like the idea that we had the Virgin Mary of

Guadalupe on the picket line. They didn't like that. To César, religion was a very practical thing that you used in your work. It was part of you. It wasn't something that was distant and way up there. It was something that was very, very much a part of you.

Farmwork is Sacred Work

I like to tell people when I speak on the campuses, on the college campuses, I always tell students that, if you're a professional and you have a degree, your job is to go work with—to serve working people. To serve people who work with their hands. This is what professionals do, not to take advantage of them. You have to go work and serve the people who work with their hands. Because they're the ones who create the wealth, the farmworkers, the auto workers, the garment workers. They create the wealth.

I like to tell people, if you had to be on a deserted island and you could only take one person with you, who would you take, an attorney or a farmworker? Right? I think that kind of gets it down. Because farm work is the most sacred work of all and yet farmworkers are so looked down on.

I gave a speech in Dekalb University in Illinois and this one young man came up to me afterwards and he said, "My mother works in the fields. She's an onion picker." He says, "And I was always ashamed of my mother until today." In Michigan, the farmworker children there are ashamed to say that they're farmworkers or that their parents are farmworkers. That's got to end. We have to get farmworkers the same types of benefits, the same type of wages, the respect that they deserve because they do the most sacred work of all. They feed our nation every day.

20

Testimony of Dolores Huerta

Mrs. Huerta: My name is Dolores C. Huerta. I reside at 320 South Sutter Street in Stockton, California. I appear before you today on behalf of the Community Service Organization consisting of 29 chapters within the State of California, four in Arizona, and one newly organized group in Texas, which has not yet been chartered. The CSO concerns itself with self-improvement among the Spanish-speaking people and encourages programs of education by active civic participation in citizenship, voter registration, voter education, labor relations, etc. Our most recent voter registration drive produced over 35,000 new voters in the State of California since January 1, 1960, and 600 in Texas. Hand in hand with the voter registration, chapters of CSO "Get out the Voters" in precincts where Spanish-speaking people and other minorities predominate.

Since a large percentage of our membership is directly employed in agricultural labor and as our Service Program handles individual problems without charging for them, the problems of the agricultural workers are becoming more and more a part of our working program. The CSO nationally has taken the position of being against the further importation of labor from other countries.

The complete lack of protection and vulnerability of farm workers should not be minimized. The recent recruitment of 474 laborers in Texas for the asparagus fields in San Joaquin County clearly points up the above statement. The men from Texas were recruited by means of radio announcements, television announcements, press releases and paid recruiters who were flown to Texas for that purpose by the San Joaquin Farm Production Association. The radio and television

California State Legislature, Senate, "Hearings of the Fact Finding Committee in Labor and Welfare," June 15, 1960, pp. 117–22.

announcements promised $1.25 per hour and twelve to sixteen hours per day of work.

The first group of 35 men recruited individually without the benefit of the following publicity were brought to Stockton in a semi truck without seats. The door was wired from the outside so they could not leave when the truck passed through various communities. They were told not to say that they were being charged for the trip which they later had to pay $22.00 for.

On arriving in Stockton in the first week of February, they found that the asparagus harvest had just started. The men were then put to do other tasks which were sorting asparagus roots, weeding, etc., at .90 cents per hour. The promise of $1.25 per hour in their case and subsequent arrivals pertained only to asparagus cutting, it appeared.

An interesting sidelight of the arrival of the first group of Texans was the dismissal of the local farm workers that had been occupied doing asparagus sorting and cutting. The day the Texans arrived their jobs ended.

Senator Cobey: Would you say these are a Violation of Public Law 78, the Bracero Program, and were they reported to the United States Department of Labor?

*Mrs. Huerta:*Yes, these were reported. I do believe these are a violation of Public Law 67. This is interstate recruitment.

Senator Cobey: These are just the ones from Texas?

Mrs. Huerta: If they were a violation, I think they would be under interstate recruitment.

Senator Cobey: The regulation of the Secretary?

Mrs. Huerta: These were reported to the Department of Employment and the Department of Labor.

Another important consideration in this case was the fact that no effort, and I wish to emphasize this, no effort had been made to recruit local workers in San Joaquin County for this work, but rather those few workers that had been working were laid off.

Mr. Art Lang of the local Farm Placement Office in Stockton stated at a general membership meeting of the CSO in Stockton that his department was not in any way responsible for this situation, as not one order had been placed in the Stockton office for asparagus cutters. He stated, "Somebody in Sacramento goofed." Our feelings are sympathetic with those of Mr. Luis Verdugo of El Paso, Texas, who stated at the meeting to Mr. Lang—"I regret, sir, that your Department and the Department in Texas made that mistake. The miseries and suffering that your mistake has brought upon our families cannot be measured."

On writing letters to the Department of Employment and Department of Labor, the Departments concerned with this situation, the answers received were that an "emergency situation" existed. An emergency situation? What type of emergency exists when local available farm workers are not being called to work by the Department of Employment and yet this same Department places an order—in Texas—with the Employment Commission for out-of-state labor?

Since the asparagus harvest was not yet ready, the hundreds of men recruited by the San Joaquin Farm Production Association soon found themselves only partially employed—in one camp on Rindge Tract they worked seven out of seventeen days—they began to leave the camps in large groups. Testimony attached to this one will verify this, along with numerous complaints filed with the Labor Commissioner in Stockton.

Those men that chose to stay in the camps were soon encouraged to leave. Some were fired for talking on the job, but the larger majority were informed that they were now to be placed on a piece-rate basis of pay. If they did choose to work at the piece-rate, they were free to do so.

Some tried, but found they worked harder and averaged the same amount of pay. But they were not given a choice and had to leave the camps. To what agency do these laborers turn to in such apparent injustices? The level to which farm work has sunk leaves little room for human rights or dignity. If the employer stays within limits of the existing laws, there is little recourse for the worker but to seek employment elsewhere. Growers themselves do not try to make conditions favorable so as to make their workers remain. The recent illustration above of the Texans clearly indicates this. These men came from thousands of miles to work and then found on arriving that there was not full employment and that deliberate efforts were made to make them leave by growers who were anticipating the certification of Mexican Nationals. The question arises, do those growers who wish to be part of a Government subsidized program have a right to expect imported labor when they do not recruit and actually discourage local workers either by extremely low wages and adverse working conditions?

Would our Government by any stretch of the imagination furnish imported labor to any other occupation if the working conditions were anywhere near the condition of farm workers? Where do we begin to correct conditions? The present economic state of a large amount of our population is a disgrace to the American standard of living and our ideals. If we openly detest oppression as a nation, let us not condone it for just one group—the agricultural workers—and then do this with Government assistance.

If growers choose to recruit labor, their recruitment efforts are overly successful as can be illustrated by the recent efforts in Texas of the San Joaquin Farm Production Association and the recruitment effort of the Podesta Ranch in Linden. Workers came from Monterey and Santa Clara Counties to pick cherries in the Linden area only to be turned away because there was enough labor available.

These trips cost the people time and money. This is the same ranch you have been hearing about before. We are concerned about perishable crops. We should be more concerned about waste as it affects people in their labor, time and personal economy.

I have personal knowledge of growers in Stockton who have hired hundreds of people. Yet one grower's office staff makes it a practice never to take names or addresses of people seeking employment, knowing full well that they are anticipating a harvest. On some occasions as many as fifty people in one day approached one office seeking employment in farm work. Some were local and some from other communities. Upon being told they would not be hired, they had to leave to some other place. Yet these growers are the largest employers of Mexican Nationals in San Joaquin County.

The above points out that growers themselves deliberately contribute to the chaotic disorganization in the labor field for reasons of their own convenience. If they do not list names of applicants for jobs, it would appear as if there is no labor available. Since growers create this disorganized situation that lends to the present state of the labor force, certainly, it is up to them to make recruitment efforts and better working conditions to keep local farm workers before they can declare an emergency situation in the press.

At the membership meeting last night I talked about today's hearing and one of our members gave me a short statement. This is a sworn statement and she did want to say this. They had been working in onions in Linden, California, last week and they were being paid 12 cents a case or 100-pound sack for an eight-hour day, and this is the business of picking onions, and the sack, they averaged $3.75 for eight hours. Out of that $3.75 they had to pay 50 cents for the ride to work and they had no bathroom facilities in the field and no drinking water in the field. I would like to see this Committee make some type of recommendation. Whether this can be done through the Department of Employment or legislation, I do not know, but I think the recruitment effort as such should be spelled out and not just recruitment efforts. We could have men downtown to work in asparagus but they cannot walk 10 blocks in Stockton and they will go down one mile to recruit those same people for the same asparagus fields. Something is wrong with this recruitment. I think this should be spelled out in detail. Certainly, some responsibility should be placed back on the growers. It's not fair that they should declare a labor shortage when they make it impossible for people to continue working for them.

Thank you very much.

Senator Cobey: Any questions? Has everybody testified from a written statement? If you don't mind, we would appreciate having copies of those statements.

Huerta: Mr. Chairman, I do want to say one more thing. I forgot to mention this point. This lady that gave me this little statement about the onions here, her husband is a foreman of the Mexican Nationals and he is presently employed as an arbitrator for a group of Nationals in one of the largest camps in Stockton that are averaging right now about $3.00 a day. They are being paid on a piece-rate basis. This is in the asparagus season and there is very little for them to pick; they went on strike three days ago and refused to work any more unless they gave them more time. The foreman told them they would have to go back to work. He couldn't get them to go back to work, so he sent for the owners to talk to the Nationals and the Nationals were told if they didn't return to work the crop would be lost and would also be taken out of their pay checks.

Senator Cobey: Who told them this?

Mrs. Huerta: The supervisor. Needless to say, they all went back to work. Another thing, I remember last year at this time there were, later on in the year, there were Nationals taken from the Farm Production Association and these men wanted a change of employer and they were not getting full employment and only working four hours a day and they were told they'd either return to their employer where they were at or they could go back to Mexico and they chose to do the latter and were sent back.

I would also like to see the Senate Fact Finding Committee see what opportunities are offered the Mexican Nationals, what the rate is. I know at the De Waglio Ranch last October they were coming in 40 or 50 every two weeks. They'd have some come in two weeks and another batch leave and following two weeks a whole new bunch of people. This makes it hard on commissary facilities.

These Mexican Nationals come and they do not have full employment. Also, it seems we have got to have some kind of answers on the labor problem. Labor is a part of the CSO problem. We do immigration work and it is sometimes impossible to immigrate someone's relative from Mexico unless you get producers to fix their papers and we need supplemental labor. We should let these people come in as residents and be citizens instead of having a captive labor supply. Thank you.

Dolores Huerta and UFW President
Arturo Rodríguez (left), March
in Watsonville, California, for Strawberry Workers, 1993. Courtesy of
John A. Kouns.

21

Letters Written by Dolores Huerta
to César Chávez, 1962–1964

Wednesday, October 3, 1962

Dear César:

I hope you have fully recuperated from the meeting last Sunday and are ready to roll on ahead.

I know that I am. Ambrosio has been haunting the office here, and has taken two pledges and he wants to move ahead. Lupe and he were at our board meeting last night. I thought we might have a meeting of all of our helpers and give them the results of [the] Fresno meeting, Sunday, then pass out the pledges and see how many they come back with.

However, I shall wait for your commands, General. So give me the word on the next line of tactic. The troops are restless.

The fellows from Hughson called me about an hour ago, and they just received their credentials today. I think the fellow who had the key to the box didn't deliver them or something. They called me Monday to "reclamar" that they had not received the credentials and I told them they had been mailed.

I spoke to Joseph Tapia, the promoter who has worked with us on a couple of dances about the possibility of having a benefit for the Association, and he said he was willing to let us have all of the profits on one of his bookings. Probably it would be good to try this in Fresno at some place like the Rainbow, if we could get the proprietor of the hall to give us the hall for free and give him a percentage on the beer. What do you think? I told Tapia we would let him know. . . .

Also I spoke to Attorney Funke, the guy who handles most of our Industrial Accident work, etc., and asked him about how much

---

UFW Archives, courtesy of Wayne State University.

he would charge to file our Articles of Incorporation. He is just going into business with another attorney named Russell Cook who is supposed to be a researcher. Anyhow to make a long story short, since these boys are newly received, he said he would make our papers for us for $150.00. I told him we could probably get them drafted for free. However he told me he had taken a lot of labor law in law school, that his office (where he is now) represents the teamsters, they recently handled the Teamster's Insurance. Anyway, he sure wants to do them for us in the worst way, and he warned me of all kinds of pitfalls that we may encounter if our articles are not drafted properly, etc. I told him I would relay all of this to the General, and would let him know our decision. One thing, though, he said he realized we did not have any money and he would not charge us *until* we had funds with which to pay. I told him this might be many, many months. But he said that was OK, but he would like to feel he would be recompensated when the organization had money. He sounds like he has faith in our group too. This attorney is a very hard worker, and he is frank and honest and all that stuff, as Gil can tell you, as he discovered him.

He tells me he will look up other contracts and articles like teamsters to make sure we get the best. In this I believe him because, as I said, he is a hard working attorney, of which there are few.

César, there is a good possibility the local chapter might start giving me a bad time soon. I hope not.

Also I want to know if you will lend me your station wagon. It makes me sick of the time I have lost because of my junkie cars, yet I hate to get in debt for a better car when I'm not sure where my next month's check is coming from.

If you can lend it to me, let me know, and I can go after it. I will take out the insurance on it, if you will let me, and as soon as I can I shall get another car.

The CSO car burns too much oil and is very unpredictable.

I'm going to cut this short now. Please write and let me know the next plan of action.

Give my regards to Helen and Manny the Many.

Sinceramente,

Dolores

Viva La Causa

Mary says she is sorry she could not attend the meeting. Genevieve said the meeting was very good and if there is anything she can do, she will (I just told her I'll give her the orders, ha ha).

Augustine Angel, one of our Stockton members, said to give you his best regards.

Attorney Funke, Room 515, Board of America Bldg. Stockton

◆ ◆ ◆

Nov., 1963
Mi Estimado Lider:

Con respeto, admiración, y desperación le dirijo esta carta esperando que Ud. y su familia se encuentran en la mejor salud.

I know that you and all of those dear to you are as shook about "the Mexican's" death as we were here in Stockton.

It does not seem that things like that are possible, and when they happen, one keeps waiting for something to happen that will undo the tragedy, but it does not happen, and only the adjustment to reality is left. Our local Franciscan Fathers held a requiem mass yesterday, the day of the foul deed. It was a beautiful mass—this they dedicated openly, with prayers said aloud, to the president and his family, also special prayers for our new president Lyndon B. Johnson. Please, if you have not done so, send condolences in the name of our little association, and inform the members you have done so, I think they would appreciate this.

Just heard Castro's statement stating the sadness of Cuba in this mess.

César I am sending you a book with this letter that was given to me by Mr. Barrett, my friend in Washington whom I told you was the editor for the machinist's paper gave me. Probably the most important part of this book for our purposes is the section on layouts.

As I told you in the my last letter, I came right back from Washington to a house meeting, which turned out to be cancelled, as was yesterday's because of our President's death.

In Washington, I saw Henning briefly and he denied he will oppose Burton in the congressional race. I spoke to Fred on the phone, he is pretty depressed on the whole CSO right now, and I also called Burton, he wants me to phone Wedemeyer to have him give me a job.

I am not interested in a state job though. I am going to apply for my U.I. next week, and will be hoping and praying they don't send me out to work, but if they do I am afraid I must. I have not paid my rent for six months and also have many bills all piled up around me, so I have to move. The support money Ventura and Ralph are giving me ($80.00) this month, barely keeps me in groceries and pay utilities.

If I do go to work, it will be just long enough to get me out of debt. It may be that my performance for FWA will be better, if I am not bogged down with financial problems, those who will suffer are of course the kids who will not see me day or evenings, but I guess they are conditioned to this by now.

Next week I plan to leave this ratty town to go and start working in Tracy to see if I have better luck in house meetings. In Stockton, I can't seem to have any of these meetings turn out any results, in fact I've even been having trouble getting people to the meetings. In fact, in the last two weeks, all I have had are cancellations. I have another one tonight, I sure hope this one works out.

I'm sorry I made a mistake in the M.O. I sent you, I bought an M.O. because of the 50, if not I would have sent it in cash, but I guess in my rush, I made a mistake, but will include this in the next batch I send. I am going to close this now so I can get the book in the mail.

Regards to all, Dolores

P.S. Can you send me some cards and literature?

Also AWOC organized a bean sorting shed where Ramón Reyes-Barron works and he is asked to pay their dues, what do you think. No increases were made on the wages though, they had effected this increase prior to AWOC's arrival. He asked me whether he should pay. I told him he didn't have to. Please comment. Total number of works in shed, 8. If I can help on the credit union, please let me know (I should say try to help).

◆ ◆ ◆

Dear César,

I'm going to write you a short note to let you know some of the developments. I hope to go to Delano either Thursday or Friday, probably Friday, so we can discuss my moving also other problems.

Some new happenings, I have a girl staying with me, the daughter of one of our members, who was going to be sent to Perkins girl school. She is a terrific worker, but "poquia veldt" but anyway the way things look now she will move to Delano with me. She is in my custody until January, and although I do not know yet whether I will have her baby sit for me, I haven't been able to see how she treats the kids yet, even if she works out, she can help watch them in the evenings, this way I can just have someone come in the day time, and if we can get child care center going I can stick all the kids except the baby there.

I will call Salas tonight, I hope to go to Sacramento tomorrow. Right now I am on the way to see one of our members who is in critical condition in the hospital, Porfirio de los Santos of Hennig Tract, also to see if his wife needs any help.

I hoped we could wage a battle on the welfare front. As you know they cut off all the welfare recipients because work was available, but many are only making five and six bucks a day. There are so many people here you would not believe it.

But in Alameda County, they are sending them out to do farm work and continuing their assistance anyway.

What I hoped we could do was issue a release saying, "The need for a minimum wage is clearly brought out by these etc., etc. treatment of farm labor and so forth." We can discuss this when I go down. I am making definite plans to move down just as soon as school is out and I think I will apply for ANC just to make sure Ventura and Ralph help me through the D.A. This would be OK as long as I was working don't you think:

Enclosed is a loan application for a member—Ernesto Buzo.

I forgot my notes I left the other day on delinquent members. Send them to me.

Till later alligator. Dolores

[Handwritten]

Have you gone to the hospital? Mr. De Los Santos had an arm torn off and is in a coma. Will the company give him a write up for life policy?

Have not been able to contact Salas, and have called day and night.

◆ ◆ ◆

Dear César,

Just received your most welcome letter with the CSO Convention latest. Sorry to hear about them stealing our program, and makes me very suspicious of especially a couple of our "joint" members and/ or those CSO persons present at the Convention (FWA Convention). However, I know you feel as I do on this score. Unfortunately these programs cannot carry themselves alone, and . . .

On the oil, so help me, I do not know what you are talking about. I gather that you have some oil that can be sold for 22 cents a quart. Yes I am game, but will it be too expensive to send via greyhound, but you figure that out. Also, can we sell to anyone or just members. I know, just members.

Re-read the letter Auto-Insure and contacted California Casualty about the group auto, and they are not very interested think our membership is too small (I told them 1,000) and said they are limited on writing group auto because they have Teacher's association 38,000 members. The fellow I spoke to has promised to set up a meeting for me next with the "man in charge" who was not available Friday, so I will have to go back to Frisco next week. He suggested we try Cal-Farm (Farm Bureau Federation).

I inquired about the AFR teachers Union, who have a small membership about 2,000 members, and found that they have a broker's arrangement, whereby they buy their auto insurance. I am going to do some weekend work on both types of policies and see how much savings the CTA has. By the way, the premium is not paid on a group, master contract basis, but I paid on an individual basis by member. So from here right now I cannot see the big difference between the Broker and Group arrangement, but probably will after more study.

Had a busy time in Washington, Jeffrey Coheland's secretary saw me and said Jeff wanted to talk to me. He wants us to keep on the alert, because he says farmers will probably try to reinstate PL 78. Naturally, I saw Phil Burton for a few minutes before he went to hear a speech by Johnson that all Congressmen were going to, he asked about you, about the association, but more than anything he wanted to know how AB 59 was working out and still remembers his personal sacrifice of time and energy. He said he still felt very gladly about not being able to pass U.I. for us, and also said he was glad to be away from pesty me. Sala, his wife, likes Washington and helps him out a lot. We were talking when he received the long distance call announcing Salinger's decision to run, sounds pretty much like a conspiracy between Big Daddy and the Kennedy boys doesn't it. (This is my own private opinion) but dates back to CDC Unruh Machine infighting.

Well dear leader, the time has come to stop this chatter, and I will set my nose to the grind-stone and dues collection. I left my list and receipt books with José Soto and Gabino, but have not seen them yet to see how they made out as collectors of delinquent dues.

I will see Porfirio Sedano tomorrow, was unaware that he was having troubles, which gives me good reason to go to the islands, I got the word through Lucio Gonzáles that a CSO on the islands has been telling everyone that our Association is no good and the insurance will not succeed but will fail as did that of CSO.

I will probably have a lot more to say, but have run out for the minute. Enclosed is $3.50 for Manuel's dues. I am sending this without a receipt because as I said the boys have my book. Also, before I forget Gabino asked that you send his mail to 828 So. Monroe, he has not received anything for a long time because of interception of the mails.

I am sending back your receipt book for stamping. It is not so much the book I was worried about, I can buy the book, but I do not have the Association stamp. Maybe I should order one with your P.O. number on it, what do you think? Give me your OK and I will, I will probably have more uses for it in the future. If you do not think it is wise, money wise to send me the oil through the greyhound bus, get a few cases together and I will go after it, that way I can take you some asparagus.

Hastey Lumbago—Causa.

Secret Agent number D.C. TWA

1/2 + 3 = 7734

Manuel's dues in separate letter.

◆ ◆ ◆

Dear César:

Just a few short lines to send you some of your favorite paper $$$ and also to propose some ideas to further my moving—if this is still what you want, me to help and move down.

I get some extra sensory vibrations that maybe you do not believe that financially I should move down because of what it may cost me to live down there and the doubt that maybe you will not be able to pay me, so I have this proposal.

I am now working on having my kids stay with various assorted relatives for the next month and one half until school starts. If all goes very well, I will still be left with maybe one or two kids, depending on whether Ventura can make arrangements to keep the boys, anyways Vincent I would not leave anywhere because he would miss me too much. Then do you suppose I could make living arrangements with someone to put me and my one kid up for a month and one half, then I could pay room and board. That means I would not be paying rent, or a baby sitter or utilities, at least until school begins. Then if some money could, or rather whatever money you could gather I could use for board and my car payment. If after the end of two months before school starts it looks like we can't make it, then I will come back to Stockton and go to work. I thought maybe Josefina and Julio would let me [stay] with them, or somewhere where one more wouldn't make that much difference.

I had hoped to get down there to Delano to discuss this plan with you possibly either Friday or Saturday if I can get down to Delano. However, if you do not think there is any need for me to go down there as you stated in one of your recent letters, let me know right away.

I saw Fred and Francis along with all the CSO board members and I spoke to Francis afterwards on the phone. She said you and Fred decided you could not raise enough money for his expenses so he could help you. She said she thought Fred would rather help you than take on this job in New York.

Mozosson still has not gotten my license and said it will still take about 60 days before he can do this, it seems there is some difficulty in the firm. However he says we can send xxxx in the applications, just to send them to him, at home—His home address is 209 Upper Terrace, San Francisco. The rating book my brother had was not the right one, so he is going to send me one (he says), also the names of the adjustors, and we can have the 10%.

César, I am enclosing $13.50 for myself, $10.00 on my loan, and $3.50 for my dues. I have a feeling my payment is $15.00, I don't remember, but this is all I can pay now.

All of Stockton

Also enclosed:	Jose Soto	$3.50	
	Ernesto Buso	$7.00	($3.50 dues, $10.00 C. Union)
	D. Huerta	*$13.50*	
		24.00	
	Total	$24.00	

I am reading insurance books my brother lent me, I also have the IAC materials, now if I do not move to Delano, I guess I better send you these books, so you can handle the accident cases you have down there.

If the good Lord wills, I will see you Friday or Saturday.

Dolores

◆ ◆ ◆

1964

Dear César:

Since I had not heard from you I was worried about whether you were angry with me because I did not stay to finish the minutes. You probably noticed I was peeved at the last meeting because of the motion that was made at the C.U. meeting before my arrival and I was not to take the minutes unless authorized or some stupid thing, that will teach me not to stick my nose in where it does not belong. I was also peeved because you accepted the money from the citizen's committee because I had already told Lou Haas (the governor's secretary at whose house the deal was at that we did not want any of the money). Especially since you have rejected all of the donations I have sent from income tax expenditures. Furthermore Emmy Gunterman told me that she had heard in Sacramento that the

Citizen's Committee had goofed up our meeting with the governor, so you can see it was not just my vivid imagination. To further finish up with my peeves, since I am not the quiet long suffering type, I also resent it when you are not honest with me, and in this I refer to the newspaper thing with Tony. When we discussed this prior to meeting with Tony I had the idea that probably Tony could not do it, but yet Sunday, when the three of us met to discuss this, you made it look like it all depended on me, if I said yes it would work. I do not mind playing the part of the heavy if I know why and when I am supposed to take on this role—please remember this for any future conspiracies. This is what I mean by your "honesty" of sincerity if it sounds nicer that way. All of this is old business, but now I want to get to the newer developments.

Last week was taken up with cases and running to San Francisco. I went to one meeting of the State Social Welfare Committee of which I am a member, Wedemeyer says he wants to talk to me about the work rule for farm labor. So this week I will try to get up to see him. I did not stay for all of the meeting only for the first three hours than I came back to Stockton. I spoke to the insurance guy and he says it may [be] one or two weeks before he gets down to see you and then on to Los Angeles to see these other companies. He wants a "fuller report" of our organization, and i just don't know how much to give him considering how close the Teachers Union is to AFL-CIO, so i am still sticking by my original lie that we have 1,000 members. Please tell him the same when he gets down there to see you. If possible I am going to try to arrange my schedule to be down there in Delano when he gets down there to see you. I'm supposed to see him Thursday again, *pero me estoy awitando* because there are "no new developments." I told him we could get 50 politicians in one year and 750 at the end of two years, what do you think? Is this too high a figure?

I spent half a day talking to Bob MacLane about the coop, and he gave me a lot of material to read. One of the reasons the coops organized on a share basis was to keep them honest and to encourage member participation. Bob said that one of the problems in having an organization business is that you can never tell what will happen in the future when other people are running your organization. In a way, you have to compare the coop with the credit union and the way that it is formerly established and administrated counts a lot for the success or failure of the coop.

Rene Rodríguez of the Manteca FWA suggested when I was mentioning this to him that we get a bus and run out to the campus and sell things, he feels we could do well this way. Maybe we could do this and then give each member a discount on his card (membership card). I think Rene would be a good one to take on this work he is currently on AFDC and is slightly disabled but he is very honest. I did not mention this to him, just to you right now. We could probably make money right off on selling to the braceros (nylons, hair oil, soap, etc.)

I wouldn't mind trying it for an experiment right away anyway Rene if he could do it could do so without having to have a salary. I mean a fixed salary. I am going to wade through the material on the coop and will give you any more ideas that develop, OK. If you want me to send you the stuff say so so you can read it yourself. Maybe I can go through it and mark it. I think it would be wise if we could set up a few say two or three "buses" or panels as you suggested and we could probably pay them off with the profits. Under AFDS and the work relief program, the recipients only work 36 hours, and if they have a "parttime" job, they are still eligible, so if you have anyone else down their like Regalado, they could do this ambulatory store and still get their aid. You probably will not like this any more than my other wild schemes, but there it is. We could even get articles to begin with "on consignment" whatever we did not sell we could return, if they were not perishable to whatever whole sale house they came from. By the way Bob MacLane said there is from 16% to 20% mark up on groceries except for "necessities." We got to get that money during the summer months.

I don't know what we are going to do about the newspaper. It all really hinges on you and what you are going to do. If you want me to move down there and take over your duties of paper work, I guess I can but probably not till after school is out. In the meantime, I hope to start this next week in setting up meetings again to try to get members. I met a young couple from Victor who are related to the Salazar's [sic] the members in Acampo, who are unbelievably honest, so much so they refused to give them welfare assistance because they would not stretch truth, and they have promised to set up a meeting in Victor with the other shirt tail relations. I guess the only alternative to freeing you for the newspaper is to get more members so we can hire some clerical help. Am I right in this assumption? If you have other thoughts let me know.

Dolores

◆ ◆ ◆

Dear César:

You probably think this end of the rope has raveled, but I have been rustling dues.

Enclosed is the net effect of a few days collection, i.e. all of Thurs, Fri, Sat, Sun, Mon and Tues. Thursday and Friday I did not go to Sacto, but for all the good it did. Contrary to what you heard, the rain brought nothing but trouble.

Most of the guys here have not worked enough to be able to pay their dues, as you know around Stockton, the work is not steady work, but the net result here goes.

Of the ones that did not pay, as you know a few are in Mexico, some have moved and three did not want to pay. The three that did not pay I attribute directly to dear Ambrosio. He is still helping out in the office, so with some of these guys they think he is important.

Legislation: You have probably been keeping abreast of the PL 78 thing [Bracero Program]. We sent the governor dozens of telegrams. I think he played a very dirty trick on us, and I have let his secretaries, and Mr. Tieburg know it. I sent a telegram in your name, which you find also enclosed.

There is now a resolution in the house and senate (I mean assembly) state to memorialize Congress to extend PL 78. I shall [do] my damndest to kill it. If you can help by sending a letter to Myron Frew please do. He is on rules committee, and rules committee decides where the bill is going to be sent. If we get this in a good committee, the chances of it not passing are so much better.

Burns from Fresno is also on senate rules, as you know. It may well get out of the Senate, but I have good hopes of killing this in the assembly.

Frankly, I'm so damnded [*sic*] disgusted with the whole setup, I even hate to go to Sacramento.

Henning called me from Washington. Herman submitted my name for an economic development meeting for minorities in Washington. My only interest in going is to lobby against PL 78. Henning said they would announce the meeting next week. On PL 78 he said to get letters in to the Secretary of Labor. He said if PL 78 gets through, it will probably be only for 1 more year.

As you will note I picked up two old guys, both over 50 from CalPack. One of them, Abel Preciado only looks about 45 or younger, but as you will note he was born in 1907. I would consider him a good risk, the other Pulido, I picked up also by mistake. I know you may have to send me these back. The only reason I am submitting them is in case you get desperate for members.

With this guy Preciado in, I have a good chance of getting the other workers in CPC because he is a foreman, and very well liked. I know all this does not cut any bones with the insurance company rates, so feel free to reject them, I am expecting you to.

I held some additional meetings, one in a camp with about 30 guys but they had just barely started working that week, Monday so I hope to get some Saturday. I will keep sending these in daily until you tell me not too. I am still hopeful of picking up some more before the 1st, but I know the time is terribly short now. I hope you were more successful than I was. Till then, I am,

Sincerely yours,

Dolores

Regards to Helen, the kids and Manuel

The receipts are mixed up because I split the book up in three parts so Manuel and others could help me collect. I will send Manuel's receipts in later. He forgot to leave them.

◆ ◆ ◆

Dear César:

This typewriter is not very good, but I want to answer your letter and thank you for the lovely card you sent.

As to all the questions in your letter, it would seem that you would be satisfied with my telling you before I would be willing to work for the association, money or no money. I cannot take on any other jobs at this time anyway, so it looks like working for the association is just the job I need. Whether my assistance will be of any value, is another question. You decide what it is you want me to do. What I think might be wise is to follow up on the pledges I have from before and see all the guys that were out of the country before. For mientras.

However, I bow to your better judgment and experience and will do as you say. Right now I have three handicaps, no car, no typewriter (just two). As for the money, let me remind you that since the first of May we have been getting along on nothing, and doing it very successfully. I imagine the more we do, the better we will get at "getting along [on] nothing." If I can make it thru August, and I know the Good Lord will not let us starve, then in September I can apply for my substitute teacher credential, and work one or two days a week teaching at $20.00 per day, hours 8:30 to 3:00 pm. Furthermore in substitute teaching you can pick your days to work, if you don't feel like working on [you] just let them know you are not available that day.

Enclosed is $10.50 from Dario Duran. I also went to see Eustalalio Juárez and he says he definitely wants to keep up the insurance and the Association, and will send in his dues before the first. Please let me know about Lucio Gonzáles, we went to see him but he was not home. Also has anyone else sent in their dues.

I will try to see the rest of the delinquents. Also, I have been home every day, so have not had time to inquire about the newspaper (third handicap, no phone). I agree with you 100% that we have to start the paper right away. We can make hay and claim credit for passage of AB 59.

I received a letter from Dept. of Social Welfare on services for many Americans, they want my opinion, and I do certainly want to go to Sacramento and tell them about policy decisions on the families of the new immigrants as far as eligibility for ANC UP. Don't you think that's worth a trip.

Chris Hartmire and Hank Anderson stopped by to see me. Hank is his usual jerky self, Chris his usual sweet self.

I'm cutting this short so I can get this in the mail. I'm still on the day shift (big kids) and night shift (baby) and will probably be on this schedule for another week until little Eva (how's that for a name) learns to sleep all night. So have not taken time to do any book or paper work. Ernesto was in Fairfield, but I see across the street that he is home this afternoon, he had not been home before today. Will run across and get him to sign.

Hope I have more dues next time I write. Waiting to hear about the elder members, if we don't get cancelled out first. I bet you are having kittens, and I don't blame you. It is the same old story, we the officers let you do all the work and worrying about the welfare of this organization. Hope I can help more now. By the way, you guys should have another baby. They are so sweet and make you feel like you are close to the angels.

Until next time, Viva la Causa, (y la Seguranza).

Dolores Huerta

◆ ◆ ◆

1964

Dear César:

Enclosed is $10.00 for dues. The price I gave you on the paper the other day was wrong, it is .50 per package, a package which contains about 5 reams. How about that.

How did Manuel come out in his fight with the County Hospital, does he still need my able assistance? Did Westgate ever send the films? My typewriter is acting up as you can see, won't space.

Fred, (this I forgot to tell you the other day), said it was a good thing Tony did not take the paper because he thinks in a strange way. I have two house meetings set up, Friday in Acampo, and Tuesday in Linden with Daniel Ramos. Daniel says he will pay all up Saturday, will give you the news on the rest.

I am going to San Francisco to see the insurance guy tomorrow, will let you know what develops. Will send gas tags with money for gas, if you suspected why I had not sent them, that is why. I can afford to pay for it now.

Before I forget I am baptizing my baby Sunday for sure, and our shindig is going to be at Dad's Point, if you can stand to see that place. The baptism is at 1:00, party beings [sic] right after so please try to come and bring the kids, we have plenty of room, invite Manuel and his Mrs. Also tell Tony, Gil, Julio, Mike etc., if you see them. I am sending them a note anyway. If you can come Sunday, will see you then, if not hasta next visit, or your next letter.

Dues: Genaro Aguayo (my address) Stockton $5.00

Teresa H. López 640 E. Fifth Street, Stockton $5.00

Credit Union—Card plus 8 for membership of Joe D. Gonzáles, 816 Garden Stockton

By the way, one of our members Serna has a sick baby. Would you consider it illegal if I advised him (1) to take out a separate policy under convertible clause or (2) put money in Credit Union in baby's name. Would either of these procedures injure our cause with the insurance company or CUNA?

Please advise.

Later Alligator

do

Dad's Point is where we had our ill fated barbecue. If you come bring some oil.

◆ ◆ ◆

February 29, 1964

Dear César:

I received your penitent letter, much to my surprise, and as the natives say, "No hay fijon." I deserve the recriminations which you were concerned about, especially since the information which I send you I have had in my possession since the 4th day of Jan, or thereabouts. Furthermore, I think I am still ahead when it comes to losing tempers. Frankly, I did not give it a second thought, and please feel free to express your opinions as far as my work is concerned, even though they may not always be in praise, because as you know, I always work better under pressure and "guided instruction." You will further blow your top with the following:

I did not get to call or go to Sacramento today as planned: my baby sitter went home for the weekend at the request of her parents and as they say, you never miss the water till the well runs dry, and I find I am absolutely grounded. I thought I would be able to get away after the girls came from school, but a few unexpected callers took care of that. I had hoped to get to a phone and call Sacramento today to find out about the welfare cases. Please let me know if they have called you. However, I have written the boys a letter, so that may help. Anyhow if they don't join, I wouldn't dare, they don't look like a very good element to me.

The Union had a big meeting (of wios and palapatoys) in St. Mary's Hall. Teresa López (one of my unexpected callers) was so inspired by the Union's proposals of "Strike now, eat later," "call on us and we will go talk to your boss to increase your wages," etc., that she came right over and paid her dues to us. Furthermore she said some of the other ladies that were present at that meeting also want to join us the non-striking Union.

Another bit of information. I am going to be on a panel representing the Farm Worker's Association at a conference of the County Welfare Directors in Sacramento on March 6. The object of the discussions is on improving relations and removing discrimination from welfare practices. If you have any thoughts on this, please let me know. Erica will be gone all weekend, but I'm going to call Ventura to come after the little kids so I can get out tomorrow evening, I have a couple of members in Acampo that are going to join for March. Also tomorrow several have promised to come in and pay their dues. Ramos and Ambriz are to pay tomorrow.

By the way, I am enclosing a loan application for one of our member's wives. She and her husband are having marital difficulties and he took off leaving her with just a little cash, $16.00. They are paying off their home and have several old cars (three, I think). Father Finian wants me to take her over to welfare, but I suspect that his feud is not permanent and I would like to keep him on as a member, which I think he might object if we go through the welfare rigamorole of Dist. Attny, etc. Furthermore, as you know they will not help her on ANC for 90 days and general relief is such a hassle for the junk they give that I thought it best to get her some money for rent and food for the 60 day waiting period for ANC. Also, if in that time her husband returns, I think it will be a better solution, don't you. If you have less than the amount asked for, could you send her that? Also, if you think it will be too long before the loan can be made, let me know. The important thing is to help her out on food, she has six kids. She says the owner of the house she is buying will wait for the payments. So, if you can fill it if it is only with $50.00, that will help. She will be starting work (with luck) in about two weeks in the asparagus packing sheds, so it's just a carry over to avoid going to the welfare department.

More later

[handwritten] Gave you Isaac Torres dues in Delano or sent these, don't remember what, check your receipt back and let me know. Whatever you do do not charge him for July because he definitely paid.

Dolores

Sorry about the welfare, will give you my thoughts.

◆ ◆ ◆

July and August 1964

Dear César and Helen,

I am writing this letter from the hospital.

I still don't know when I will be getting out. Maybe tomorrow or the day after. The doctor just said they were going to keep me "for a while."

They gave me one transfusion but I had a bad reaction to it, so now I am on pills and shots. Anyway, to make a long story short, I am in pretty bad shape yet.

I hadn't written sooner because I did not have a pen or pencil or paper.

I hope this illness of mine does not foul things up too much. But then, I really wasn't helping that much anyway.

César, if you get a chance, (1) write to Mario Soto to ask him if he has gone to work yet, and if he hasn't to try to work. (2) Write to the Dr to get his report = that is if he has released him.

Some of the members have been in to see me. News gets around fast.

I can't think if anything else to say except to apologize for being under the weather.

Dolores

22

Statement of Dolores Huerta, Vice President, United Farm Workers Organizing Committee, AFL-CIO, to U.S. Senate Subcommittee on Migratory Labor, July 15, 1969

My name is Dolores Huerta. I am the Vice President of the United Farm Workers Organizing Committee (UFWOC), AFL-CIO. It is a pleasure to come before your committee to discuss a very serious matter for our union and for all farm workers—federal obstacles to farm worker organizing.

As you know, UFWOC has undertaken an international boycott of all California-Arizona table grapes in order to gain union recognition for striking farm workers. We did not take up the burden of the boycott willingly. It is expensive. It is a hardship on the farm worker families who have left the small valley towns to travel across the country to boycott grapes. But, because of the table grape growers' refusal to bargain with their workers, the boycott is our major weapon and our last line of defense against the growers who use foreign labor to break our strikes. It is only through the pressure of the boycott that UFWOC has won contracts with major California wine grape growers. At this point, the major obstacles to our efforts to organize farm workers are obstacles to our boycott.

Our boycott has been met with well-organized and well-financed opposition by the growers and their sympathizers. Most recently, several major California grape growers joined with other agribusiness interests and members of the John Birch Society to form an employer dominated "union," the Agricultural Workers Freedom

UFW Archives, courtesy of Wayne State University.

to Work Association (AWFWA), for the sole purpose of destroying UFWOC. AWFWA's activities have been described in a sworn statement to the U.S. Government, which Senator Mondale placed in the Congressional Record.

In spite of this type of anti-union activity, our boycott of California-Arizona table grapes is successful. It is being successful for the simple reason that millions of Americans are supporting the grape workers strike by not buying table grapes.

After six weeks of the 1969–1970 table grape harvest, California table grape shipments to 36 major United States cities are down 20 percent from last year, according to United States Department of Agriculture reports. The price per lug for Thompson Seedless grapes is at least $1.00 less that it was at this time of last year's harvest.

It is because of the successful boycott that, on Friday, June 13, 1969, ten major California growers offered to meet with UFWOC under the auspicies [*sic*] of the Federal Mediation Service. UFWOC representatives and ranch committee members met with the growers for two weeks. Progress is being made in these negotiations, which are presently recessed over the issue of pesticides.

U.S. Department of Defense Table Grape Purchases

Now that the boycott has brought us so close to a negotiated settlement of this three-year old dispute, we learn that the United States Department of Defense (DOD) has doubled its purchases of table grapes. We appear to be witnessing an all out effort by the military to bail out the growers and break our boycott. Let me review the facts behind this imposing federal obstacle to farm worker organizing.

The DOD is doubling its purchases of table grapes this year. DOD bought 6.9 million pounds of table grapes in the fiscal year 1968, and 8 million pounds in the first half of FY 1969, with an estimated "climb to over 16 million this year" (according to an article in *The Fresno Bee*, 4/25/69 by Frank Mankiewicz and Tom Braden).

DOD table grape shipments to South Vietnam this year have increased this year by 400 percent. In FY 1968, 550,000 pounds were shipped to S. Vietnam. In the first half of FY 1969 alone, these shipments totaled 2,047,695 pounds. This data on completed FY year purchases of table grapes comes directly from a DOD Fact Sheet entitled "Use of Table Grapes," dated March 28, 1969.

Commercial shipments of fresh table grapes to South Vietnam in 1968 have risen nine times since 1966, according to U.S. Department of Commerce statistics. In 1966, S. Vietnam imported 331,662 pounds of U.S. grapes and was the world's 23rd largest importer of U.S. fresh table grapes. In 1967, when the UFWOC boycott of Giumarra table grapes began, S. Vietnam's imports of U.S. table grapes jumped to 1,194,988 pounds, making it the world's 9th largest importer. Last year, 1968, S. Vietnam became the world's 5th largest importer of this luxury commodity, by buying 2,855,016 pounds of U.S. table grapes. "This could not have occurred," states the *AFL-CIO News* of June 14, 1969, "without both DOD and Agriculture Dept. encouragement."

These are the facts as to how the Grapes of Wrath are being converted into the Grapes of War by the world's richest government in order to stop farm workers from waging a successful boycott and organizing campaign against grape growers.

The DOD argues in its Fact Sheet that "The total Defense Supply Agency purchases of table grapes represent less than one percent of the U.S. table grape production." Data from the California Crop and Livestock Reporting Service indicate, however, that table grapes may be utilized in three different ways: fresh for table use; crushed for wine; or dried as raisins. It is clear that DOD purchases of table grapes *for fresh use* represents nearly 2.5% of all U.S. fresh table grape production!

Table grape prices, like those of other fruits and vegetables are extremely susceptible to minor fluctuations in supply. DOD purchases of table grapes are probably shoring up the price of all grapes and, at a critical point in the UFWOC boycott, are permitting many growers to stand firm in their refusal to negotiate with their workers.

It is obvious that the DOD is taking sides with the growers in this dispute. The DOD Fact Sheet states that "The basic policy of the DOD with regard to awarding defense contracts to contractors involved in labor disputes is to refrain from taking a position on the merits of any labor dispute. This policy is based on the premise that it is essential to DOD procurement needs to maintain a sound working relationship with both labor and management." Nevertheless, many unions in the

United States are decrying this fantastic increase in DOD table grape purchases. *AFL-CIO News* of June 14, 1969 notes that "union observers point out, however, that DOD does not become involved in a labor dispute when it so greatly increased its purchase of boycotted grapes." It seems that the DOD is violating its own policy and endangering its working relationship with labor, and we hope that the committee will explore this fully.

DOD Table Grape Purchases: A National Outrage

The history of our struggle against agribusiness is punctuated by the continued violations of health and safety codes by growers, including many table grape growers. Much of this documentation has already been submitted to the Senate Subcommittee on Migratory Labor. Such violations are so well documents [*sic*] that Superior Judge Irving Perluss recently ruled that a jobless worker was within rights when he refused to accept farm labor work offered him through the California Department of Employment on grounds that most of such jobs are in violation of state health and sanitation codes.

If the federal government and the DOD is [*sic*] not concerned about the welfare of farm workers, they must be concerned with protecting our servicemen from contamination and disease carried by grapes picked in fields without toilets or washstands. Recent laboratory tests have found DDT residues on California grapes. Economic poisons have killed and injured farm workers. Will they also prove dangerous to U.S. military personnel? Focusing on other forms of crime in the fields, we would finally ask if the DOD buys table grapes from the numerous growers who daily violate state and federal minimum wage and child labor laws, who employ illegal foreign labor, and who do not deduct social security payments from farm worker wages?

The DOD increasing purchase of table grapes is nothing short of a national outrage. It is an outrage to the million of American taxpayers who are supporting the farm workers struggle for justice by boycotting table grapes. How can any American believe that the U.S. Government is sincere in its efforts to eradicate poverty when the military uses its immense purchasing power to subvert the farm workers non-violent struggle for a descent [*sic*] living wage and a better future?

Many farm workers are members of minority groups. They are Filipino and Mexican-Americans and black Americans. These same farm workers are on the front lines of battle in Vietnam. It is a cruel and ironic slap in the face to these men who have left the fields to fulfill their military obligation to find increasing amounts of non-union grapes in their mess kits.

In conclusion let me say that our only weapon is the boycott. Just when our boycott is successful the U.S. military doubled its purchases of table grapes, creating a major obstacle to farm worker organizing and union recognition. The DOD is obviously acting as a buyer of last resort for scab grapes and is, in effect, providing another form of federal subsidy for anti-union growers who would destroy the efforts of the poor to build a union. UFWOC calls on all concerned Americans and on the members of the Senate Subcommittee on Migratory Labor to protest this anti-union policy of the military and the Nixon administration.

Washington, D.C.

July 15, 1969

Dolores Huerta with San Francisco
Mayor Willie Brown and Rep. Nancy
Pelosi, circa 1990s. Courtesy of
John A. Kouns.

23

Teamsters and UFW Debate, 1973

Moderator: Ms. Huerta will be the chief debater for the United Farm Workers. Ms. Huerta will start the program. She will have 30 minutes from when she walks to the lectern.

Dolores Huerta: I wish to thank everyone who made this possible. The organizing of farm workers in this country has a long and bitter history. Every effort that has been made has been broken by the powerful force of the growers with violence against the powerless, most of the time ethnic groups, such as the Chinese, Japanese, Filipinos, Mexicans, Mexicans, and Mexicans again. The Teamsters Union in 1961 tried to organize farm workers. They set up an organizing office in Stockton, California, my hometown, put out a lot of effort and a lot of money and their effort failed. They had to close down the office.

One of the other groups that tried to organize farm workers was the Agricultural Workers Organizing Committee. They had a group strike in the lettuce fields in the Imperial Valley in 1961. The Teamsters moved in there during that strike and signed a backburner deal with the Bud Antle Company, allowing them to keep their foreign Mexican workers, the braceros. It was a straight sweetheart deal and the Teamsters gave the Bud Antle Company $1 million to keep that company from going bankrupt.

César Chávez has been working with farm workers since 1952. Himself a farm worker, he decided that he was going to start a union. He started that union in Delano, California with the workers almost on a one-on-one basis in house meetings night after night, until the people got enough courage in themselves and enough faith in having an organization of their own that they finally had a union. The result of that was the first grape strike back in 1965. The Teamsters came in

UFW Archives, courtesy of Wayne State University.

again. We had a strike and boycott against the DiGiorgio Corporation and the Teamsters came in behind our picket lines and began signing workers up. We got them to agree to an election. We had that election because Governor Brown, the Democratic Governor of California, ordered that election and we beat the Teamsters Union two to one in that secret ballot election. They signed another backdoor deal with Moretti, a wine company, we had a boycott against Moretti.

But then the Teamsters decided they didn't want to have any more elections. They made demands on Gallo, on Almaden, on Christian Brothers, all of these wine companies where we had been organizing farm workers. But when Governor Brown said you've got to have an election, a secret ballot election the Teamsters pulled out, they pulled out of Gallo, they pulled out of Almaden, they pulled out of Moretti and they signed an agreement with us saying they would never again step into the field of farm workers.

We went ahead with the first big boycott and all of you who are sitting out here who didn't eat grapes helped the farm workers achieve, for the first time in this nation, the right to have a union; the right to go to work and know you're going to get paid a minimum wage. When our contracts expired the minimum wage was $2.25 an hour. They were allowed to have toilets, drinking water, freedom from pesticides, a farm worker medical plan that covers the farm worker, his wife and his children for a nine month period of time and requires that they only work 50 hours. This plan only cost the employer 10 cents an hour because the farm workers paid, the money goes directly to the worker. We have paid out four and one half million dollars for the farm workers in three years. We had a credit union for the farm workers that lent out two and a half million dollars. We had five clinics in three years. César Chávez was such a bad administrator that he was able to set up five clinics for the farm workers without a single cent of taxpayers' money, not one cent of taxpayers' money. Any farm worker can go into our clinic and get a full medical examination for $3 and have a baby delivered for $75.

We set up service programs, a retirement village for old Filipino farm workers who've been so brutally discriminated against. All of these dreams we've committed our lives to for farm workers in one sharp blow have been smashed.

The labor contractors are back again, and hate is exploiting the labor contract system. The West Coast Teamsters signed an agreement with the contractors to go back into the fields. Child labor, which was eliminated in the United Farm Workers contracts is back again. Pesticides are being used and illegal aliens are being brought in to take the jobs of the people who were on strike. We have some of the grape strikers here who were in jail. They were on strike working on the boycott, as were farm workers across the country, working to get their union contracts back.

In the Cannery Workers Union, which the Teamsters have represented for forty years, my mother was a striker to get a cannery union, was turned over to the Western Teamsters. Those union officials have been found guilty of 34 counts of racial discrimination against Mexicans. The cannery workers don't have clinics, they don't have credit unions, they don't have service programs. The Teamsters Union has been known to discriminate all the way down the line against Mexicans-Americans, and of course the bulk of the workers in California are Spanish-speaking people. So that's why we don't want the Teamsters Union, not even talking about the violence and all the other terrible things they have done. They are in here to protect the growers. The Teamsters Union was brought in by the growers. A Teamsters official has pleaded no contest to accepting a $10,000 bribe from a lettuce grower in California.

The whole thing is so filled with corruption we want our own union, we want our own leaderships and the farm workers are willing to come all the way across the country to fight and ask you for help to begin their own union in a non-violent method in our boycott of grapes, iceberg lettuce, and Gallo wine.

I think one of the biggest things of our union is that we do have Alex López here—he is President of the Ranch Committee. We have a steward system so that if a law passes that says there shouldn't be pesticides, we can depend on the law. There shouldn't be child labor; if you don't have a union steward out there in the field enforcing that law, that law doesn't exist. We have union stewards; we have union committees; we have ranch committees that are elected by the workers. We have challenged the Teamsters time and again to have elections and they refuse to have an election because they know that we'll win.

They know that we will win and we will challenge them again. Now they say to us, why don't you get under the National Labor Relations Act. They've been under the NLRB [National Labor Relations Board] all these years. They're supposed to be under those laws. So why did they do illegal things such as signing backdoor contracts with the growers without notifying the workers or having any kind of election. They claimed that they had petitions signed; we saw those petitions. We saw the same handwriting signing pages and pages of workers' names. There were Arabian workers in Detroit, Michigan that appeared on those pages. While they were in Detroit, Michigan they were signing petitions in California.

The evidence is overwhelming and we have it all documented. In terms of representation, if there is an issue of representation, then why don't they have an election? They can't say that we should be covered under the NLRB because they know that that may take five years or longer before we can get any planned congressional action to make it. Last year we had a bill in California that would've made it mandatory, AB 3370, that would've made every ranch have an election. The Teamsters and the growers defeated that bill. We passed it in the Assembly and they defeated it in the Senate. Now if they were so interested in having elections why did they defeat that bill in the state legislature? Why aren't they using that money that's destroying farm workers to make life better for their members they have under contract? Why are they using that money against the farm workers? For just one reason: to help out the big agricultural growers who own 1.5 million acres of land in California; I don't think they need their help.

Moderator: Thank you Mrs. Huerta. She will be followed by Chuck O'Brian [COB], International Brotherhood of Teamsters.

Moderator: Now we are moving to rebuttal. Dolores will be given five minutes to rebut anything that the opposition has talked about.

DH: It's very hard to answer the innuendo that was made during the Teamster's presentation. I would also like to say, though this may not come out right, I was elected at a convention of farm workers to represent them by many thousands of farm workers. We have here today farm workers who are grape strikers. People from Delano, people who know Josie Capaton and the women who are on strike right now and came out on strike in 1973. I know them very well, they're members of our union. I think if we want to know what the farm workers think we should hear from the farm workers and not somebody who speaks for the farm workers and they are with us this evening. As you know, the National Bishop's Committee has established a committee of five bishops to engage with the growers and the farm workers in negotiations. These bishops were with us in our negotiations that we had right from the grapes to the lettuce. The recommendation of the bishops was for the National Conference of Bishops of America to endorse the boycott. César Chávez met with the Pope [Paul VI] in Rome a few weeks ago. I don't think the pope would've met César if he was the type of man described to you this evening. We have also been endorsed by the Synagogue Council of America, by the American Jewish Congress, and the National Council of Churches that constitute the major denominations.

I think that it's unfair to show a grape field that has been farmed for 40 years and is no longer producing and to say that this is because of the farm worker's union. As a matter of fact, we did have an election in DiGiorgio, we did win that election and it was supervised, one by the American Arbitration Association and by the State Mediation Service. All the land that DiGiorgio had that was still producing was taken over by other growers. There were workers working on those ranches and you saw many of those workers on strike wanting the union back at the ranches.

If he thinks that $1.65 an hour was an adequate wage I'm sorry, we don't. That's why we had our first strike and boycott and when we raised the farm workers' wages to what they were.

In terms of the Teamster's contracts all I can say is what the workers were making under those contracts, they're not making what is shown on paper. The workers are working under labor contractors and having exorbitant amounts of money taken from their paychecks, sometimes they end up with just $20, $30, $40 a week. There are a large number of illegal aliens working there, many of them are not getting any social security deductions turned in for them. If anything, conditions have gotten way worse.

We are winning on the boycott. The grape growers have about $8 million of grapes sitting in cold-storage that they can't get rid of. They had a very good few years—contrary to what the Teamsters say. If he did some research in this area he would see for himself that the grape growers themselves said that in 1971 and 1972 declared publicly that those were the best years that they had had in terms of the grape industry since the 1950s, and that was under UFW contract. Likewise, in terms of wine, they had fantastic domestic wine sales under our contract. By the way, we do have under contract besides the Coachela contract which covers about 1500 workers, we have a contract in strawberries, we have a Interharvest contract in lettuce that covers about 2000 workers and we have many other wine contracts that have been renegotiated and resigned by those growers. What he didn't say was that the plan to kick out the farm workers was cooked up in Nixon's office, between President Nixon, the Farmer's Federation and the mover behind the plan to destroy the United Farm Workers was none other than Charles Colson. His research didn't include that big plot to destroy the United Farm Workers.

Moderator: We're going to move to the section of 30 minutes of cross between the two parties.

Teamsters: We hear so much about violence. I wonder if I could give you a copy of a check signed by César Chávez, a copy of an indictment against the organizers of your UFW who shot two of our organizers and the check amount for $11,000. I wonder if you could explain to me this act of violence, an act of violence okayed by the United Farm Workers.

DH: I know the incident you refer to and yes it was an act of violence and no it was not supported by the United Farm Workers. The man who shot the Teamster organizer was a farm worker. He was not a United Farm Workers staff person. He was a person with the strikers. It was a lettuce strike in Santa María. Yes, the union did take responsibility for the damages because it happened on our picket line. Just the same way that we took responsibility for the 19 farm workers who were killed in the bus accident in Blythe, California in a labor contractor's bus. We buried every one of those workers even though they were working under a Teamster contract and had no safety protection in that vehicle that caused them to die. And I just want to say something, O'Brian was saying something about the truth, let's talk about the truth. We have a statement here saying that the election held in DiGiorgio was conducted by a Catholic clergymen; that is simply not true. The American Arbitration Association and I'm sure the Teamsters officials here know that, is a professional firm, it is not a religious organization. The DiGiorgio election was conducted first by the American Arbitration Association, they had neutral observers. The second one was by the State Mediation Services in the state of California and not by clergy, so Mr. O'Brian has his facts a little mixed up. The people who came to vote in the DiGiorgio election had to show that number one he had been a DiGiorgio employee and number two that he came up on strike from that ranch during that period. There was a cutoff period of time; any one who had come out on strike in response to the picket line at the DiGiorgio ranch before they agreed to have an election was given the right to vote. And yes, the DiGiorgio had gone to El Paso, Texas to bring in workers and they had gone all the way to Mexico to bring in workers because the DiGiorgio ranch, like most of the corporate growers in California won't send a bus 30 miles to Fresno to employ farm workers but they will send buses into the interior of Mexico to bring in people so they can bring them to work at slave wages.

The other thing is, you've made a statement about signing a contract with apple growers in California. There were 11 people working when the Teamsters signed the contract with the apple growers. Since then there's been a strike at that ranch and every single farm worker has come out on strike at that ranch. This is not recorded by me, it's recorded in Salinas, California and the *Fresno Bee* and in all of the papers.

COB: Probably the most pressing question for people in organized labor, and I don't know how many people supported you but I do know one thing, the AFL-CIO would never support a product by workers under a contract for a particular industry or a particular company that is a scab company or a non-union company. That question comes to mind and that we're pushing for and that we'd hope the United Farm Workers would help us get the bill that Senator Tunney introduced that you say would take 10 or 15 years and that's not true. It's already been read once, it comes up again in January in the Senate, where hopefully and we're praying very hard that this bill would give the workers the right to an election. I'd like to ask why don't you and César Chávez fight as hard as you can to get that bill passed? You say you're interested in elections, free elections.

DH: In terms of the bill in California, which would've been passed, the Teamsters voted against it. It was a fraud. I think, especially when you're on the boycott, you always hear the guards say, well the farm workers don't want Chávez's union and why don't all the farm workers belong to the union if they want the union? I think the White River strike is a really good example of what farm workers are up against when they're just trying to save what they've got. I think that a lot of the people that work at White River thought that they were safe, that they would never have to go on another picket line again for a long time and they thought that the battle was over and they could just do their work in peace and not have to worry about going on strike. But I guess they got fooled. Maybe the White River strike was a blessing in disguise. There's a letter that a farm worker sent me from Calexico, he said sometimes we have to do God's will and we don't know why or how but we are trying to do it. And maybe it was a blessing in disguise because a lot of the farm workers in Delano are now suddenly aware that maybe their contracts aren't so safe after all, that maybe they will also be in the position of the White River strikers. I think this is what really spurred people to get out and work for Proposition 22 [in 1972 Proposition 22 was defeated by the voters in California]. In all of the history of farm labor organizing, what happened at White River, history has repeated itself again and again. You have the growers with their private security police force. The reason the people couldn't get close to those machines was because the people who were operating the machines had shotguns by their sides and they had a security guard with a gun. We heard an interview with Mr. Allen who was the head of the growers and they asked him what would you do if any of these strikers come in and he said "I'll shoot 'em. My men have been instructed to shoot if any of them come into these fields." Then this reporter said, "Aren't you afraid you're going to kill somebody?" He said, "Well they should know better than to come into the fields and that's what we've been instructed to do." It was just amazing, this is what the people were up against and there was all of the sheriff's office. They brought in some kids to work and they said there are children in the fields and the sheriff said, "that's not my department, I don't worry about that." On the day of the mass arrest there were people being taken out of their cars and being thrown in jail.

What do the people have to fight with? Nothing, just a picket sign and a flag and that's it. Now it was interesting to see that they had filed a lawsuit against Proposition 22 because of their intervention in the White River strike and some of you know this and maybe some of you don't, the two men who were involved in breaking the strike at White River, one of them was Harry Cooble, the head of the Nisei Farmers League in Fresno County who was the chairman for Proposition 22 in Fresno County. The other guy, Bill Taber, from Tulare County, who was the chairman for 22 in that county, was also instrumental in trying to recruit scabs. And not only that but Bill Taber was the guy who organized the hoodlum squad, the goon squad that crashed the office and broke the windows and went into the UFW office and wanted to eat some of the people up there. I made this speech a lot in San Francisco because I was telling everyone in the Bay Area about it, but the Tulare County officers were sitting right on the corner watching the people as they were advancing on the [UFW] office with their guns and shooting bullets and throwing rock and throwing bottles. They were watching this happen and they didn't bother to arrest anyone. That deputy sheriff knew every single person that was involved in that assault on the office. He knew every single person but he didn't bother to arrest one person because afterwards, when it was reported to the press and the Tulare sheriff, they said it was a figment of the union's imagination. I guess they have a pretty good imagination.

These are things we have to remember. This is how they crush the strikes, by putting the leadership in jail, by deporting them before when people were trying to organize and by using all of the force of the courts and the community against the strikers. Of course we have something now that we didn't have before. What is it?

Audience: The boycott.

DH: The boycott, yeah. We all realize that the only way the farm workers can get justice is through the boycott. That's the only way that the White River strikers are ever going to get their contract. It's really interesting to note, when we were in negotiations they told us that the picking cost would be about $400,000. The company claimed that they didn't have one penny more. We said you've got to pay what

Christian Brothers was paying and Paul Masson in Almaden, and they couldn't afford it because they were renovating the ranch and putting a lot of money into it and they couldn't pay one penny more. I don't know where they found the million and a half dollars that it cost them to break the strike. They were chartering buses every day and sometimes the buses with just a few growers in it. Some of the Japanese growers were so good-hearted that they helped them pick some of the grapes. The day the Japanese growers had their barbecue they had 16 Tulare County Sheriff's officers protecting them while they were eating their steaks in front of the White River strikers. They had 16 patrolmen protecting them and being paid by taxpayers. And yet when we had trouble at the office we couldn't get one deputy to go out there and protect the people at the office.

It's interesting where they got that money. You can see the employer is willing to pay even better wages, to spend a lot of money as long as it can break the union. That the main thing they want, they don't want us to organize. They don't want the people to get together and that's what the whole thing was about. I know we're going to get them, especially now that the Prop 22 has gone down the drain.

24

Keynote Address before the Annual Convention of the American Public Health Association, October 21, 1974, New Orleans, Louisiana

Thank you very much Dr. Kerr and Mr. McBeath, Executive Director of this conference, and to all of you delegates. I wish to tell you that Mr. Chávez's illness is his recurring illness that he has had over the years which is that of his back. And he had just come back from a three week tour to Europe, had been in Washington to testify about the use of illegal aliens in the government committee, went to a board meeting. We traveled all the way to Yuma, Arizona where there are 2,000 farm workers on strike and he was unable to get out of the car and address a rally of workers who had waited for him for four hours. We don't know how long he is going to be laid up. He's in a hospital right now in San Jose and we hope it won't be too long before he will be able to be back on his feet.

I wish to bring you greetings and a hope for a very successful convention on your hundred and second convention to all of you who have dedicated your lives to making life better for the world, for America. I think that your goals are very much like the goals of our union. We got into the business of organizing farm workers for mainly health reasons. It is no accident that farm workers have an average life span of 49 years. And those of you who have worked in rural communities, I think know the reasons. Those of you that don't, I just want to give you a little picture of what health is like for a farm worker in a place where he does not have the United Farm Workers to represent him.

UFW Archives, courtesy of Wayne State University.

In Delano, California, I remember 3 specific instances: One, a worker who had his hand broken on the job and he was sent to his local doctor, who by the way is also a grape grower. The doctor prescribed some ointment to put on his hand. The worker's hand started swelling. He came later to use our X-ray machine which at that time was just a small trailer. We had this old X-ray machine from the year one and we found out that his hand was broken. There was another farm worker, Chala Savala, who another local grape grower doctor said . . . she was ill. He said, Why, you're pregnant. About six months later she found out she wasn't pregnant; she had tuberculosis. But by that time she had to have a lung removed. Farm workers who are poisoned with pesticides are told they have sun stroke. And it's always the same thing, you have no money, the doctor can't see you.

When we first won our contracts as a result of our first strike and our first grape boycott, we made some very fantastic changes. I'd just kinda like to ask, how many of you didn't eat grapes between 1965 and 1970? Raise your hands. Well, I'm glad to see that there were a lot of you. And I'm going to tell you some of the changes that you brought about in health for farm workers in Delano, California, this very same place that I'm talking about.

The first thing that we got when we got our contracts was a medical plan. And we named it the Robert F. Kennedy Medical Plan after our good friend Robert Kennedy. The plan was paid for by the growers. We made them pay 10 cents an hour for every hour that the workers worked. And the workers, we took the plan to the workers so that they could vote on it, so that they could decide what kind of medical care they wanted. And the workers decided that they wanted doctor visits paid for; they wanted maternity benefits; they wanted hospitalization benefits; they wanted an X-ray lab; they wanted prescriptions paid for under their medical plan.

And so we developed a really fantastic medical plan. Because every migrant worker, his wife and all of his children are covered under our medical plan. If they only work 50 hours for the migrant medical plan they were covered for a 9-month period. Nine months, no matter where, they can make a medical claim and get paid for it. And the money goes directly to the worker. Our major medical plan is 250 hours. Under this plan they get hospitalization, and surgical benefits, ambulance benefits, a minimum dental and eyeglass prescription care. Again no matter where they are at.

See, the beautiful thing about our medical plan and the reason that we were able to do this fantastic medical plan for ten cents an hour is because we did not go through an insurance company. Now when we first tried to get this plan passed, many of the growers were very upset about it. They said you have to go through an insurance company. We are very lucky that César Chávez is a grammar school drop out. And he hasn't been educated to think that insurance is a way of life. And he said he wasn't going to give any of his money to an insurance company, any of the workers' money. So the way that our medical plan works is that the money comes in and it goes out directly to the workers.

It's a non-profit plan and it's administered by the farm workers themselves. The person who administers our RFK Medical Plan is out of the first grape strike, María Saludado-Magaña. When she first came into the union, she couldn't read or write English. She now administers the full Medical Plan. She's been audited many times and our plan is perfect.

But once we got the medical plan we found that that really didn't stop the abuses, because the doctors were still not giving the workers good health care. So the next step was then to build a clinic. So the workers started to build their clinics. During the period of the last 3 years we have built five clinics. Five clinics: four of those were in the state of California, one of them is in Mexico and we are building another one in Florida, which will be opening soon.

I think our clinics are unique in that we call them people's clinics. The people built them, we raised the money for them. There is no government money at all in our clinics. And the kind of work that the clinic does is primarily, first of all educational. And we don't have mickey mouse clinics. Our clinics are really beautiful. I mean there is good medicine in our clinics. The workers are taught about nutrition, to combat diabetes, which is very common among farm workers. They are given pre-natal instruction, to have healthier babies and healthier mothers. They are taught about inoculations. You know it's a really funny experience to go into the waiting room of our clinic, and you will see a group of farm workers sitting around talking. And one worker will say to the other one: well I came in to get a shot. And the other worker will say: why, you shouldn't get a shot if you just have a cold because you know you can build up an immunity to penicillin. And these are farm workers teaching each other, you know, about health.

Our health workers go into the labor camps. They've done a vast service on tuberculosis and on other diseases that are contagious. And when we find a sick farm worker, someone that has tuberculosis, someone that has another disease that shouldn't be in the labor force, we take that farm worker out of the labor force. And he is put on some kind of disability compensation so that he doesn't have to work until he becomes well again. We do home visits. We have a team approach with the doctor, the health worker, the nurse, and we go right into the homes of the farm workers.

Needless to say, this kind of preventative medicine that we are now undertaking has saved so many lives that the statistics of Tulare County in California have changed. Last year I had my tenth baby in a hospital in Tulare County, and the doctor who was delivering my baby, who happened to be a specialist along with our own doctor from our clinic, told me that our health care was so good that we had actually changed the statistics of Tulare County—I think that's pretty fantastic, because our doctors are so dedicated, and because their medicine is so good.

Now, some of you might wonder how come I have ten children, right? One of the main reasons is because I want to have my own picket line. But all kidding aside, it's really nice to be able to go to a clinic when you are pregnant with your tenth baby and not have people look at you like you are kind of crazy.

Or like you don't know where they come from, or put pressure on you not to have any more children. Because after all you know, Mexicans are kind of poor people and you shouldn't have all that many kids. So that's another good thing about our clinics. Because unfortunately, that pressure not to have children translates itself in county hospitals and places where people have no power because those babies aren't taken care of and into very hard labor for mothers because they are trying to make it as hard on the mother as they can to have another one. And I guess I feel a little bit strongly about that because I've been in situations where I've seen children die, babies die, because somebody there thought they shouldn't have been born in the first place.

Now another great thing about our clinics is that we train farm workers as lab assistants, lab technicians, nurse's aides, we train farm workers to do the administration of the clinic. The receptionist is a farm worker. We have two of our clinics right now being administered by farm workers. One of them, the Delano Clinic, is administered by Esther Uranday who was a grape striker, from the first grape strike. Juanita Ortega from Calexico administers the other clinic that we have. So what we're doing is we're not only just giving good health care—fantastic health care—but we are training our own people to be able to do the health work and to administer the program.

The amazing reason that we have been able to build these clinics in such a short period of time is because our clinics are non-profit. The doctors that come to work with us work the way that we do. We work for no wages. Our doctors get a little bit more for some of you out there that might be interested. But nevertheless it is a sacrifice. And that's important. Because you can't help poor people and be comfortable. You know, the two things are just not compatible. If you want to really give good health care to poor people you've got to be prepared to be a little uncomfortable and to put a little bit of sacrifice behind it.

Now there are other ways that the Union has changed things in terms of health care. And I'm going to talk a little bit about the pesticides. Because that's something that we raised the issue many years ago and a lot of people have been concerned about but it was sort of a "no, no." Nobody could talk about it openly. What we have in our union are Ranch Committees. Where we have a contract we elect a ranch committee. The workers elect their own committee. That committee is responsible to make sure that no pesticides that can be harmful to them or harmful to the consumers can be used in that ranch. They check out to see what kind of pesticides are going to be used, what the antidotes are, what the re-entry periods are . . . everything that there is possible to know about that pesticide.

Do you know that we were amazed to find out, you can get all kinds of information about what's harmful to a pet, but you can't get any information about what's harmful to a farm worker. Because there has been very little research done in this area. And when we were negotiating contracts, I was in charge of the contract negotiations for the union, we called up a friend of ours who worked with the Los Angeles County Health—Industrial Health, and he gave us some information on one of the organic phosphates that we wanted to know. Well, one of the growers who was in on the negotiations tried to get him fired for giving us that information. And this man worked for the Los Angeles County Health Department. But this shows you, and I'm going to talk about that a little bit more, about the kind of repression that I know a lot of you are faced when you do try to make real changes or when you try to get into those controversial areas where you have conflicts, you know, of power.

In our contracts, we banned DDT, Aldrin, Endrin 2,4-D, 2,4-T, Tep and many of the other,—Monitor 4—many of these other pesticides. We banned these pesticides in our contracts starting from 1970. It is interesting that just recently, the government has come out against Aldrin and Endrin. And the Farm Workers Union banned these pesticides many years ago. We find that the only way that you can be sure that the so called laws are administered, that the so called laws are carried out is when you have somebody right there on the ranch, a steward, a ranch committee, somebody that can't get fired from the job, somebody that has the protection of a union contract to make sure that these things are carried out.

All of these great things that we were able to do and all of you that didn't eat grapes helped us to accomplish are being wiped out now. And they are being wiped out because last year, as many of you know, we lost our contracts. The growers brought in the Teamsters Union, they signed backdoor contracts with them, 14,000 farm workers went out on strike. Four thousand farm workers—this was not a war, this was a strike—4,000 farm workers were jailed for picketing, 200 farm workers were beaten and injured by Teamsters and police, and two farm workers were killed. It is sad for me to report this, but the clock has been turned back and California agriculture, with the exception of a handful of contracts that we still hold, we now have the labor contractor, the crew leader system back again, we now have child labor back again.

There was a bus accident, to talk to you about health standards and safety standards. There was a bus accident in Blythe, California on January the 15th. This was under a Teamster contract. Nineteen farm workers were drowned when their bus turned over into an irrigation ditch. This was a school bus. It had no business transporting people, you know, 70 miles to work. The seats of that bus were not fastened to the floor. The people got tangled in the bus. They couldn't get out of the bus. They were crushed to death and they were drowned. Among those that were drowned was a 13 year old child and his 15 year old brother. There were four women that were drowned. The labor contractor who owned that bus got a 50 dollar fine for the death of 19 farm workers. I'm sure that many of you didn't read about it in your local newspapers because this is common among farm workers, these kinds of accidents. Twenty five farm workers have been killed because of lack of safety precautions in the fields since the Teamsters took over the contracts.

We now have a return to pesticides—40,000 acres of lettuce were poisoned with Monitor 4. This lettuce were shipped to the market. In California it was sold as shredded lettuce in Safeway stores. That's nice to have Monitor 4 with your shredded salad, huh?

And you know we have a return back to the archaic system that we had, primitive system that existed before and still exists where we don't have United Farm Workers contract. People working out there in those fields without a toilet, people working out there in those fields without any hand washing facilities, without any cold drinking water, without any kind of first aid or safety precautions. All of this has come back again. The California Rural Legal Assistance just did a spot survey of about 20 ranches in the Salinas and the Delano area, just a couple of months ago. And every single instance they found either no toilet or a dirty toilet, and you can imagine. And this is something consumers don't understand. That that lettuce, those grapes are being picked right there in that field. If there's a dirty toilet it's right next to the produce, and that produce is picked and packed in that field and shipped directly to your store. The way you see the grapes in your market, the way you see the lettuce in that market, it comes directly from the field. It doesn't go through any cleansing process. It's direct.

I remember talking to the head of the Food and Drug Administration in San Francisco. You know I found out that there was a law that says: No produce can be shipped for interstate commerce if it has been picked or packed in a way that it might become contaminated. Well, if you've got a field there you've got several hundred people or a thousand people working, and there's no toilet, that produce can be contaminated. You know what he told me? He said, "I've got to enforce the Food and Drug Administration law in four states. I can't go out there and check every field to see if there is a toilet or not, or hand washing facilities." You know these are those little tiny things that are kind of overlooked. And they're so serious. But I'll bet that if any public health person brings this up there are going to be repercussions because they bring it up.

The Teamsters have brought back illegal aliens. And now when I say this, I want to tell you what's happening to these people. Today President Ford is hosting with President Echavarria in Mexico. And they're going to talk about a bracero program which is a slave program for workers, for Mexican workers. And Mexico needs this because they've got a 50% inflation rate in Mexico and they've got a 30 or 40% unemployment rate. So they want to get rid of the people. They want to get rid of the problem. But what does it do to people over here? They want to bring in one million Mexicans from Mexico. We've already got close to a million people here illegally. And how are they being treated? They are paying 300 dollars each to come over the border. They are being put in housing where you have 30 or 40 people in a room without any kind of a sanitary facility. We have one report of an illegal alien who was picking peaches on a ladder; the ladder was shaky, it broke. The ladder went right through his anus. And they didn't give him any medical attention. Luckily one of our members found out about it and brought him to one of our clinics for treatment. We're having illegal aliens who are coming in, who are being blinded by pesticides, for treatment. This is slavery. And it's wrong. And we've got to see what way we can stop this.

We can't really wait for legislation. You know there's a lot of things that we can do right away. I think that the one thing that we've learned in our union is that you don't wait. You just get out and you start doing things. And you do things in such a way that you really help people to lay the foundations that you need. We don't have to talk about a charitable outlook. You know people come in with a lot of money and they give people charity. We've got to talk about ways to make people self-sufficient in terms of their medical health. Because when they go in there with charity and then they pull out, then they leave the people worse off than they ever were before. We've got to use government money to help people. And I don't think that this is so radical. Lord knows that the growers are getting billions of dollars not to grow cotton, you know, all kinds of supports and subsidies. Well, if any money is given for medical health it should stay in that community. It shouldn't just come in there at the pleasure of the local politicians and be pulled out at the pleasure of the local politicians.

And I don't think that public health people should be repressed. It worries me when I see a clinic in a farm worker community that is afraid to put out a Farm Worker flag or put up César's picture because they are afraid that they are going to get their money taken away from them. And yet this has happened. And this is wrong. But the only reason it happens is because we let it happen. We've got to take the side of the people that are being oppressed. And if we can't do that, then we're not doing our job, because the people in that minority community or in that community are not going to have any faith in the medical program that is in there, if you can't take their side. They're going to suspect you. You know, we've got to be able to stand up and fight for our rights. We can't any longer cooperate with any kind of fear, any kind of bigotry, any kind of racism, anything that is wrong. We've got to be able to stand up and say: that is wrong. And it's going to take that kind of courage, I think, the same kind of courage that César has taught the farm workers, to make the kind of necessary changes that are needed.

Health, like food, has got to be to cure people, to make people well. It can't be for profit. Food should be sacred to feed people, not for profit. Health has got to be a right for every person and not a privilege. You know you would be sad to know that many farm workers before we had our clinics had never been to a doctor in their lives. In their entire lives they had never been to a doctor. And I'm sure like farm workers, there are many many other people who have never been to a clinic or to a doctor. And many times that is even out of fear because they see the doctor or they see the medical person not as their friend but they see that person as their enemy.

Now I hope that what we have done, our experience, will serve some use to what you're interested in and what you're doing. I hope that you will help us get back what we have lost which are our union contracts so that we can continue this fantastic health program that we have that we started in California. And you can do this very easily just by not eating any grapes, until we win, by not eating any lettuce, until we win, and by not drinking any Gallo wine. And I'm saying that lightly. It's not light, it's a very serious situation. Within the next year they are spending millions of dollars to destroy the United Farm Workers. They are spending millions of dollars to tell what a bad administrator César Chávez is. Have you seen these articles in the *New York Times* and *Time Magazine*? They say César Chávez is a bad administrator. What they really mean is: he is the wrong color. And if he were a good administrator . . . can you imagine five clinics, a medical plan, a credit union, a retirement center for farm workers, fantastic increases in wages, the removal of the labor contractor system. All of this César did in a few short years. What would he do if he was a good administrator? We have a booth here, booth 1020, where we're giving out information about our clinic. I implore all of you, if you can give up a year of your life or two years of your life, drop out and come and help us. The only reason we haven't got more clinics is because we need doctors. In our Delano clinic right now, we only have one doctor working. Please come and join the people and help us build health care for everybody and we will give you a little bit of money, not too much. But we all work for $5 a week. None of us get paid. Even César gets $5 a week for his personal benefit. We get $5 a week for food. We live off of donations. All of the money that we need to run our boycott and our strikes. We have a button table where we invite you to buy a button and please wear our button. As I say, all the contributions that you can give will be greatly, greatly appreciated because we do need money very desperately.

We're also going to be showing a film, the film of our strike, of the bloody strike that we had in California last summer. It will be shown at one and two o'clock in the auditorium. I'd invite all of you to come and see the film. You'll never forget it. And you will really see . . . when we talk about the principle of non-violence, you still see it in action. Because you will see farm workers getting beaten and killed and you will see that the farm workers do not fight back with violence. We are using a non-violent action of the boycott, so we really need your help in that.

Let's say a few Vivas now, okay? You know what Viva means? That's what you're all about: Long life. Long life. And we always say that in the Spanish community, we say Viva, which means long life. So we're going to say a few Vivas and we're going to say some Abajos. You know what Abajos are? That means down. And then we will say one other thing: *Sí se puede*. Can we have this dream that we are talking about? Health for everyone, brotherhood, peace? It can be done: *Sí se puede*. And we'll all do the farm workers' handclap together to show that we're united in thought and action and in love. And the farm worker's handclap starts out very slow and then it goes very fast. So let's try it. We're going to say first "Viva la Causa" which is the cause of labor, peace and health. "Viva La Justicia" which is justice, and then we will say Viva Chávez, for César, may God give him long life. And then we'll say down with fear, Abajo, and down for lettuce and grapes, Abajo, and down with Gallo wine. Because Gallo is on the boycott too. Abajo. By the way Gallo has some other labels like Ripple, Thunderbird, Madria, Madria Sangria, Joe Steuben. Anything that says Modesto, California is Gallo wine.

Okay, let's try it now. All together, huh. I'll say Viva La Causa and everybody yells, Viva, really, really loud, okay? Viva La Causa! Viva! Ugh, that was very weak. This is very important. This is like kind of praying together in unison, you know, so it's really important. Let's try it again. Viva La Causa! Viva! Viva La Justicia! Viva! Now so César can hear us in the hospital—where he's at and the growers can hear us where they're at. Viva, Chávez! Viva! Okay, now we'll try Abajo. Down with fear! Abajo! Down with lettuce and grapes! Abajo! Down with Gallo! Abajo! You know, this really works. We did that at the impeachment rally in Washington, D.C. and we said Down with Nixon, Abajo! And it worked. Can we live in a world of brotherhood and peace without disease and fear and oppresion! *Sí se puede*, right? Okay, let's all do it together. *Sí se puede*. Clapping. *Sí se puede, Sí se puede* . . . (with clapping). Thank you very much.

Dolores Huerta and Richard Chávez, 2005. Courtesy of Carlos LeGerrette/ César Chávez Service Club Archive Project.

25

Speech Given by Dolores Huerta, UCLA, February 22, 1978

Terri Fletcher: My name is Terri Fletcher, I'm from the Campus Farm Worker's Support Committee here, and first I'd like to thank the Women's Resource Center and MEChA for co-sponsoring this with us and also the professors who donated money and also all of the other people who helped us out because we really needed it. We went to the Speaker's Bureau to ask for funding for this and they said, "Well we never heard of Dolores Huerta, so she couldn't be that important." That really shows how little they know. Dolores has been with the union since it started in 1965 [*sic*]. She is an executive board member and a first vice president in the union. She has been on the New York boycott; she's worked in Florida; she is currently the head of the Delano field office and is negotiating seventeen contracts right now. She is the leading woman in the labor movement in this country today; she is a very busy person and we are really lucky to have her here. So let's give her a big welcome.

Dolores Huerta: Thank you very much for that kind introduction, and I thank all of you for taking the time for being here with us this morning, and I appreciate the invitation to be with you also. The union has been around for quite a while now, and when we first started, a lot of you were still maybe in junior high school or grammar school. I know my own children, I have eleven children, and some of them were little teeny ones—you know when we first started the union—and now of course, they are growing up to be leaders in the organization. I saw the Martin Luther King movie the other day, how many of you saw that? The film that they have on the Martin Luther King struggle, did any of you see that? They had it on NBC the

Transcribed from audiotape and with permission of the UCLA Chicano Studies Research Center Library and Archive, Chicano Studies Research Center, UCLA.

other day. In seeing that they were showing all of the things that had changed in the South like integration, people having the right to vote, and the tremendous changes that were made in a twelve-year period. And I remember we were organizing the union at the same time that these civil rights, the big organization was going on in the South, and we were almost organizing simultaneously when King was organizing. And I thought to myself, of all of the things that have changed for the farm workers in the last twelve years, and you know it's hard to believe, but when we first started the union there was no food for people. When farm workers were out of work they had no food period. Farm workers were earning fifty cents an hour when we started. When people ran out of work they had nothing to eat, people literally had to go into garbage cans to get food because they had a program in California called Surplus Commodities. You know all of the food that they had in storage they would give it out to poor people. But in all of the rural counties of California, in the San Joaquin Valley, the Imperial Valley, all over the places where farm workers were at, they could *not* get surplus food—the only places that got it was San Francisco and Los Angeles. So one of our first fights we had was to get food for farm workers, just to get the extra food that they threw away to give it to farm workers, and we won that fight.

Farm workers had no unemployment insurance. It wasn't until Governor Jerry Brown got in and there was an Assemblyman here from Los Angeles, Jack Benton, who really helped push that bill. [Governor] Reagan vetoed the bill four times. We first got it out of the Assembly back in 1961. I remember one of the farm workers said at that hearing, "They are going to get a person to the moon before we get unemployment insurance for farm workers," and they did. A man landed on the moon before farm workers got unemployment insurance. Isn't that incredible? But we finally got unemployment insurance that we finally have now. And César said, "We won't get unemployment insurance until we organize the union."

There was a time when farm workers couldn't get any kind of welfare. Again, if they were out of work, they couldn't get it. Back in 1963, we did a big campaign and we got farm workers covered under welfare so if farm workers were out of work they could at least get welfare. Of course they had no kind of job security. When Robert Kennedy ran for the presidency back in 1968, farm workers who had a Robert Kennedy bumper sticker on their cars were immediately fired from their jobs. And they couldn't take any kind of activity, like registering to vote, or do any political action because they were fired. So, when you see where we are at now, we have come a long way in the changes that have been made. The minimum wage for farm workers now in the places that we don't have the union are two dollars and fifty cents an hour and two dollars and sixty cents an hour, right? Of course where we have union contracts now the farm workers' wages are three dollars and thirty cents, three dollars and forty-five cents and three dollars and fifty-five cents an hour minimum. We have union contracts where some of the farm workers are getting up to six dollars an hour for the kind work that they do, which is backbreaking and very hard work. So we have come an awful long way, we have a medical plan now for farm workers, a Robert F. Kennedy Medical Plan, where farm workers are under union contract, we have paid out six million dollars to farm workers in medical benefits, isn't that incredible? And this is money that we make the growers pay into a fund and then it goes back to the workers. Our credit union that we have, we have this little bank for farm workers. The farm workers put their own money into the bank and they borrow from themselves, and, of course, everybody says, "Oh, farm workers can't learn a credit union, they are migrant, they don't know anything, they don't have an education, they're too dumb to run a credit union." Well César didn't believe all of that, so he set up a credit union back in 1963. Our credit union has lent out five million dollars to farm workers, of their own money, isn't that incredible?

Now the other incredible part of all of this is that we only have right now, we are only covering, I guess less than ten percent of California farm workers are under contracts right now. There's about three hundred thousand farm workers in the state of California, and we only have under union contracts about ten percent, about thirty thousand. But wherever we have—the reason that the wages go up—even when we have a lot of election activity, the growers are trying to beat the elections so that the workers won't vote for the union so they jack up the wages. Like in Delano last year, we were negotiating with about seven grape growers, there's about forty grape growers in the area, but we had all of this election activity and so the growers are trying to beat the union so they raised the wages forty-five cents an hour. Which is a great benefit to the farm workers, right? You know we still have to try and go back and have those elections, seriously, because we concentrated down in the vegetable industry last year and we're going to try and get the grapes this year. The grape growers are still not wanting to sign a contract.

Now when we think, you know, how did all of this happen? How were these changes made? When we think of how the changes were made, the way that you make change, social change is so simple, but people don't believe it. You know I've been in the movement now since I was twenty-five years old, maybe some of you are younger than I was then, and I look back and I see all of the things we've done, and even to myself it's hard for me to believe how we made the changes that we made and how we made them. The changes that were made were made by people that were like the poorest of all, people that didn't know how to read or write, people who had no resources, and when we think of the changes that we were able to make for farm workers, it's really kind of a mindblower. Because the kind of action that has been taken, the kind of political action has always been very simple things. About this time ten years ago, César Chávez started his first fast. He did this because we had been on strike at that time for about five years, no for three years, and we still didn't have any contract and the contributions stopped coming in, everybody was living on Campbell's Tomato Soup and Pork and Beans because that's what we got in donations. Tons of Campbell's Soup and tons of Pork and Beans, and a lot of the farm workers were getting kind of desperate. So César started his first fast for nonviolence in 1968. He did a twenty-five day fast and he didn't eat for twenty-five days, and this was to commit farm workers in all of our movement to the philosophy of nonviolence. And of course a lot of people thought he was crazy. Some people said that César was trying to play God and some people who were very anti-religious were furious over the fact that César would do something so crazy. They thought that doing the daily work of the union was more important than fasting. This was some of our staff people. And a lot of people left the union because they didn't agree with César fasting, they tried to pressure César to stop fasting.

Myself, I was in New York working on the boycott and I kept getting calls from Delano where people were saying "César's crazy, he's trying to have this fast but you should call him up and tell him to start eating." I said, "Well look, this is his decision." I didn't do what they asked me to do, and we let César continue his fast, and, of course, it was a very glorious thing that he did. The day that César ended his fast, Robert Kennedy was there with him, and there was something like nine thousand farm workers. But that was a very simple thing that César did, he just fasted. We sort of picked up on that idea of César's fast, and then we thought, why couldn't the whole country do a little fast? Let's ask everybody not to eat grapes. That's a kind of a simple thing, right? It doesn't take a lot, just don't eat grapes. And so we asked the whole country and the whole world not to eat grapes, and they didn't. And as a result of that, people not eating grapes, we had our first big national grape boycott and we got our first contract. That was a really simple thing, but it had a tremendous impact. Because we were going to the heart of the growers, and that is their pocketbook. And we have to remember that when you are dealing with corporations and you are dealing with businesses you can't, like when you go to school you are taught to be rational, to be objective, to believe what you read and to weigh things, and do all of these things. You have to be very careful when you are in school and learn all of these things because it can be an entrapment. Luckily, farm workers many times—because they don't have school they go by their guts—they know what's right and they know what's wrong and they aren't afraid to take action.

That's a very important thing when you are in school, that you never lose that, don't ever forget to go by what you think is right and wrong down deep inside of your gut because all the time that you are in school you are going to be taught how to conform. And I am saying this from experience because I was in college, and I was a schoolteacher, and I quit teaching schools to come back and help César build a union. So I know where I come from, and I had to unlearn about being rational, objective, and being logical, right? Because when you are dealing with a big social fight and trying to make changes, the people that you are dealing with are not going to be rational and they are not going to do things on the basis of justice—they respond to only one thing and that is economic power. So somehow, you have to hit them in that pocketbook where they have their heart and their nerves and then they feel the pain. Otherwise, they can give you a thousand arguments on why something can't be done. This is why, going back to the King story, the Montgomery Bus Boycott was effective, right? Because it hit them where? In the pocketbook.

When I talk about the boycott—there were about fifty farm workers—if we took this part of the room and I would say to all of you let's all go to New York Monday morning and do a boycott, would you be willing to drop everything and go? Probably not, right? You'd have to think about it a little bit, maybe somebody would. This is what the farm workers did. They got on a bus and went to New York—people who couldn't speak English, people who couldn't read or write, and they went to speak to people and tell them to boycott grapes. They did this in 1968 and they did this again in 1973. In 1973 when the Teamsters came in—only this time there weren't fifty farm workers there were one thousand farm workers. After two of our farm workers were killed, Nagi Daifala and Juan de la Cruz, one thousand farm workers got into their cars and drove to New York City, to Chicago, to Montreal, Canada, to Toronto, Canada, to Florida. They left their houses, they left everything behind them, that takes guts right? They took their kids out there, people who had never been out of Delano, Fresno, and Lamont went out there to do a big boycott and they stayed out there until they got the Agricultural Relations Law. A lot of the work that was done was done by picketing. What is picketing? That is just marching, its just walking up and down in front of a store asking people not to buy grapes or not to buy lettuce, or not to— whatever it is we happen to be boycotting. Now that doesn't seem like that could be powerful, but it is! It's just amazing how powerful it is. Just walking up and down in front of a store. I always relate picketing to praying in a way; when people pray together they say that it has a lot of effect, except you are not praying just by yourself, you are praying with your feet and your hands and your whole body. Because it is like a petition you are out in front of the store and you are asking, trying to reach that man's conscience, or the people's conscience, trying to give them a message and you do this by displaying your whole body and that is the thing that counts the most. It's your own body, your own person; this is what counts more than anything else.

Probably some of you think to yourselves that I'm not a Martin Luther King, I'm not a César Chávez, I'm just plain old me, and what can plain old me do? Well, this is where you really have to think about it and about what plain old you can do. Plain old you can do a lot of things, you can make real great changes for this country, just plain old you—if you make a commitment. Just like farm workers have done, all of the changes that have been brought and farm workers have done is because farm workers have made a commitment and they lent their whole bodies to go out there and do something. It was, again, like during the Civil Rights struggle when people went in and sat in and got beaten up and what have you—it was their bodies that made that difference. So don't ever think that plain old you can't make the difference; it's like dropping a little stone in a pool; it's just one little stone, a little pebble, but it makes all kinds of waves that reach way out. That's what your action does, what you do goes way way out. Sometimes this may be hard if we haven't been in political action before or social action, and you think, "How can I do this?" or think, "I don't know how," because you've never had the opportunity to learn or been lucky enough to be on a picket line or a sit-in or some type of demonstration to make change. And we have to do these things, it doesn't happen by osmosis, you know, or long distance, you've got to be present and it's got to happen to you.

When we are small a lot of us are baptized into some faith or another, well, there is another kind of baptism that has to take place as you go along in life and that is the baptism of fire. When you are on the picket line or in a demonstration, you get insulted, people make fun of you, people tell you things like if you are Mexican "Why don't you go back to Mexico?" and then you have to remind them that this is Mexico. If you are Black then they will say, "Why don't you go back to Africa?" and you have to tell them that my grandparents were here before yours were! If you are a religious person they will ask why aren't you in church preaching where you are supposed to be. Your own relatives will make fun of you and say are you crazy or something, why don't you study and forget about all these other crazy things. I know, because I've been through all of this. When I first joined César and

quit my teaching job, there were very few Mexican-American teachers when I was teaching—I was maybe one of five or six in my whole
community—and all of my family thought I had gone crazy. In fact,
one of my relatives bought radio time to announce how crazy I was.
They thought they could pressure me into leaving the union and
going back to teaching again. They thought, here she's giving up a very
good teaching job to work for five dollars a week because this is what
we get in the union, five dollars for food and ten dollars for personal
expenses. That's another kind of a lesson that we have to learn.

The same thing happened to César when he was organizing—they
would make fun, and tell his wife Helen, "Your husband is out there,
you don't know where he's at, you don't know what he's doing; he tells
you he's having a meeting but who ever heard of people going around
having meetings at night? How come he doesn't go out and work like
other people do?" And Helen would be out there picking grapes all
day long and have to come home and make dinner for the family, and
she had to put up with this ridicule for years.

It wasn't until our union became a very big national thing that
people stopped making fun of her and the biggest pressure that she
got was from her own family. Almost everybody who has worked in
the union will tell you that they have to go through that, that you never
really know if you are a hero or a fool. Your family is always trying to
make you feel like you're a fool and of course you know that you're a
hero because you are committing your life to social change. That's a
decision that a lot of people have to make. Maybe not everybody can
make that decision and say that I'm going to throw my whole body
and my whole soul into it like César Chávez does or like a lot of the
people who work for the union do, but we have to make a commitment somewhere along the way, and if you can't do it all the way then
for God's sake do it at some level. Decide at some level that you are
going to do it.

You know sometimes we wonder why the conservatives in our
country, the people that are the reactionaries, why do they have so
much power? Poor folk always say because they are working at it all
the time, and that's true. See they work at it all the time—how they
can take advantage of people, how to consolidate their power, how to
enlarge their power and people, who are good people, just do it once

in a while when they think about it. They go on voting day, or when there's a big demonstration of some type, but we don't make a commitment to do it full time. And there's got to be a continual working program to make changes, not just once in a great while. You've got to plug in, you've got to be ready, and you've got to work. And you've got to build up those muscles; it's like an athlete in training, he's doesn't go out there and try to be in a boxing match—you've got to do some training. Inside of yourself you've got to look at your spiritual strength and your spiritual power and your physical strength and your mind strength to do these things. It's not going to happen any other way. You have to go through that baptism when people yell at you and tell you you're a "Commie" or something like that. Insult you and say why don't you take a bath? All of these things, this is what they tell you and you have to go through that and then you realize how the people that are yelling at you are ignorant and how they don't understand what you're doing, and then when you see how many people do that then it sort of appalls you because you think of the ignorance in our country and how many people are ignorant and how easily they are led by the people that exploit them. And so here we are a whole nation of people that are being exploited, just like the farm workers, right, because we don't know how to fight back; we don't know how to fight.

And when you come to school, you come to school to get the abilities to learn and to strengthen yourself, but you don't learn how to fight. In fact, you learn how *not* to fight. They teach you just the opposite. Don't make waves, don't make noises, don't take any risks—I know friends of mine who went to school and graduated and had positions, and you try to go get them to help you and they won't; you know why? Because they are afraid they will lose their positions, they are afraid to take risks. And poor people, they don't have to worry about that because they don't have anything to lose anyways. So when you go up to the picket line in front of a field and you have people that are earning very few wages they'll come out on strike and they'll leave that job behind and they'll join the picket line. They don't know where their next meal is coming from. They don't even know where it's going to come from, but they have enough faith in God to know that it's going to come from somewhere. And some of them will go to school and become really conservative, so—be on guard—be on guard—we have to be on guard so that you don't fall into that trap of being afraid, because we are dominated by fear; this is how we are controlled, by fear. Fear of losing our jobs, fear of being ridiculed, fear that we'll get a bad grade even sometimes. Sure we've got to keep our grade point average up there, but that is also bad.

We people need to forget all of this fear and how it controls our minds. We see this in the fields a lot when the growers control workers by fear, like if they live in a camp and they say that they are going to evict you, even though that's illegal, or they threaten them that they are going to beat them up or threaten that they are going to fire them, and some people are afraid. The job that we have to do in the union is to remove that fear and remove that ignorance from people's minds. That's really what an action program is, is to remove fear and remove ignorance from people's minds. And to get people strong, and I guess this is sort of the cause that we have is to do that. To go out and get people strong make them strong and make them get involved. Some people say that they don't like to get involved in politics, right?

I remember seeing this figure that in Russia only three percent of the population, maybe it's fifteen percent, that are involved in action party politics and I remember some people saying, "How appalling!," "How terrible that is!" And then you think about our country—how many people are really involved in party politics? I'll bet it is less than that. Because people feel—you know politics are no good and I don't want to get involved in politics. It's like water—you know I don't really care about water. Well, what happens when you don't have any water? You die of thirst, right? And if you have too much water you drown, right? So, you have to learn how to handle water. Politics is the same way. Decisions are made for people by politicians. We are so out of it—we are so out of it we don't even know what is going on, and I am going to prove it to you right now. There is one college, the University of California, that is financed by the taxpayers; of course, all of us are taxpayers, except for those of us in the union who work for five dollars a week. We don't have to pay any taxes because we don't make enough money. But what happens to the taxes that we pay? We know a lot of the taxes are going to bonds and claims and those kinds of things, right? But there is also—our taxes go to exploit farm workers—you know? They really do. I am going to show you how

that happens. The University of California—back in 1919—they organized the Farm Bureau Federation. The Farm Bureau Federation is a
four billion dollar organization that manufactures pesticides, fertil-
izers, farm equipment, and has an insurance—in fact maybe some of
you have even contributed to the Farm Bureau—Allstate Insurance.
That is their insurance company. And what does the Farm Bureau
do? The Farm Bureau has always been against any laws to protect
child labor. They have been against unemployment insurance. They
have put money in to break strikes. They have been totally against
the Farm Workers Union. The Farm Bureau met with Richard Nixon
and the Teamsters back in 1972 to get the Teamsters to come to the
fields in California. That is who the Farm Bureau is—very powerful
lobby group in Washington, ok? In 1933, the Farm Bureau organized
the Associated Farmers, which is an organization that was very much
against the unionization of farm workers. There were a lot of strikes
in cotton then. Eleven farm workers were killed by the Associated
Farmers, the organization that was started by the Farm Bureau
Federation. It was a vigilante group. I know you are not getting any of
this in school because they aren't going to teach you anything about
labor history.

This is another thing. You should insist on having a very good
labor history class about California, and you would be surprised
about how many organizers were lynched in this state and were killed
by Associated Farmers, the group that the Farm Bureau organized. In
1943, the University of California organized the Bracero Program. This
was to bring people in from Mexico that were kept like slaves behind
barbed wire to work in the California fields and were exploited so terribly. We, by the way, worked in that program, César and myself and
the others in our union, but I saw checks of people who had worked
for two weeks of sixteen cents after two weeks of work. It disrupted the
family life in Mexico. That program ended after twenty years and that
was organized by the Farm Bureau. They put a lot of the local people
out of work. The University of California opposed that—the ending
of the Bracero Program—but we overcame on that one. In 1970, the
University of California joined the Farm Bureau to support the use of
pesticides on farm workers. In 1970, when we had the lettuce strike in
Salinas, the University of California decided to give the growers a little

hand, so they started developing a lettuce picking machine so they wouldn't need any farm workers.

In 1973, we had a strike of the melons and the University of California brought out a little melon picking machine to break our strike. Now we have the ARLB thanks to all of you that helped on Proposition 14; we have our money; we have our law, so in 1977 the University of California gave the growers classes paid for by the tax-payers on how to defeat the union in farm labor elections. In 1978, as of this point, the University of California has twenty-nine research projects to remove—to get rid of—farm workers. The projects that the University of California has going on right now will eliminate the jobs of two hundred and ten thousand farm workers. Two hundred and ten thousand. Maybe some people say, "Well, what's wrong with that?" You know? The farm workers shouldn't have to pick those melons and grapes and tomatoes. How are they going to eat? How are farm work-ers going to eat? How are the children ever going to be able to go to school if they don't have jobs? And who uses these machines? It's not the small family farmer because his plot of land is not big enough to use the machines. The people who use the machines are the big grow-ers like Superior Oil Company, Tenneco who has one million six hun-dred thousand acres of land. These are who the farmers in California are—Tenneco, Blackwell Oil Company, Getty Oil Company—these are the people who have the land. These are the people who are going to use the machines and put the farm workers out of work.

And what is going to happen to the farm workers? Let's see what happened to the farm workers that worked in the cotton. Between 1955 and 1960, they brought in the cotton picking machines. They elimi-nated the jobs of about one hundred thousand farm workers all over the South because most of these farm workers were in South Carolina, Texas, Arizona, California—just here in California alone there were about twenty thousand farm workers who were put out of their jobs. And where do those farm workers go? Most of those farm workers by the way were Black farm workers. The grape growers of Delano actu-ally hired armed guards with guns to keep the Black workers out of the fields because they refused to hire Black workers because they said their fingers were too fat and they can't pick grapes properly. I mean that is how horrible it is. The cotton picking machines eliminated twenty thousand Black farm workers and where do they go to? Watts? Hunter's Point? Oakland? That's where all the farm workers went—what is going to happen to the other two hundred and ten thousand? Who is going to support those people? Welfare? You know, are they all going to go on welfare because the oil companies have to make more money? I mean as if they didn't have enough already.

So it's like a very, very serious problem. We have been having a series of workshops all over the state; I don't know if you've read about them or not. We had one in the Bay area. We had one here in Los Angeles on the eleventh. And we are trying to develop an action program to stop the machines. And the farm workers had some great ideas. They wanted to have a march to Sacramento. They also thought it would be great if every oil company that eliminates farm workers by machines should give every farm worker a plot of land to farm—like a thousand acres apiece. And that they should divide all the profits that come from the machines, right, among the farm workers so that they could set up their own cooperative programs, their own clinics, their own schools, their own furniture shops, their own housing—you know—wouldn't that be great? So they had a lot of really good ideas. I am sure that some of you have some good ideas too.

But we are going to start an action program to stop and we are going to do it just the way we have been talking right now. It is going to be nonviolent action. It's probably going to be an awful lot of letter writing. Just a lot of very simple people kinds of action. We would like to invite all of you to come and join us when we do that action—when we start doing those kinds of programs. And if you have never done this before we have some other action programs that are going on right now to build up your muscles for that time. But let me tell you it is an education. I also went to college as I said, but I never learned as much in school as I did working with the movement for the union because it is hard to keep an organization together. The attempts at breaking up organizations—everybody tries to break up an organization—you have seen that. When César started the union the first person that knew he was starting a union was David Rockefeller, and he sent César a telegram offering him a fifty thousand dollar a year job in Venezuela. So, César graciously turned down the job. And the next person that got into it—just to show you how organized they are—I mean the growers didn't even know we were organizing but David Rockefeller knew, the Teamsters knew—Jimmy Hoffa sent out a representative and they offered César a big wad of money and César said, "No thank you. I will let you know when I need your money." He kept on organizing without any money.

I want to talk just briefly about that. One way that they break up organizations is that they buy people off—they break up leadership and buy people off. They give people big jobs and he forgets about everybody else. He just thinks about himself. When you better yourself, who are you bettering? Just yourself, right? But you're not bettering anyone else out there. We sort of got to think in terms of what we do with our lives as a service, a time to help other people, you know? Just think whatever you are studying for—just think to yourself—how can I use what I am learning to help poor people? How can I use what I am learning to help make changes? Think about that, ok. If you think about it, you will find a way that you can do that. Of course, as I said before, we would also like to welcome you to come and join us, even maybe just for a year to learn how to organize and to learn how to do the things that we do. We have a summer program and a winter program that we have just tailored for people who want to come on for a short period of time and a spring program. We have three programs. Believe me it is quite an experience to just come in for a year. One of the things that you are going to learn and this is probably the biggest thing that you will learn and that is how to live without money. That is a very hard thing to do in our society, right? Because our whole country is oriented towards buy, buy, buy, buy. It's like an addiction. Some people if they don't buy they have—they get jittery—they sweat. It's almost like getting off of heroin or something—you have withdrawal pains. That's another thing we have to learn how to do—not to buy and conserve our resources. Poor people are getting better, sometimes. Sometimes once they get money— they want to get more to spend. But learning how to live without money is a tremendous resource. That really is tremendous strength. It takes a lot of courage not to buy things. It takes a lot of courage not to spend money. And to live poorly and to live simply. And this is what we have in our union and everybody in the organization and it is in our constitution. Everybody in our organization gets five dollars a week for food, if you are single, you get ten dollars, but if you have a family you get five dollars for each person and then you get ten dollars a week for your personal expenses. Plus we house you and if you need medical attention—we have a lot of clothes from donations. All of the clothes that we get are from donations. We have fantastic wardrobes with histories. All our wardrobes have histories in them, you know. But nobody ever goes around naked because everybody has a lot of clothes. And we always have plenty of food and we always have shelter. But to live very simply, and sometimes you have to do this because you cannot help poor people—remember this ok? Because a lot of people say, I want to go help the poor or I want to go help my Raza and they forget about it because they are too busy getting a big house, two cars and a color T.V. and trips to Mexico or Europe or Hawaii. And they forget about the poor, you know? It's kind of like they are just pretending to help the poor because they are really helping themselves. All that money that is supposed to be going to help the poor people is going to them. A lot of people need help in our country. A lot of people need organizational help. People need help to learn how to be strong, how to fight back, and how to make the changes that have to be made. So we won't continue to be exploited.

We would like to invite you to join in the action program and we have some action programs going on right now and they are really exciting. We have a picket line going on in the morning from five o'clock to nine o'clock in the morning—four to seven—and you get off in time to make it to your classes. We are picketing down in the Terminal Market and it is very colorful. The language is colorful—you get called all kinds of colorful names. We have police protection down there so nothing will happen that is violent and there is a lot of good singing going on. It is a really exciting picket line because it is in the dark. Four to seven—you can see the sun come up. It is out at the Terminal Market. We also have a really good action program going on against Coors. Adolph Coors out of Nazi Germany who is now in America making beer and exploiting people and refusing to sign a contract. We have another exciting boycott going against J. P. Stevens. J. P. Stevens is a company in the South—hires mostly Black workers and many people have been maimed and injured in that plant. Those unions—the textile workers and the amalgamated clothing workers—they have not merged. They have been trying to get a contract with that company for almost twenty years! Twenty years and they fired people and they refused to obey the law. So now there is a boycott. People just giving something up—giving up those nice shoes—those nice pillowcases to make them come to terms. So we are helping those unions. Like they helped us—we are helping them with the boycott. We are going to have some really exciting stuff happening with the mechanization causes. So, I would like you to come in and join in. Join in on the action and help make the changes so that when your kids go to school and they start saying, "Look, I read about this boycott going on," and then you can say, "I made that history." We are not just going to sit here and read about the history; we are going to make the history so other people can read about it. We can do that. All of us right here in this room, if we were to go out right now and go down and picket some big store—the Broadway—if all of us were to just walk out of this room and go right down there in front of the Broadway—they would tip off J. P. Stevens just like that (snaps her fingers) fast. That is how important our bodies are. But we probably won't do that, but we would like you to sign up and help. Think about that and we would like you to make a decision to sign up and help. Build up those muscles because you are going to need them, you are going to need them. This country needs a lot of changes and we have to make them. We can't say, "I am going to wait for somebody else to do them," say, "I am going to do it. In whatever way I can, I am going to do it." In Spanish, in our union, we have a saying called— whenever we start these impossible tasks like they told César—"You can't organize a union, César," and "You can't start a national boycott." The unions told us we couldn't do a national boycott; now they are doing it. We always say, "*Sí se puede.*" Who knows what that means, "*Sí se puede*?" It can be done, right? *Sí se puede* means it can be done. I am going to ask all of you to join me in the farm workers handclap to show that we are together and we are organized and we will say "*Sí se puede.*" Also we are going to make some "Vivas." When we end the farm workers' meeting, we always shout "Vivas!"—that means long live. I am going to say, "Viva la causa." Causa means the cause of labor and the cause of poor. Everybody shout "Viva" together—it means long live and then we will say one for César—"Viva Chávez" for our great leader that we have so that God will give him a long life. What should our third one be? "Viva la causa?" Should we say, "Viva los estudiantes?"—the students. OK, let's get it together—say "Viva" and then we will say a couple of *"Abajos"*—*abajo* means down. We did this in front of the White House when Richard Nixon was in office and we had this big rally and we said, "Down with Nixon" and everybody yelled, *"Abajo!"* and it happened.

This is part of the stuff that we are dealing with here. Let's try it—we will say the "Vivas" first and then the "abajos" and then we will all clap together. We will all clap together to show that we are organized and we are working together—*Sí se puede*. And I want everybody to shout and if somebody doesn't shout that means that you have fear inside of you and remember that fear is bad—it's damaging and keeps you from doing what you have to do. So everybody shout really loud—

Huerta: "Viva la causa!"

Audience: "Viva!"

Huerta: A little bit louder so that the Regents can hear us.

Huerta: "Viva Chávez!"

Audience: "Viva!"

Huerta: "Viva los Estudiantes!"

Audience: "Viva!"

Huerta: "Down with Coors!"

Huerta and audience: "Abajo!"

Huerta: "Down with J. P. Stevens!"

Huerta and audience: "Abajo!"

Huerta: "Down with racism!"

Huerta and audience: "Abajo!"

Huerta: "Down with oppression!"

Huerta and audience: "Abajo!"

Huerta: "Down with sexism!"

Huerta and audience: "Abajo!"

(applause)

Huerta: Can all of us sitting here, can we build this world of brotherhood and sisterhood, peace and justice? Can we do it?

Audience: *Sí se puede*!

(continued chant of *"Sí se puede!"* and the farm worker's clap)

End of speech.

26

Dialogue on Leadership and Popular Movements

The UFW Experience, Center for the Study of Democratic Institutions, March 12, 1985

Huerta: It's interesting that I am here today because just last week I was with Mr. Fred Ross, Sr., who was sort of the godfather of the farmworkers' movement, and we were looking at the movie, "Grapes of Wrath," and Fred Ross had been a manager in one of the migrant camps, in fact, the camp that the movie was about, down in Arvin, California, which is just about twenty miles from the headquarters of the United Farmworkers, and this was kind of what the subject [was] about, you know, seeing that movie, seeing what had happened to farmworkers in that era, and then comparing it with what is happening to farmworkers today. And in this discussion that we had at the University of California, I kind of wanted to steer the comments towards organizing, and of course, everybody else wanted to hear about what happened to the people that came in, the Okies that came in from the Southwest. So, it's kind of appropriate, that we are talking about the subject today.

There is another event I participated in, which was a theological meeting of several hundred theologians, religious people, and this was their topic, mass organizations. Well, I guess the big conclusion that we came to is that there aren't very many of mass, grassroots organizations right now in existence in the United States, and God knows that we need them very desperately right at this point in time. And speaking from the point of view of the Hispanic community, of course

---

Transcript courtesy of Special Collections, The Davidson Library, University of California, Santa Barbara.

they are desperately needed in our community, and the thing is that we really don't have too much of it happening.

I'd like to go back in time a little bit to talk. I've often kind of compared in my own mind the type of organizing that Fred Ross did, and the kind of organizing that we have done in the farmworkers' movement, and the kind of organizing that César has done, and that all of us have done in the union, both of which are mass-based organizing.

Fred Ross, and I want to just talk a little bit about the way he organized. Fred went back in the early fifties, and he desegregated some of the parts of California where they still had Mexican children in one school and the Anglo children in another school. I think one of his first projects was down in Tustin, in Orange County, and the Farm Bureau Federation came and tried to run Fred out of town. And that's when he developed his whole way of organizing, which is what they call a "house meeting" approach of having a meeting in one house and going to another house. And the farmworkers are the one that suggested this to Fred. He was talking to a group, and then one of them said, "Look, let's go over to my compadre's house, you know, my friend's house, and we'll have a meeting there with some of the other workers." So Fred started having these series of meetings, and soon he called them all together, and they started on this voter registration drive, got people elected to the school board, and eventually ended the segregation in that town, of the school system.

Well, this pretty much is the same system that we later used to start the Community Service Organization, which was the first mass-based organization of Spanish-speaking people in the state of California. And, in the forming of this organization is when Fred found César and taught him the basic type of organizing. Which I just have to sort of emphasize that Fred sort of stumbled on, you know, because he had gone through all of the other, all of the other types of trying to get the professionals together, trying to get the business people together, trying to get the religious people together, and it never just ended there.

And then we used the same type of organizing when we started the United Farmworkers, by having house meetings, I in the north, César in the southern part of the Central Valley, until we were able to get together a thousand farmworkers that were willing to put their names on the line, and start paying dues, and this was how we started the union, with a thousand. That was our goal, to get a thousand farmworkers together, and we got them through house meetings, and got them to commit to pay a due system of $3.50 a month, to which we attached, by the way, a little death benefit. We contracted with this insurance company and so part of our dues money went to pay this death benefit, and of course, workers then were making like fifty cents and sixty cents an hour when we started the union. So this death benefit, which covered the whole family—one thousand dollars, I think, for the head of the family, and five hundred for the dependents—was very, it was like a little gimmick in a way, but it was also very helpful. And of course everybody, every time somebody died, we had a big barbecue, right?, to celebrate the death and to let everybody know that if they joined the United Farmworkers they could also get this little death benefit.

And so that was pretty much the way that we started, until we had the grape strike in 1965, and then our dues structure fell apart, and then we started living on donations and the contributions that we got from outside.

I want to make a notation here, because when César first started the organization, the people that knew César back in the fifties would not recognize him as the kind of a leader that we have today. He was a very self-effacing person, and I had been in the Community Service Organization for several months before I met César, although Fred always talked about him, and five minutes after I met him, he disappeared and I couldn't find him again because he looked like everybody else, you know. I mean, he just was not the kind of a guy that would, at the meetings that we had he was very soft-spoken, never called attention to himself. He was a tremendous organizer because wherever he was at just tremendous things happened. You know, there were thousands of people marching, and he did this big campaign right here in Oxnard to get rid of the bracero program, and pulled some strikes with the braceros themselves, the Mexican contract nationals that had been brought in. And you know, he was in the papers, and he was doing all this stuff, but César was a very quiet person.

Well, after we started the UFW, we sort of analyzed a lot of the things that we felt were wrong with the Community Service Organization. Part of them, number one is, no economic base. You know, our dues in the CSO were like five dollars a year, and here in the UFW, working with the poorest of farmworkers, we were charging $3.50 a month.

And you could imagine, these are people that didn't have really money to eat on, because we had no unemployment insurance, we had no surplus commodities, we didn't have foodstamps. So going to those people to say, we want you to pay $3.50 a month, was very difficult. And I kind of want to dwell on that because I think that that's kind of the crunch about organizations of poor people, right? And César, I remember we used to talk about this when we first started [talking] about the possibility of forming a union. I kind of thought, wow, it was so overwhelming, you know, how can you possibly start a union.

We had already worked with the AFL-CIO agricultural workers' organizing committee, which I had organized that started in Stockton of the black, white, and Hispanic people, and we had a group of about four hundred people under another organization called the Agricultural Workers Association, and when the AFL-CIO sent a representative out, I got this meeting together with them and they couldn't believe it. You know, we had a whole hall full of farmworkers. And then they subsequently started to fund it.

But one of the things that César always used to say is whoever is paying is going to determine what's going to happen to the organization. And so when he started the union, he wanted to make it very clear that the workers would be paying. We were living off of those dues of those one thousand workers. I mean, that's what we were living off of, and whatever came in we would use the money for the gasoline, took a very small salary, something like sixty dollars a month in the summertime. In the wintertime when the workers couldn't pay their dues, we would take like twenty dollars a month, or, you know, we were just barely making it. In fact, Helen Chávez's sisters used to go out and collect food from the welfare department to bring it over to César and myself—I had seven kids; César had eight kids—so that we could keep eating while we were forming the union.

But at some point in time, I think just about the time the strike started, César decided, it was like a conscious decision, that somehow there had to be an identification of the organization. And so we started. I remember the first time we made a button with César's picture on it—I think it was the "Non-violence is our strength," or one of the buttons—he had a fit. I mean, he had a real fit, because he did not want us to be putting his picture on anything. You know, he didn't want to be like the focal point of the organization. But because of the strike that we got into, because of the boycott, the rest of us in the organization felt that we had to start identifying the organization around César, especially since we had the other organization, the Agricultural Workers Organizing Committee—which was the AFL-CIO group—was still in existence. You know, that was before we had merged. And we had to really identify César as the head of our union. And so we, kind of did it for him, right?

And I think it was, it turned out that that was a good decision because down the line a few years later, we had the grape strike in 1965, and subsequently we merged with the AFL-CIO in 1966, which was very good at the time, because it was a survival thing. Had we not merged, the Teamsters would have wiped us out because they moved into the fields in 1966. And again, having César really identified as the head of the union made it very easy in that fight that we had with the Teamsters, because here we had an indigenous leader, you know, a farmworker himself who was the head of the union, as against the Teamsters, right, who were all outsiders who had come in there to try to destroy us. I just have to say that he suffered a lot with that, and I remember when we used to go into meetings and all of the workers would be yelling, "Viva Chávez," and César would just groan. He would say, these are the guys that wouldn't give me house meetings, that are now yelling "Viva Chávez." But he kind of accepted that as part of organizing.

Then of course César, I have to also mention this, some of the things that he used, again, always thinking of organizing and always thinking of, you know, making the people stronger, well, we got the concept of trying to organize without violence, which is something that he was very afraid of because he felt that if people started, if we got into a violent situation, people would start killing each other off. I mean, it would not end. And so he had his first fast for non-violence, and that of course was publicized nationally. Bobby Kennedy came down to break the fast so that was like a very big breakthrough in terms of trying to get national attention.

Even today, the farmworkers refer to the United Farmworkers as "Chávez's union." You know, "La Unión de Chávez," that's the way that they refer to it. And that's, of course, to distinguish between something that the Teamsters or somebody else might be trying to do and "La Unión de Chávez." I, as the first vice president of the union, am in a difficult situation. The workers, I think, trust me ultimately, and I can go in there because they know that whatever I represent is going to be what César is thinking. The workers have an ultimate belief and an ultimate faith in him.

Now, you know, one thing in our society—I'm talking here about the American educational system, the American society—you always have this kind of, I remember when I went to high school, when I went to college, you know, people say, you got to be wary of the man on the white horse, you know what I mean? These are the demagogues, these are the false leaders, etc. I want you to know that working people and poor people don't have that problem. They recognize leadership, and they're willing to follow whom they consider is the leader. I mean, it's almost kind of a simple kind of faith, you know—and I think that they can also turn on that leadership, we've seen that in history—but they don't have problems with that. They want leadership, because leadership really means people who are responsible, people who are willing to take the risks, people who are going to be out there in the front fighting. And so they want leadership, and they respect the leadership, and they know that when somebody, say even in a ranch, where we have our ranch committees, they elect their leaders to that particular ranch, they expect them to take leadership. They really like the structure of leadership.

Now, I don't know whether that's because a lot of our membership is from Mexico, but they just don't have these liberal types. One of the things that we always say in the union is that many times our liberal supporters want to feel our heads to see if we have any horns, if we have grown any horns since the last time they saw us, you know what I mean? That somehow, and I don't know, maybe that's because we're Hispanic, but somehow they expect us to convert into bandits or something, or to convert into some kind of a dictator or something of that nature.

It's somehow like somewhere along the line you're not going to stay the same kind of a person. You've got what [President] Carter referred to as the "curse of Montezuma," but supposed to be like some kind of Hispanic curse. You're supposed to become corrupt. And of course, and people are really fed up because in our history books that we get Pancho Villa is never listed as a great leader of Mexico like he is in Mexico, right? He's always a bandit, right? I mean a lot of the people think of Pancho Villa—if they even know about him, because most American children that go to school don't even know who Pancho Villa was—as a bandit, and that's the way he is depicted, even in a lot of books in our colleges. He's depicted as a bandit, and not as a great leader of the Mexican Revolution. And so they kind of expect that to happen.

I want to just digress a little bit now, and just kind of talk about what is not happening in term of mass organizations. Fred did some work back East with Saul Alinsky when he was still alive. He trained some leadership in organizing. One of them was George Wiley, who started the welfare rights organizations, and subsequently died. Fred recently has been working with the nuclear freeze people. Now, people don't know, who is Fred Ross? You know, they don't know him. Fred Ross, I guess talking about self-effacing people, believes in organizing, training the leadership, and then just kind of stepping back. And that's, I guess, the true, quote, unquote, true organizer, because he trains the people and then he steps back, and he doesn't really believe in, or his whole idea is to find leaders and to train them. That's what his whole life has been. And I think it's a shame, Fred is seventy-five years old now, and he's not going to be around very much longer, but I think it's kind of a shame that recognizing the great work that he has done in finding people like César—I'll include myself, because that's how I got into this whole movement thing, was at a meeting that I went to with Fred Ross, where he talked about what poor people could do if they got together and got themselves into an organization—and a lot of Fred's skills are not going to be around. I kind of think it would be nice if we could have an organizing center where really organizing could be taught.

Now, there is the Industrial Areas Foundation that trains people, out of Chicago, and I know some of the people who used to work for our union have gone through their training and they are now doing some organizing—like Jim Drake, who is organizing in Texas; Ernie Cortes who has initially organized in Texas as one of our organizers, and then went on to become an organizer—you know, they've done the work in Los Angeles, UNO, they've done some work in Orange County under the name of SANO.

The only comment I can make about that is what I know about the IAF organizing. It's not, I think, as political as the kind of organizing that Fred Ross taught us. One of Fred's first programs that we ever had was voter registration, right? The next program that you had was to get out the vote, and voter education in between that to get identified with the issues. And so Fred's premises were always, are always, the politicians work for us and so you put as much heat on them, you put pressure on them, and you always find the pressure points and then put the pressure there to accomplish what you want to accomplish. I don't see that in the IAF organizations, and I don't know whether it's because they get money that's non-profit or whatever it may be. But in CSO we are very definitely political; it had a very strong political axis to the work that we did. And I don't see that with the other organizations like UNO and those in East L.A. I mean, they're doing a lot of, kind of what I call kind of safe work, you know what I mean? And it's not, I think, the really strong political. But if we look at the situation in which, say, the farmworkers find themselves in today, having trouble with the Republican Administration, [Governor] Deukmejian's administration, where they have cut our budgets, really wiped out the budget for the ALRB [Agricultural Labor Relations Board], not replaced staff so they have lost something like fifty-five staff positions, so the law isn't working now for farmworkers and we are having to resort back to the grape boycott and some of the boycott tactics that we used in the past. I think you really have to have a political base.

And again, you know what's happening to unions in general, with the Reagan Administration's whole attempt to de-unionize America, which is really what's happening. And this is a very dangerous thing, because any time that any totalitarian government, or fascist government, takes power, whether it be Poland, or Chile, the first thing they do is, they wipe out the labor leaders. They kill them, they get rid of them, they put them in jail. And so what's happening in America today is a very dangerous kind of situation.

I didn't talk too much about labor unions as mass organizations, but they really are when you come right down to think about it. Labor is the only institution that represents working people. And probably is the largest representative of minority people in mass organizations, the labor movement. You know, we have large numbers of minority people in an organization.

The most difficult tasks still today, I think for mass organizations to be able to survive is how do you get your economics. You know, how do you get the money? And in a labor organization you can get a dues check-off, and the members all pay a dues percentage to the organization. That's how you function. That's how we run, with the dues that come in from our members, we organize, we do all of the other stuff that we have to do. But in a community organization, to really form a strong community organization, how do you manage to pay for it? You know, the Community Service Organization that we had was a volunteer organization. We just had very few staff people. César was one of the staff people. He was the executive director, I was a staff person. We had about maybe three or four staff people for the whole organization to cover the whole state of California and Arizona. And I think that's like the big question about how you can have a strong community organization that has some political clout to it, and yet can be politically independent. I don't think that has been answered yet. And maybe this is why a lot of the community organizations just fight in the "safe areas," because they are dependent upon foundations or other people for their money, and they really can't get involved politically because they are afraid to lose their tax-exempt status.

We've got all these people coming in from Mexico into the cities, from Central America, Asians that have come in, you've got a lot of people on welfare, you've got a lot of unemployed workers. The need for mass organization is now probably bigger than at any other time in our history, maybe since the fifties. But we just don't seem to have the resources to be able to support, say, the organizers and the organization. We don't have the formula of how to do it to get the money so that they can support themselves.

Jeffrey Wallin: Thank you very much, Dolores.

Donald McDonald: I have a question for Dolores. A couple of questions. One is, what is the status of the mass support of the UFW now, across the board, the American public opinion. Also, in connection with that, what about the workers' support of César and yourself in your own union? Are those things that have to be won each year, because of the nature, you are dispersed, your workers are dispersed so much geographically? And do you have to win their allegiance year after year, or is there a steady continuity that you can build on? It seems to me you have a real, real problem there with workers who are always picking up roots and following the crops and so on. How do you keep in touch with them? That would seem to be a very difficult problem.

Huerta: Well, we are sort of working, right up to this date we have sort of kept in touch with them sort of by word of mouth, so to speak. And I would say that the allegiance of the workers to the union is very, very strong. There is a lot of fear, of course, because people have to eat, you know what I mean? And so when it comes right down to an election, if that employer convinces the workers that they are not going to have a job if they vote for the union, then you are going to lose workers, even though they are loyal workers, see what I mean? to the organization, because they are worried about—

McDonald: And you have no strike benefits for them, do you?

Huerta: Yeah, yeah.

McDonald: Or very little.

Huerta: No, we could have strike benefits. But you never win with a strike. I mean, we have found that out, because there's always ten workers to take the job of the one. What we have happening right now is, you have large numbers of people that are being brought in from Mexico. I mean, they are bringing in people from Oaxaca, I mean large numbers of Indians from Oaxaca, Mexico, that don't speak Spanish. I mean talk about having trouble communicating. And they are brought in by one crew leader, and he is the only one that negotiates for them and speaks for them. And everything. It's very hard to reach those large numbers of undocumented workers. I think that the loyalty to the organization is there with the ones that have been here for a while. You have to constantly, as you say, reach the new ones that are coming in all the time.

I mean even a ranch, say, where we had an election a couple of years ago, and where we haven't got a contract, because the employers aren't bargaining right now, because they know that they can get away with it. Nobody's going to do anything to them if they don't bargain in good faith. Then you have to go back in there and reorganize that work force, to try to get a contract. So it's a continual thing.

And what we're going to do to counter that is, we are having a new sort of a campaign. We call it the hi-tech, doing stuff on mass media, on television, on radio. And we have a big direct mail operation now that we have started at our headquarters, where we are going to write, we are writing directly to workers and also to supporters.

McDonald: Public opinion, mass—

Huerta: Public opinion, I think that the support is just tremendous. We have been sending letters out all over the country telling people about, say, the new grape boycott that we are starting, and about some of the other boycotts that are going on, and the response that we have is incredible. I mean, people send back that they want to hear from the union. We just get, really, cards, we enclose in our mailings a little card and people send them back, and they want to get on the mailing list or they send money. We are having an extremely, very, very good response from our mailings.

Then we are also doing surveys to follow up on the mailings to see whether people got the letter. Did they answer it? Did they respond? Are they boycotting that particular store or that particular product? And so we are trying to do it on sort of a scientific basis, right? And really trying to get that worked out. And it seems to be going very well.

But the first problem in the first grape boycott, and I think that was kind of a mass movement, too, when we think about it, because we sent, you know, farm workers all over the country, and then they got supporters to help them picket and do boycott work, and that sort of became a mass movement in itself. The people are still out there. And there's a lot of them that are really happy that we are giving them something to boycott again, you know? Something to do again. That's kind of the response that we get.

Our first problem in our first boycott was, first of all, letting people know that we existed. Secondly, getting them to understand that a boycott could work. Because everybody, including the people in the labor movement, said, hey, boycotts don't work.

And when we talked about a consumer boycott like the grape boycott, I did the boycott in New York City. I organized the boycott in New York, in all of New York, Boston, Chicago. And people said, it can't be done. I mean, we'll help you, we'll support you, but, you know, we don't think, you know, there's a little kook, you know? But, so when it did work, people were just surprised. And of course now people use the boycott as a weapon all the time. You know, Nestle, there was the Nestle's boycott, the J. P. Stevens boycott, and people know that boycotts work. The big battle was getting people to believe that a boycott could work.

Ralph Turner: It would be interesting in that connection with the boycott, the support, of course, from outside through the boycott was crucial, I assume, to the initial success. These techniques like that really call upon people who already have some background, some sympathy, some interest, or some experience, frequently, in this sort of thing. You had a sort of, I take it, a New Deal tradition still. You had the younger generation of the sixties coming along. I wonder if you have a new generation of young people who understand this sort of technique and are sympathetic to the cause, and who also resonate to the symbol, the charismatic symbol, that Chávez presents, or whether you are still largely appealing to the older and aging constituencies that supported the original boycott.

Huerta: Well, I think it is really both. The young people, while a lot of them don't know about the farmworkers' movement, because they were just babies when it was happening, once that they know about it I'll give you a good example of this. César spoke at the nuclear freeze rally that they had in Los Angeles—it was the big giant one, I think they had like eighty thousand people, or something like that—and he got a tremendous response, and there he asked them to boycott Dole. We were having a little fight with Dole going on at that time for one of their mushroom plants. And the response was incredible, just incredible, and naturally we, Dole settled within weeks after César spoke at that rally. So, they grasp it very, very quickly. They know something about farmworkers, while they might not always identify the organization, once they know the response is just almost immediate.

I also spoke at one of the previous nuclear freeze rallies, and I had a lot of trouble in Sacramento then. They had all these bills in to try to stop the organization, to change the laws so that we couldn't organize, to change the Agricultural Labor Relations law, and so I had people pass out leaflets, to sign, to send telegrams, to authorize us to send a telegram in their name. You won't believe this, but we picked up close to seven hundred, which, we could have gotten thousands had I had more people there. But we passed out little leaflets saying, would you please authorize us to send a telegram in your name to your assemblyman or your state senator, and we picked up seven hundred authorizations to send a telegram, which was tremendous.

Just recently, in the last couple of months, we got some wind that the Teamsters might be coming back into Salinas. Within one week we were able to get a rally together of, a march of twenty-five thousand farmworkers. Twenty-five thousand farmworkers in the Salinas Valley. And this was all farmworkers because we didn't have time to organize any supporters from San Francisco or anyplace else. It was strictly farmworkers, and we had twenty-five thousand that got together on a week's notice. We had another march in Calexico to celebrate the anniversary of Delfino Contreras, one of the farmworkers that was killed, and that was February the tenth, and we had there about five thousand farmworkers that gathered there to march.

By the way, we are having to sort of let people know that the movement is hitting the streets again, so to speak, we are having marches all over the state of California, so we'll be having about six or seven of them throughout the summer to let people know what's going on.

César was just on the "Night of the Stars" the other night. I don't know if anybody saw him on ABC Sunday night, and he was one of the eight people that had been invited there. But his report when he came back was that everybody, all of the stars who were at that event said, "César if you need our help, we are here to help you." So he got a very good response.

Luiz Ortiz-Franco: In working with similar social movement organizations, we found that organizations go through cycles in terms of their organizational dynamics, and that many social movement organizations begin with the leadership of a charismatic, powerful visionary, like César, and that after a period of excitement and growth, where everyone is working for the cause, commitment is very high, creativity and energy is almost explosive, that once an organization gets past that first stage, when it is grown some, has a name, etc., the imperatives of growth require new management skills. When you have thirty people, it is very different from when you have a hundred and fifty people. And that so many of the groups that I work with really falter as they try and move from that first charismatic leadership stage to a larger organization, because the leader himself or herself does not have the management skills, because people start forgetting about the cause and be concerned about their status within the organization—things like salary, things like titles, etc.—and I've seen that stress, from that first phase into a more traditional kind of organization, tear up organizations all the time. How did you make it? How did you get past that?

Huerta: Well, those are very important issues that you raised because we did have to, at some point, start structuring the organization, and we did have a lot of tearing, internal tearing. One of our conventions, I think it was the 1977 convention, the farmworkers at that convention passed a resolution, and what their resolution said was that they wanted the organization to be run by farmworkers. That seems like a very innocuous resolution. Of course, if it is a farmworkers union it has to be run by farmworkers, right? But we in our organization, because of the work that we had done initially and on the boycott, we did have a lot of non-farmworkers that were in the organization—people that had come in to help. And so we really started taking that seriously and, the idea of starting to get farmworkers to take over the leadership, to train farmworkers to become the attorneys of the organization, train farmworkers to become the accountants of the organization, and so we had to start doing that. And it was not very well received by other people in the organization, because a lot of people had had a vested interest. They had spent a lot of their lives in the organization.

And then we had to think also about structurally how are we going to organize a national union? The way we had divided the union is that we had regional districts, for instance our Oxnard director in Oxnard was in charge of all of Oxnard, be it citrus, vegetables, strawberries, whatever, the nurseries, that person was in charge of all of those operations. The same thing in Delano and Salinas. And that became a very big problem, because that director was always busy with one problem or the other, plus whatever little work was being done in the community, or with boycott supporters, etc. So, César met with Peter Drucker, who is like a management expert, and we all got Drucker's book, *Management Tasks, Practices, Responsibilities* and we started having, I mean literally, weeks and weeks of meetings on management, and reading the management books, talking about the tasks of the union, the responsibilities of the union, and then trying to get to some kind of structure.

So we finally came out of all of these meetings, César's meetings with Peter Drucker, we came out with a whole new structure for the organization. And the new structure is that we are structured on crop lines. So our person who is in charge of the citrus division is in charge of both the citrus in Florida and the citrus in Oxnard, and the citrus in Porterville. You know what I mean? He's got the whole citrus area, which means he can concentrate on that, about the marketing, the prices. And then he develops his own leadership, he develops his own staff, he handles his own boycotts. And likewise with the vegetables, likewise with the grapes. And so that was a very big decision.

And the second after that came to be to get farmworkers and start training them to be in the leadership, say to be the organizers, the negotiators. And that was very hard, because a lot of the farmworkers are terrific organizers, but not very good at negotiations. They have a language problem. So then we set up a school at the headquarters where we taught a lot of farmworkers how to speak English. And then we sent them back to the fields, and then tried to get them to come back on staff. Another difficulty that, I think in terms of the management part of it, we spent like about the last, anywhere from 1979 to the present, just working on the management structure. But we have spent like an awful lot of time on that. And I think we're getting there. It's still going to have to be changed and adjusted, but we're getting there.

Just one other point I have to add is that we are volunteers. In our constitution for the United Farmworkers, we have in there that we don't get wages. I mean, people work on a volunteer basis. And that is a big, it's a big thorn in many ways, because, and people kind of joke about this, if you want to work for the farmworkers' union it means you have to commit yourself to poverty for the rest of your life, literally. The union pays our rent, we get food stamps, or we get a small stipend for food, and if you are ill or anything, of course the union pays your hospital bills. We have a big medical plan for our members but the staff is not covered. We don't have our own medical plan for our staff. All of our farmworkers are covered with a major medical with dental and vision.

But if you get sick, whether it's an operation or whatever it is, a baby, the union covers the full medical for the staff of the union. But we still don't get, I mean, that's kind of a little contention, because a lot of people felt, well, we should be getting salaries, right? But we do have it in the constitution that people who work for the organization, who are volunteers, that you do not get a salary. You get a stipend, you get your rent, you get a clothes allowance, we get a clothes allowance for the kids, for the children, but you do not get a salary. And so I guess that makes César the poorest, all of our board members are like the poorest paid officers in the whole country. But, you know, it's always been kind of a philosophy that you really can't help farm workers if you are so much richer than they. We have good cars, which we didn't have before. We have little Volkswagon Rabbits [*sic*] that we run around in, so that we have adequate equipment. But we don't get money. You can't get money in the union.

Wallin: You mentioned a couple of times your enthusiasm for mass movements in general, and also mentioned, I think twice, your involvement in nuclear freeze. And I am wondering, what is the necessary connection here, or is there one, between the UFW and something that is clearly much more political? Is there a connection between all these things? Do you see mass movements in general as having a certain kind of political characteristic that would not be apparent, say on the surface, if one were simply to look at a movement that seeks to get some fair treatment and higher wages for farmworkers? Is there something in there, is there something sort of not obvious on the surface about this that we should be aware of?

Huerta: I'm not sure I understood your question. Are you asking, what is the connection between the farmworkers and the nuclear freeze movement, or what do I think about the nuclear freeze movement as a mass movement?

Wallin: Or, what I'm wondering is, is there some kind of ideological connection here that I certainly wouldn't have seen right off the bat? I don't know if there is or there isn't. But the fact that you mentioned that a couple of times just makes me wonder whether there is some sort of connection, or at least in your own mind, is it that, in saying, for example, that we need more mass movements and so on. Is there a sense that mass movements tend to have the right kind of political agenda and that they are all associated some way, at least in their ultimate goals, or—

Huerta: Well, I said that Fred Ross was training some of the people in the nuclear freeze movement, which is not the union. And I said that César had spoken at a nuclear freeze rally. He had been invited to speak at a nuclear freeze rally as a speaker, along with many other stars that were there. When I think, in the kind of mass movement that I would be interested in is movements of poor people. I'm talking about working people and poor people. Like people in East L.A., people in the ghettos, people organizing to better their own condition. And I think that one of the great things about Fred Ross is that he had, and César and all of his faithful poor people, that they can organize themselves, that they have the intelligence to solve their own problems, if they can get themselves into an organization where they have a voice and they can let the world know, the community know, what it is that people need to do for them so that they can get out of their misery, have some control over their own lives. That is what I refer to as organizing and mass movement.

Wallin: All right, so do you—

Huerta: To me, the nuclear freeze issue is like an issue organization. It was like the Vietnam war, right? There was a big mass movement that was created ending the Vietnam war. But once the war ended it fell apart. It just didn't exist any more. And to me that's not an organization. That's like organizing around an issue, which I think it's easier to do than it is to try to build an organization like a union or like the Community Service Organization, something that stays on for years and years and years. And we can just look back at all those organizations that came up during the sixties. Very few of them are around. Especially those that were built on poor people.

Franco: Switching gears again, back to the question, general question of leadership, many of the groups I work with are led by women leaders. And one of the things that I am discovering is that women seem to have more trouble than men with accepting the ramifications of leadership in a number of respects. In particular, they are very uncomfortable with the phenomenon of being objectified in the way that you describe César being uncomfortable with that. And I want to know from you what your own experience has been with, how does it feel to be Dolores Huerta, not the individual, but the symbol of the union? And did you yourself have any difficulty with adjusting—to being a symbol and having your movements watched by other people, and judged by other people, not as an individual, but as a symbol.

Huerta: Well, I am certainly going through that stage right now, because for years I never thought about it because we were so busy in the fight. You don't notice what's going around you. And all of a sudden I am invited to speak here and there as a symbol for the women's movement, as an Hispanic woman. And it has been difficult. But I am also sort of a born-again feminist. All of a sudden you find out that, I look around at my sisters that were leaders in the early days of the movement, and they are home taking care of one of the organizer's babies, you know what I mean? It really makes me angry, because I feel like they should have stayed in there. And a lot of the young women had high seniority. They were in the movement since they were seventeen or eighteen years old, and stayed with the movement throughout their entire lives. And then all of a sudden they should be in leadership positions, but they're not, you know. They got organized into being in jail at home surrounded by the four walls. And so I am kind of taking that up as a banner right now. The women have got to stay involved. And I am putting the responsibility on the women. They've got to see themselves in leadership positions, and they've got to, because I think that the energy of women is extremely important. I mean, who knows, we might have had a potato boycott instead of a grape boycott, right, if it hadn't been for my role in the organization as a woman. And there's a lot of basic foundations of our organization that I fought for and that we now do, like the retirement village for the Filipino workers, our dues structure, our ranch committee structure. These are all things that I developed. Our collective bargaining agreement, I wrote the collective bargaining agreement. And I know that the history of our union would have been very different had it not been for my involvement. And I am trying to get more of our women to sort of hang in there. We do have some women in top leadership positions.

Wallin: Dolores, you talked a lot about César Chávez's leadership, with his abilities. Has the union given much thought to what is to be done if he is not around?

Huerta: Of course, you're not going to replace César Chávez any more than you're going to replace Mahatma Gandhi or Martin Luther King. Some people are just irreplaceable. César happens to be one of those people that is irreplaceable. The man is a very unique human being. And I have been working with César since when I first met him, 1955, and I have worked with him all those years on a very close basis, and I can just say to you that the man is always a very creative human being, and he is always creating, he is always thinking of new things, and he is always doing things. He's just got a tremendous amount of creative energy. And I don't think he's replaceable. I think the movement would continue because so many farmworkers—their lives have been bettered by the union. Workers have become enamored of what a union is now. You are not going to erase that, I don't think ever. You are not ever going to get rid of the union. It may not be the same kind of a union with somebody else, but the union will continue.

Wallin: Is this something that César has ever addressed himself?

Huerta: Well, I think it's probably a constant fear because his life has been threatened several times. But he also, I think, figures that it's kind of God's will right? You know, whatever will happen.

Dolores Huerta, circa 2000s. Courtesy of
Carlos LeGerrette/César Chávez Service
Club Archive Project.

27

A Life of Sacrifice for Farm Workers

Dolores Huerta

"To me, racism, chauvinism, is part of the air you breathe, the water you drink. It surrounds you, so you have to learn how to fight it, deal with it, work in spite of it. You can't let it get you down or paralyze you. You have to do all you can to change it."

Dolores Huerta, Vice President of the United Farm Workers Union and the first woman to hold such a lofty position, is five foot two, weighs 110 pounds, and regularly puts in 18 hour days. For more than 26 years she has struggled like a woman inspired for a better quality of life for migrant farm workers.

Besides working in her office in Delano, California, she spends many hours speaking at farm workers' rallies and negotiating contracts with the growers, and, when a strike hits, she travels all over the United States seeking support for the farm workers, managing on the same small salary as all other union workers. And yet, she has been called "A Model of Non-Violence." She does not advocate being submissive or subservient, but her utter dedication to a just cause leaves no room for the fruitless distraction of revenge. Dolores has said, "We couldn't have a Union without the women. Their sacrifices have been invaluable. The participation of women has helped keep the movement non-violent."

I asked Dolores to talk to me about her relationship with her mother, her father, the movement, and about leadership within the Hispanic community.

"I was born in New Mexico in a coal mining town. My father was a coal miner. I lived there when I was very young. My mother

Unpublished interview by unknown writer, July 1990, in UFW Archives, courtesy of Wayne State University.

and father are divorced. They took us to Las Vegas, California, and Mexico. When I was about six, I lived in Stockton, California. We started the Union in California, and we moved to Delano in 1962. We bought this place for the headquarters and moved here in 1972. I lived in New York for four years, and I've been all over the country. I was in charge of the first grape boycott. My father was a migrant worker as well as a coal miner. My mother was a very good cook and when we came to California, she worked in a cannery and as a waitress. It was during the Depression. She eventually borrowed money and opened her restaurant, and, when World War Two came, she opened a hotel and catered mostly to farm workers. We were close—like sisters. She was a very gentle woman, but a very strong woman. She died young—only 51 years old. She was absolutely influential in my life. She was very strong and she called the shots. I should have followed more of her advice than I did. She wanted me to go into law, but I thought I'd turn crooked. My mother raised us by herself.

When I was 11 years old, my father came to California. It was difficult. My mother was a very assertive woman—not aggressive, assertive. My father was a very chauvinistic male. He was the only son and spoiled rotten. Very intelligent. Went to college and got his degree in his 50s. He got his CPA. Very skilled, very intelligent, but very chauvinistic. I was in Girl Scouts until I was 18. I was in the choir, took music lessons, dancing. I belonged to the church organizations. In high school, I didn't belong to anything—it was pretty much racist. We traveled to New Mexico; then, when I was about 17, we went to Mexico. My brothers were raised to be self-sufficient. We all had to wash the laundry, clean. My mother always worked. We had to chip in and share the work. From very young, she taught us how to work. She brought us up all the same.

My mother married. It was a disastrous experience. Their marriage didn't last very long—about five years. Later on, she married another man. We had a good relationship with him. I was already married and had children. I had two sisters from those two marriages. They were a lot younger than I was. One of my sisters was born when I was thirteen, and the other was born when I was in my twenties. She's the same age as my two children. There was a Girl Scout leader, Catherine

Camp, who was very influential in my life, and, to get into the actual organizing, there was Mr. Fred Ross.

The first time, I married a very nice man, very responsible. We had two children. After three years I divorced him. Then, I married Sr. Huerta, a Mexican-American. That was a terrible marriage. I have a liaison now—kind of a partner. I have eleven children. I must confess I never really wanted to get married. My mother used to say that men are all alike; they just have different faces so you can tell them apart. I feel I get more tolerant about men as I get older. I put everything into my relationships. Most of all, I have to do what I have to do.

In terms of home responsibilities, I feel it's very hard. I'm not as fanatical about the house as I used to be. My children are quite grown up. They've survived and are doing quite well. All of them are strong and all are achievers. My one daughter is ill—she is schizophrenic.

Most of my ideas about how to bring up my children came from my mother. She did not oppress us. To me, a child's mind is even more sacred than the body. It's more important to have a free mind than shoes. It's important to explain the injustices, especially now with television. They get brainwashed. I believe experiences are more important than things. Let them be in demonstrations, marches, picket lines. I want them to be around ethnic groups. Not to feel the stigma of racism while they are growing up. I expect them to follow their dreams, to change the world, to make the world a better place. Not to follow other people, not to be materialistic.

When I think about Hispanics, I like the fact that the term unites everyone who speaks Spanish. I like that. I don't like what some people in the administration in Washington have done. Maybe we need another word to identify us, since the word Hispanic sounds so colonial. I think it's very important for us to be united because we all have the same problems. "Hispanic" has a lot of connotations: positive (reunification), negative (colonialization)—the fact that we are speaking a language which is not native to all of us, we are *los indios* (Indians). We speak a colonial language. That is the Indian side of me speaking. The Spanish side of me says I should be thankful to be here. I wasn't in a mass genocide like the Native Americans because the Spaniards were there, and they intermarried, and the race still exists.

When I think about Hispanic leadership, I think of a person who makes sacrifices, has ability, has perseverance, the desire to do things. Someone that people will follow. That's important because you have a lot of self-appointed leaders. You get a lot of government money to manage, and they call themselves leaders. There are a lot of those especially in Washington, DC.

I no longer have problems with being a leader. In the Union, in the strike, I organized picket lines, tried to keep people from getting killed. I organized the first grape boycott which was very successful both on the East coast, from Chicago to New York, and here in the West. César was very sick for a year—in bed—during that time. After we won the boycott, I came back, and I negotiated all the contracts for the Union. I had written contracts before. I used to do all the arbitrations for the Union. I did a lot of political work in Sacramento, Washington, passing legislation for farm workers. Then, I went back and did the second boycott in New York. More recently—I did a lot of things—like our new organizational structure. We have a 2% dues structure. That was my idea. We have a retirement village for the farm workers. That was my idea. We have a child care center. We have what we call an Economic Development Fund (now called the Martin Luther King Fund). That was my idea.

I'm an elected official. Being a co-founder of the Union made [my] election easier. About 20,000 workers elected me to my present position. So my authority comes from them. Internally, you know something has to be done, and you do it. You have to make decisions, and it's sometimes difficult, but you do it anyway. You have to know in advance that you will make mistakes and not be afraid. Men make a lot of mistakes, but they cover them up. And women don't realize it. They think men are always right. We just have to be able to argue our position, and that's hard. Men would automatically put down a woman's idea and adopt it for themselves. You have to get your ideas out and fight. Women are not willing to fight.

My vision is for the farm workers to have the same rights, protection, wages that other workers in this country have. My mission has crept into my life. I want to see women treated equally in the union. After we fought hard, I found some women were discriminated against. I realized, in about 1978, it was almost like a conspiracy. It's interesting that the men who did that are all gone now.

There are so many opportunities for leadership in our communities because there are so many areas where work has to be done: first, the area of child development; second, the effort to keep people out of prisons; third, the area of health and nutrition. The diets of Hispanics are atrocious—they have diabetes. The whole area of parenting needs work. They no longer have relationships with the grandparents. This other culture doesn't appreciate them and discriminates against them. They don't have the social and moral defenses. There is a really big need for a community organization. The Church is doing some work in this area but doesn't want to make it political, and you have to make it political. The Church has almost been against the people.

Hispanic leaders need to get over the idea of having money. As long as money is the goal, people won't have leadership. Because the money isn't there. They have to get along on the basics. They have to live at their level. We have leaders who go to school, get educated, and go to work for the corporations—for the bureaucrats. As long as that happens we are never going to have leaders develop.

A Hispanic leader is one that lives life to do the work that has to be done, knowing that it's going to be difficult, willing to take the pressure and harassment that come from doing it. I think if you deal directly with people, they'll tell you where they have to go. You don't have to look for the answers. Unless, when you get to the place where materialism gets in the way, then, you know that's not the right place to go; when people start to say, 'No. We want this for ourselves.'

Once you get into [leadership], an avenue opens up for you. God helps you if you help yourself. I paid my dues. One of my daughters wants to be an actress. Last summer Jane Fonda flew her to Canada . . . my kids are going to college, and they've gotten grants, scholarships, because of my work in the movement. To me, racism, chauvinism, is part of the air you breathe, the water you drink. It surrounds you, so you have to learn how to fight it, deal with it, work in spite of it. You can't let it get you down or paralyze you. You have to do all you can to change it.

I've taken one vacation in 25 years. I was assaulted by a police officer, and I spent a week in New York, but I was in a lot of pain. You have to expect persecution.

[The doctor who treated Dolores Huerta said that twenty or thirty minutes more and it would have been too late. She was rushed to San Francisco General Hospital after being repeatedly jabbed in the stomach and clubbed by baton-wielding police during a demonstration of almost 1,000 people against Vice President Bush, who was speaking at a fund-raiser at the St. Frances Hotel. The demonstration was sparked by Bush's joining Republican Governor George Deukinejian [*sic*] in gulping down table grapes and ridiculing Chávez, farm workers, and the grape boycott.]

There are some wonderful people doing what you are trying to do. The greatest thing is seeing what you've accomplished. Working for the Union, we've put millions of dollars in people's pockets. The laws we've passed, the contracts we've signed! The inspiration of things like the student movement and all that. When we first started the Union, the only Hispanic organizations were the mutual benefit type. Now there are professional organizations, too. People say, 'if the farm workers can organize, why can't we?'

In terms of negative experiences—going to jail, getting beaten up, having my children suffer—they are harsh things to live with. And not spending as much time with them as I would like to. The things you can't catch up with graduations, confirmations.

When you are organizing people, you get a sense of power because you know you are having a hand in helping them change their lives. Although that's very tricky. You have to do it in a way that they will not become dependent on you. You have to make them responsible. If you don't do that, you're just a charity organization. You make people helpless and defenseless, and that's a sin. The worst thing you can do to poor people is to make them helpless and defenseless. This is one of the things with the poverty program—when they started to get organized, they had their funds cut off. Because we have an education, we want to be paternalistic like the churches and treat the people like children. That's poison! We even have to say to our volunteers, 'You have to make them the leaders, not make you the leaders.' Sometimes, they don't want the workers, themselves, to be strong.

Hispanic women in leadership have no problems empowering others. We do have a tendency to let our emotions get in the way. That's something that women have to be taught—that you can hate somebody, but if you're working on the same project with them, you have to learn to tolerate it.

Every time I talk to women's organizations, I tell them to read Betty Jean Harragants book, *Games Mother Never Taught You.* I think that should be the bible for women because men play all kinds of games on you, and not just men in power. One needs to learn, not to play those games, but to recognize them when they're being played on you.

Work is important; it's creative. It's a creative part of you. You have to do what you like to do, not what someone else wants you to do—no matter what it is. Sometimes women are afraid to ask for help. I always ask for help. Of all the things I've learned, I always ask for help and people love to give advice. Nobody has the gift of knowing everything."

[After the interview, Dolores took me to meet César Chávez. He certainly summed up this interview when he said, "No march is too long, no task too hard for Dolores Huerta if it means taking a step forward for the rights of farm workers." (César Chávez, 1990)]

References

Huerta, Dolores. Interview with author. La Paz, Keene, California, June 23, 1989. Tape recording, Cherry Hill, New Jersey.

"Huerta survives near-fatal battling." *El Malcriado*, October 1988, 3.

"New Director, New Negotiations Drive." *El Malcriado*, February/March 1989, 3.

28

Bush's "Cowboy Mentality"

Interview with Dolores Huerta

**Samuel Orozco, News Director,
Radio Bilingue War Times,
Tiempo de Guerras, May 15, 2002**

Dolores Huerta founded the United Farm Workers Union with César Chávez about four decades ago. She served as the union's vice president for many years. Huerta has been arrested numerous times while leading non-violent demonstrations to improve working conditions for migrant farm workers and at rallies for human rights. Recently retired from the union, Huerta continues her social activism from her home in Bakersfield, California.

Q. It's been eight months since Bush declared "war on terrorism." What do you think about it?

A. Ever since he was elected, Bush has always talked about making war. He and his father have engaged in the task of making war, making more weapons and causing more conflicts. We know that millions of dollars are spent every day on war. Instead of moving forward, we're going backwards. Bush said: "You're either with me or you're against me. You're either with the U.S. or you're against the U.S." It's like saying that if you engage in criticism, then you're against your country. And that's not right, because as citizens we should criticize; we must criticize.

Q. Millions of dollars are being spent every day in the name of the "war against terrorism." How does that affect farm workers?

A. It affects the entire public. In California and many other states they are cutting back on the monies that should be spent on schools.

Instead of monies going to our children, they're going towards war. It's affecting the entire world. Also, the anti-immigrant policies that are related to the anti-terrorist laws affect many immigrants. It's going to be much more difficult to immigrate to the U.S. All of this has produced more racism against people of color, many of them Latinos. It's a step backwards.

Q. President Bush has announced plans to expand the war and attack Iraq. What do you think about these plans?

A. It's a cowboy mentality. Everything has to be done as ordered by Bush. It's always been part of U.S. foreign policy to first put a dictator in power and then to get rid of him. Like Manuel Noriega in Panama and the Taliban in Afghanistan. The U.S. trained and financed the Taliban. Same with Saddam Hussein. Now they want to remove him, too.

They always say these actions are in the best interests of the U.S. But I don't think there's a single person in the U.S., besides the oil corporations, who cares about who rules Iraq. Those are not our interests. Those are the interests of the oil companies and Bush is very well connected to them. The people need to raise their voices about this and call their congresspersons to tell them that they are against a war in Iraq.

Q. Is the conflict between Israelis and Palestinians an issue for Chicanos?

A. Everything affects us one way or the other. Our money is there in Israel, too. It's our taxes that are paying for the wars in Afghanistan and Colombia. Bombs are being dropped that kill innocent people. And our money is paying for those bombs. We have to take responsibility. We have to say: this is our money. The check that I sent the IRS is being used to make bombs. And today, with the tightening U.S. budget, we're being asked for more money than ever before to make more bombs.

We can look at it from a very personal viewpoint. When they talk about war, we're the ones who end up paying for it.

Dolores Huerta, 1999. Courtesy of
Susan Samuels Drake.

29

Interview with Dolores Huerta, Community Leader and Activist

Dolores C. Huerta was the co-founder and First Vice President Emeritus of the United Farm Workers of America, AFL-CIO ("UFW"). She is also the mother of 11 children, 14 grandchildren, and four great-grandchildren and played a major role in the American civil rights movement.

TCLA: What role do you play in the community?

DH: My role in the community is to get involved with issues, especially issues that pertain to immigrants, women, labor, and the environment.

TCLA: *Teaching to Change LA* is doing a series on the 50 year anniversary of Brown v Board of Education. Do you remember when the Brown decision came down?

DH: No. However, interestingly enough there was a decision before that that had to deal with Latinos called Mendez v Westminister (1946). One of the persons who was involved with the case and with myself in organizing it was a man by the name Fred Ross. [Editor's Note: Fred Ross was an organizer with the Community Service Organization who worked closely with César Chávez.]

TCLA: Where did you attend high school and what were the conditions like?

DH: I went to Stockton High School in Stockton, California and that school was pretty racist, as some high schools still are today. We had

Originally published in *Teaching to Change LA*, 4, no. 1–3 (2003–2004), issue 2.

a big division between a lot of the rich kids from the north side and the poor kids from the south side and east side. There was a lot of discrimination; most of the Latino kids that I graduated grammar school with dropped out of high school. So it was a struggle to get through high school because of the racism in the school. But I did graduate because it would've never occurred to me to even think about dropping out. My parents both had a high school education.

TCLA: Did your elementary school value students whose families spoke languages other than English?

DH: In grammar school, all of us came from different backgrounds—Mexican, Japanese, Filipino, Italian, Greek. The teachers were very hard on students. We had four hours of English everyday—penmanship, writing, grammar, reading—and a couple of hours of math everyday [*sic*]. The teachers were intensive and concentrated. The teachers were helping and teaching the kids. I don't think you see the same determination in the curriculum today.

TCLA: Are certain students treated with more or less respect than others today? And, if so, how would you describe these differences?

DH: Well, I think that the Latino kids are definitely discriminated against.

TCLA: So, what should be done to achieve equality in our current school system?

DH: To achieve equality in our schools, I think teachers need to be given the resources that they need in order to be able to teach. My daughter is a teacher and she doesn't have what she needs. The kids are struggling right now in the sense that they are not taught in a language that they could learn. While they might learn English, they're losing out on everything else.

TCLA: What would you recommend to students and parents who want to make changes in their schools?

DH: Number one, we have to start with the money. A lot of these school boards get money and it never comes down to students. And we need to support the whole "education not incarceration" movement, so that the money goes to schools, not to jails. Students must get involved, send letters to the legislature and the governor. And parents need to get involved and see what's happening in their children's schools. They need to support them and make them understand. Like I used to tell my kids when they went to racist schools, "You don't have to live with these teachers forever. You're just there for a little while. Learn what they have to teach you and realize that something is wrong with them, not you." The main thing is to hang in there, you know. I mean, a big part of winning is staying in there and not giving up. Remember "La Canción del Rey." A line in there goes, "No hay que llegar primero, pero hay que saber llegar" which translates to something like, "If you have to repeat classes, hang in there and you can overcome." I have a son, who is a doctor, and who graduated from UCLA Medical School. I couldn't help him with any of his studies. There's this idea that parents can help, well, sometimes parents can't help. All that we can do is be supportive of them. Sometimes all you can do is let them know that what they are doing is important.

TLCA: As a UC Regent, what is your view on the proposed budget cuts to UC outreach?

DH: It's horrible. It's terrible and we should fight it with every ounce of our strength.

30

An Interview with Dolores Huerta

Frances Ortega

"I would like to be remembered as a woman who cares for fellow humans. We must use our lives to make the world a better place to live, not just to acquire things. That is what we are put on the earth for."

Editor's note: Last fall, Dolores Huerta was in Albuquerque, New Mexico, where she announced the launch of the Dolores Huerta Foundation. The foundation aims to train grass-roots activism in the person-to-person organizing style Dolores and César Chávez made the cornerstone of the United Farm Workers (UFW). At 73 years of age, Huerta appeared before an audience in attendance at the University of New Mexico Student Union ballroom. After her address, and despite a full schedule, Dolores agreed to be interviewed by Southwest Research and Information Center staff member Frances Ortega. The interview was conducted on October 29, 2003, three weeks after California s gubernatorial election.

Frances Ortega (FO): Dolores, I have questions first that relate to California and the recent elections (Gubernatorial). I'm wondering with (Arnold) Schwarzenegger elected, people had information about him and yet did not respond. What do you think happened there?

Dolores Huerta (DH): First of all the information about sexual assaults didn't come out until about four days before the election. It was a Thursday and the election was Tuesday. I guess it was about five days before the election. That didn't come out. Although I think people

Originally published as "An Interview with Dolores Huerta," Frances Ortega, *Voices from the Earth*, ISSN: 1535–7953, Volume 5, No. 2, Summer 2004, pp. 6–7.

knew about it, but nobody brought it out. It was kind of interesting because he (Arnold Schwarzenegger) was saying from the beginning to the Governor (Gray Davis) don't use what they call pink politics or whatever, you know. So here the governor's campaign didn't bring it out. It was actually brought out by the *LA Times*. They had done an independent investigation that I think took them seven weeks to complete. Now remember, there was a short time frame for the election—from the time of the election qualifying, to the time the election took place. It was a two-month period. I'm not sure about the dates on that but you can check that out. There were 2 million absentee ballots that were cast before the election. The other thing I didn't talk about today was that they merged precincts. Especially in the minority areas you had like three thousand people in one precinct, and people couldn't find their polling places, people couldn't.

Many people registered never got their ballots. Many people of color, especially Latinos, were turned away from the polls. You know it was very chaotic and they tried to stop the election, and couldn't stop the election because they felt that many people would be disenfranchised. And actually, the people who didn't vote were the people disenfranchised in that election. And so it was very hard for the election to react. That is essentially what happened.

Schwarzenegger said the attacks were by the Democrats, but it wasn't, it was an *LA Times* article. The media never really pushed out these women. We of course had a press conference with some women's organizations and we had one women who was a maid in a hotel where he (Schwarzenegger) molested her. And yet when we had a press conference about that, we had no media on that. I think the Latino media was the only one covered, but not the Anglo media. I think CSPAN was there. So the media had a lot of impact and influence in that.

FO: Women are needed in the political process, what do you think needs to happen for that to occur?

DH: Well, women have to realize that they have a responsibility to be active.

Let's go back to the election. (Cruz) Bustamante running did not help at all. It confused the voters, especially the Latino voters. The way that they (Californians) saw that was, that Bustamante and Davis were running against each other.

FO: So do you think that the Democratic Party didn't do a good job of helping voters?

DH: It was too fast and they couldn't get it in gear. If the election time was longer, I think he would have lost. The Governor (Davis) had such a great reputation you know.

There was a gender gap of ten points by the way of women who voted against him (Schwarzenegger).

FO: Just now I was hearing someone talk about feminists and feminism. How did that come into your life and do you use it to describe yourself?

DH: Yes, in fact I am a board member of the Feminist Majority (FM) and their organization.

FO: How were you introduced to the word and its ideology?

DH: Well, actually I was introduced to it early on in New York City, because I was fortunate to be in New York when the Women's movement started and Gloria Steinem was a great supporter of the Farmworker's Union. Although, I have to say that for the first years I was so focused on the Union, that was my concentration to focus on the boycott and the Union, and at some point in the 1980s I said, "Wait a minute, something is wrong here."

FO: I will always remember you wearing symbols for women and for the huelga.

DH: Yes, *que viva la mujer!*

FO: Yes, and the question is, "Which one?" you know *"Que Viva la Mujer!"* Which one? Because as you know, so many people can identify a man (activist) by name and that's not the case so much when it comes to women.

So I am exploring the lives of Chicana activists as change agents for the environment. What is the relationship between women and the environment?

DH: Well, I know that the pesticides, you know for women who are in the fields, the chemicals that are used in industry, women are more adversely affected, because they (women) are less valued than men. The farmworkers—there are more incidences of cancer. There was just a recent study that came out about four or five months ago that women have more cervical cancer among farmworker women, and by that we say Latinas and in the Silicon Valley where pesticides are being used.

FO: You know I think I heard about that study and right away there is a counter attack about these studies, purported by science and industry—the role of science and industry. Sometimes industry is powerful and have their perspectives reflected in the results because they are able to pay for that research.

DH: Did you hear about that recent one with IBM? Where they were making the computers chips?

FO: Was this just recently, a few weeks ago?

DH: Yes.

FO: Actually I was in California three weeks ago and I was in a small town listening to a radio show where again this questioning of science of those studies finding high cancer rates among women [came up]. The talk show focused on "is there a difference between men and women?" and going back to old drawing boards and divisions between men and women from a health (biological) perspective, and I think it confuses the audience into thinking about difference rather than incidence.

DH: Yes.

FO: I think your work specifically puts the issues up front and that other groups use health perspectives to describe gender differences and can miss the point. What recommendations do you have to clarify the issues and help to get mainstream audiences to understand the complexity, and to allow your message to get across?

DH: Do you know Jane Delgado? Do you know of her? Jane Delgado is from California. She is the head of the Hispanic Council (National Alliance for Hispanic Health) and she has done so much work and she has been there for so long and is a real genuine person and very committed to her work and what she has done in the Latino communities, but all over the country, not only in California. But she would be the person to interview. Of course, the Farmworkers Union did a lot of the work on the pesticide issue. César (Chávez) did his 36 day fast to get the message across about pesticides. Have you seen the No Grapes video that we did?

The other issue I want to mention is the morning after pill. The Feminist Majority is the one that did all the work on that and to get it into this country. I mean they went to Europe, they found someone to manufacture the pill. They did all the work during the Clinton administration to bring it to our country. In California we have it and the governor signed the bill that you can get the pill in what they call behind the counter and I think there are five other states as well. You are supposed to take the pill in the presence of a doctor. In other words, it is accessible now and available to women. It was sponsored by the Feminist Majority who paid for the whole campaign. In fact right now they are paying for clinical trials because right now this pill may reduce cancers. And the Feminist Majority is paying for these clinical trials of women. We are trying to get universities and these laboratories to do more clinical trials. The National Institute of Health wants to do something. I didn't bring the paper with me. I had it with me because I was at a board meeting last week and there are a number of other cancers described in this work. If you like, I'll send you a copy so you can add it to your work. Now that we are talking about this, the Feminist Majority needs to write a whole paper on what they did, because they were using it in Europe for the last twenty years. I think in France. They (FM) had a (woman) model come over (to the U.S.) and bring the pill and get arrested in order to get the publicity and raise awareness about the issue and how the U.S. was against this pill.

FO: It is such an honor to be with you here today. In good health and strong for the rest of us. I think you are right that our country is at a crossroads.

I was wondering when I hear you talk about your Mother and how influential she was in your life and the need to take responsibility in our communities. What are some specific examples that you use in teaching within your own family about the strength of women and abilities to influence political powers?

DH: I think what we can teach our children. My mother was a strong woman. She divorced my Father and took us to California, held two jobs. This was after the depression. She was a business woman, she had a restaurant and hotel, she owned a business. So that was my role model growing up. I was not taught that women were subservient to men and women were not second class citizens. My role model was my Mother. I think it was a learned behavior in a way to say "wait a minute, I'm not supposed to serve the man." And that is not the way I grew up. My brothers and I were raised equally. My brothers had to clean and wash the clothes. I never had to serve my brothers, you know, cook for them and iron. And of course in the Latino culture that is not the way it is. The women are supposed to serve the man. My kids grew up where the girls did not have to do for their brothers. My sons had to do it for themselves because I was gone so much of the time you know. They had the privilege to take care of themselves and to be resourceful. But you know the Feminist wars, so to speak, are continual. You know women—wouldn't it be great if women had a little Geiger counter that they could use on a guy and then later could say "I'm not going to let you mess up my life!" (roar of laughter)

Because we know there are so many strong women and that they will meet the wrong person and you know . . . There is a huge percentage of men who do not support women. Then unfortunately due to the media (we) are forced to look up to males that are the Macho types instead of looking for the men who are supportive of us. Men who are supportive of us are called wimps and sissies. Women need to look for someone who will support us. Of course guys are always looking for someone who is going to support them. That is something that we need to start teaching our young women. The person you are going to marry has to support what you want to do too, and not to just support what they want to do. Like one of my daughters supported her husband when he was in Harvard Law School, and then he came back and divorced her with three kids. And that is the history of so many women who are very supportive to our men but they do not support us. So women have got to fight. That culture of Machismo is not going to change, the women are going to have to change. It is us, we have to change. Even if it creates conflict, and many times as women we don't want to have that conflict or confrontation. Of course it can be very dangerous for us too. That is why I think it is important for women to belong to organizations of women to get that support that they need to gradually educate the men in their world and in their lives. And especially we need to educate ourselves. I remember a woman at my house, she had a little boy and she was from Mexico and would say, *"ay mi'jo salgate de aquí de la cocina!"* You know, get out of the kitchen, instead of saying, "hey, get back in the kitchen and help out in the kitchen, I belong in the kitchen—you belong in the kitchen! You have to wash dishes. You have to cook."

What I said about men being independent, I meant that. But a lot of women still think "no no, that is not their place." This is my kitchen and not have their son in there. I have a son by the way who is a chef, and he is a much better cook than any of us.

FO: Where do you find your inspiration?

DH: I think that when you see inequalities and the things that are wrong in this world, that gives you energy. Struggle gives you energy. *La lucha de energía.* Especially seeing that you are able to accomplish some things when people come together and that it makes a difference.

FO: Thank you so much.

DH: You're welcome.

31

Dolores Huerta

The Vision and Voice of Her Life's Work

Julia Bencomo Lobaco

The deep, dark eyes tell stories filled with music and children, hardship and triumph. They see and share and call forth strength. These eyes belong to Dolores Huerta. At 74, the United Farm Workers (UFW) union cofounder still dances, boycotts, and raises her voice not just in song, but in defense of the oppressed, shouting *¡Sí se puede!*

Beginning in the 1950s, she and late UFW cofounder César Chávez fought for pensions for older Hispanics, livable wages, and safe conditions for farm workers and other laborers. They also fought against the *bracero* guest worker program and the use of dangerous pesticides. The list of battles—and victories—is a long one.

During an exclusive interview, Huerta spoke of motherhood and activism, jazz and justice. Her *lucha* continues.

Q: What sparked your activism?

A: My dad was a volunteer union organizer. He was very well respected and a member of the [New Mexico] state legislature. But he was expelled from the legislature because he got into a fight with José Montoya, who later became a congressman. My dad didn't tell me the story, José Montoya did. I was lobbying José Montoya in Congress and I told him that my father had been a state legislator. He asked, "What's your dad's name?" and I said "Juan Fernández." He said, "Oh, I remember him!" The Montoyas were big growers in New Mexico and had a lot of *obreros*, and he and my dad got into an argument.

Originally published in *AARP Segunda Juventud*, Fall 2004.

My mother was a very wonderful woman. When she and my dad divorced, she moved to California and worked two jobs—in the cannery at night and as a waitress during the day. But she saved enough money to establish a restaurant. When World War II broke out, because they were going to be doing food rationing, she gave up the restaurant and took over the hotel of one of the Japanese who had been relocated. That was good for her because we were able to live in the hotel. All the family lived there. It was a 70-room hotel, a real big one. We kids had to do all the work. We were janitors; we had to do the laundry and iron the towels, iron the sheets, and take care of business, and so she was able to provide for us.

I think my mother was a feminist for her time. She was what I call an "equal-opportunity" mother because even before she had the restaurant, we all three had to do the housework. My older brother and my younger brother and I split up the chores evenly. We had to do dishes. And there was a chart, and after you did your chores you got to put an X on there. We had to sweep and mop the floors, make the beds, and do the dishes and do the laundry. All of us equally. So my brothers learned that growing up. My mother never made me do anything for my brothers, like serve them. I think that's an important lesson, especially for the Latino culture, because the women are expected to be the ones that serve and cook and whatever. Not in our family. Everybody was equal. She didn't have my personality. She was one of these very quiet people who just did a lot. And she was a leader in the community. She was one of the founders of the first Latino chambers of commerce. She was just a doer. Because of the old way of thinking, when we were very small my mother would always say to us, "When you see that somebody needs something, don't wait to be asked. If you see somebody who needs something, you do it. Second thing: You don't talk about what you did. Once you talk about what you did you take the grace of God away from that act. And you never take any money for anything. When you do something for somebody don't ever accept any money, because, again, that takes away the grace of God." And that's wonderful because I think that really insulates you against corruption.

Q: Who knows you best, besides yourself?

A: Probably my kids. Because they've been with me and I think I com-municate a lot. We don't have the traditional Latino relationship, you know, where you have to be super respectful. We get into it, we argue, we discuss. They'll argue with me: "You're too busy doing that." And I'll get into it with them, about what their lives are about.

Q: You have 11 children. You've said you were not meant to be a housewife; you were meant to be an activist. How has being a mother shaped your views?

A: And a grandmother and a great-grandmother. It's a dilemma in many ways because, although I love children, I did take the activist path and I was never able to spend as much time with my children as I would've liked. And my gifts are not in the homemaking area, unfortu-nately. It is a problem, but I think my kids turned out pretty well. What I'd like to share with people is that what we have to give to our chil-dren are values, not so much material, [but] a social conscience. . . . You have to involve them at a very young age so they grow up know-ing that this is something they can do—that they have power to help people. And I think that's the biggest thing I gave my children. They had a lot of hardships—we were very poor and never had any money. Working for the union, all we had were our subsistence rent and food. They never had good clothes or toys. I do regret not being able to pro-vide them with music lessons. My son Ricky's very talented, but I was never able to give him any music lessons. I did have violin and dancing lessons growing up. I regret that, but at the same time it makes me feel very strongly that, as women, we need to fight for support systems. We need to be activists; women need to be in decision-making roles. To get there is a hard path, but our children shouldn't be neglected for us to get there. So we've got to push harder for day care—and when I say day care I don't mean just babysitting, but earlier childhood educa-tion for our young people, and support systems for women, so we can be out there doing the work we need to do. Our kids need to be not only safe, but also educated and safe.

Q: Your daughter, Juana, is bisexual. Was that a cause you always fought for?

A: When I went to Mexico, they always talked about gays. These were people that had to be protected, not abused. And in the early farm worker movement we had a young group of gay men who worked in the packing shed. They were really, really strong activists. So growing up it never occurred to me that you should discriminate against people who are gay and lesbian. I personally always felt that any kind of discrimination is wrong. I've always supported gay rights and went to all the gay rights marches that they had.

Q: Tell us about the Dolores C. Huerta Foundation. Does it focus primarily on needs that are not being addressed?

A: We received a gift of $100,000 from the Puffin Foundation. We put that money—something I'd wanted to do for a long time—into a foundation to start training people on how to do community organizing. So that's what we're doing.

Q: Are you focusing a lot on voting?

A: Registering people to vote and voting is part of it [the foundation's work]. Let me explain. You train organizers and they go into the community where there's need—we don't want to go where there's already a lot of organization, if someone else is doing it right. We do a series of meetings in people's homes. Then you set up an organization from all the people you've met with and explain why they need to get together and how they can solve their problems. Then you set up your separate committees: health, education, criminal justice, and, of course, voter registration. You get these people into those committees and put them to work, giving them the resources and information they need. We get them to do it because that way you create new leadership. Because there are people out there who want to do stuff but they don't have the knowledge. So what you're doing is training them how to be organizers, and depending on their skills and how receptive the community is, it should take two to three months to set up a community. Then you immediately start doing voter registration. You're not only registering people, you're explaining to them why it's important to get involved in the political process, *how* to get involved in the political process. So when election time comes around you have enough committees out there so you can get the vote out. Then you're looking at an 80 or 90 percent turnout. You're not looking at a 50 percent [turnout] like you are now.

Q: You were once a Republican.

A: Well, I'm from New Mexico. In New Mexico, because of the Civil War and [President Abraham] Lincoln being a Republican, people there are registered Republican. In fact, you still have in Arizona, Texas, and New Mexico a lot of people who are Republicans and don't know why. It's because it goes back in history. So when I first registered when I was 21 years old—that was part of being 21 years old, you went down and registered—I registered as a Republican. But once I started getting a little savvy about politics I changed my registration to a Democrat. My grandfather, although he was a registered Republican, always voted for [President Franklin D.] Roosevelt. He made it clear to everybody that he voted for Roosevelt. My grandparents were also born in New Mexico.

Q: Are there different political views in the family?

A: No. They all have a very strong political conscience. It's wonderful. I like to tell this story: Once I was in jail, one of the times I was arrested. This group of college kids came to meet outside the jail. One of them handed me a note and it was from my 15-year-old daughter, Angela. The note said, "Mom, sorry I can't meet you when you come out of jail, but I'm knocking on doors to register people to vote." That was a big gift for me.

Q: Why were you in jail?

A: Most of it was because you'd go talk to workers and they'd arrest you for trespassing. Sometimes we wouldn't even get inside the field to talk to them. They were already arresting us before we even got in there. That was one of my first arrests.

Q: I hear you and César would argue. Was it about style or issues?

A: I think over the years, as I thought about our big fights, it was mostly a question of tactics. It was never about philosophy, because with our philosophy we were always very much in tune, thinking the same way about direction, vision. It was always about tactics. But women think differently than men. When we had the grape boycott, César wanted to boycott potatoes, because this one big grower grew both grapes and potatoes. We had a long-distance fight, because I was in New York starting to do the grape boycott and César was back in California. He said, "We've got to boycott potatoes." But I said that when people think of potatoes they don't think of California, they think of Idaho, right? And so we had this big fight. I said, "César, I think this is an important enough issue that I should fly back to California so we can discuss this in person." But César didn't like to spend money. He didn't want to pay for the plane ticket. So he gave in. I think it's just a difference in the way you look at stuff. The whole macho thing comes in there and you want to be the tough guy or whatever. I mean, it's just the way men think. Not all men, but I always say men want to see who gets the blame and who gets the credit. Women say, "Let's get the job done. Who cares?" [Men] can't help it; they've been doing it since they were little kids playing marbles.

Q: Did you ever feel resentful of César being considered almost a saint?

A: Not really, because anybody who knew César knew that we were just very blessed to know someone like him and to be able to work with someone like him. When he did his first fast, he went five days without eating. "Oh, César, bless his fasting," I thought. I told him, "I feel so bad when I fight with you." He said, "Don't ever stop. Don't ever stop fighting with me. You're the one that really helps me think." You know, he was just a person, not a saint. He was a great person, but he was a human being, and he would make mistakes like other people.

César was always the one who was important. For César, that was also painful. When he first started organizing, he said one of us would have to be out there in front. He was uncomfortable with that role, you know. One time we were going into a meeting, with all the workers yelling, "¡Viva Chávez!" And he had this really pained look on his face. I said, "What's the matter César?" He said, "I remember some of these people that wouldn't even give me a meeting when we started." He was a very practical person in terms of his own image. He wouldn't let us put his pictures on posters for a long time. When he was in jail one time we made this button and he got really mad at us because—as he was being dragged off to jail—he said, "Boycott the hell out of them!" So we put that on the button. Ooh! He was so mad. We had to change it to "Non-Violence Is Our Strength." While he was in jail, a whole month, his cousin started running him for governor.

We had bumper stickers all over the state. He was very upset. He was not into the glory thing. It's kind of interesting now because there are all these streets and everything named after him. That was not César; he wanted people to get the work done, to work hard. He's buried right near the entrance to headquarters. I said he wanted to make sure people were coming early and leaving late. He worked very hard and set the example for everybody.

Q: If 50-plus Hispanics want to become activists, where do they start?

A: You have to start people at their level. I like to tell this little story about my daughter, Juanita. When she was three years old we were doing a training session for organizers. She was walking in and out with her dolls. When we got back to our boycott house in New York City, she was on the line with her play telephone. I said, "What are you doing?" She said, "I'm calling the people." I said, "Are you calling them to picket?" [She said,] "They're not ready to picket; they're just going to leaflet." A lot of the time activists want people to go out and get arrested right away or to go on the picket line. Maybe they're not ready to do that yet. You have to have activism at different levels, at the level people feel comfortable at, then evolve them into stronger positions.

I really realized this when I was beaten up by the police [in 1988 while peacefully protesting then-presidential candidate George H. W. Bush's views on pesticide use] and I was disabled for a few months. It's not only the physical disability, but also the emotional disability. I found that I was so emotional that during our board meetings . . . I told them, "I'm not going to be able to fight with you like I usually do." I'd just start crying right away. It took a long time to get my emotional stability back after that beating. It just did something to me. I couldn't be in crowds, I'd just panic. The physical disability healed in months, but my emotions took about a year and a half. That made me understand a lot about people, when you ask them to come and they're not ready.

Q: And then you nearly bled to death from medical complications in 2000.

A: That's right. That was even worse because I couldn't even walk. I had to learn how to walk, had to learn how to talk. I had to be fed intravenously for months because I couldn't eat.

Q: What lesson did you learn from that?

A: The lesson I learned was about dependency, because I had to be so dependent on my children. I'm very fortunate my son is a doctor and my daughter's a nurse. If not, my hospital stay would've been a lot longer. . . . And then when your children are telling you what to do. It meant something that I don't think young people understand. I've said this to some of my friends, that when I was disabled, as a parent you're not used to your children telling you what to do. It's very hard. It's very painful for a parent and people need to understand that. You know, I think a lot of people say, "I'm not going to take this, I'll just die. It's easier for me to die than have my kids order me around."

Even last night, we wanted to go see this reggae band and my daughter, Lori, who's the second oldest, but you'd think she's the mother, says, "Mother, you've got to get to bed. You've got to get up early tomorrow. I don't think you should go out." I said, "Okay," and everybody else went out dancing except me.

Q: That must have been frustrating. I hear you love music and dancing. What's your favorite music?

A: I love it all. I love classical. I love opera. I love Spanish, all kinds— *boleros, corridos,* salsa. I love to dance salsa. But of all those, jazz is really my absolute favorite.

Q: So how do we make sure people age with dignity?

A: That's so important. All cultures revere older people except for us. I don't know what it is. I guess it's the Anglo culture. But in all the Asian cultures, and in the Latino cultures, the elders are respected. The creation of more home health care workers I think is really important because they want to stay in their own homes; they don't want to go into a nursing home. They want to take care of their gardens and see their grandchildren.

Q: What do you see as your legacy?

A: I hope my legacy will be that I was an organizer; that I have passed on the miracles that can be accomplished when people come together, the things they can change. And I look at . . . when we passed the pension bill, the voting in Spanish, the getting driver's licenses in

Spanish—all these bills we've passed. The fact that you can build and you can make nonviolent change through organization; that's what I would want my legacy to be. And hopefully we'll see the day when we don't have discrimination against women, against minorities, against workers. And working for a just world. Showing people how to accomplish this, what they can do to make a difference.

32

Dolores Huerta on Fr. Luis Olivares

Interview with Mario T. García, April 5, 2005

Editor's Note: Fr. Luis Olivares was a Claretian priest who in the 1980s led the sanctuary movement in Los Angeles to provide protection for Central American refugees and Mexican undocumented immigrants. He was also a strong supporter of the farm workers and a close friend and ally of César Chávez and Dolores Huerta. He died in 1993.

Huerta: Fr. Luis was always very, very supportive of the farm workers. People have told you that already. He and César had a very close relationship. He was a person who was very common, very humble. People could always approach him. When he was in Los Angeles at Nuestra Señora de la Soledad, we used the church there [1970s]. The farm workers would meet there and eat there when we were doing our different campaigns on the boycotts. When he moved to La Placita Church [Our Lady Queen of Angels] next to Olvera Street in Los Angeles, he was somebody we could always drop in on him at any time of the day or night. It was like a second home for the farm workers union there at La Placita.

García: Would he house people there?

Huerta: As you know, he kind of turned it into a whole sanctuary. You could go to La Placita in the evening and he opened up the church so that people could sleep there. I don't remember if anyone slept there. Wherever Father Olivares was at, we were there with him. He was family to us.

García: You probably first met him in early 70s?

Huerta: Probably. It's been so long. It seems like we knew him forever.

García: Your initial impression of him?

Huerta: He was a very humble person. He was never like a person of authority. He was more like a friend. Like he was a comrade in the movement. He was just a really good friend. You were always welcome.

García: From your perspective, what could you tell of how close his relationship with César was?

Huerta: Very close. It was a very, very close relationship.

García: What explains that closeness?

Huerta: First of all, Father Olivares was wholly committed to our movement, supporting us with the housing, with food, with the church. He was just always—he was one of our strongest supporters. We could count on him for whatever we needed.

García: Was this a strong friendship?

Huerta: It was a friendship. It was a brotherly kind of friendship. It wasn't a distant or a formal relationship. It was a very bonded relationship. They could talk to each other anytime of day or night. *Hermanos de espiritu de la causa.* César was a devout Catholic. It wasn't even on a religious level. They were like brothers. Very, very close.

García: Would Father Olivares sometimes visit the UFW headquarters?

Huerta: Oh, yeah, Father Olivares would visit La Paz. He would visit César.

García: Would he say Mass?

Huerta: I'm trying to remember. I would not be surprised if he did. I cannot remember.

García: How would you characterize your own relationship with him?

Huerta: Also a very strong friendship. As I said, whenever I went to L.A. to La Placita or when he was in San Francisco. He had an open door, an open house for us. You could count on each other. When he dedicated La Placita Church as a sanctuary [1985], I was there at that

Mass. I was one of the speakers. Archbishop [Roger] Mahony was supposed to go. Mahony didn't show up.

García: Father Luis had invited you?

Huerta: Yes.

García: What do you remember?

Huerta: It was a very beautiful occasion. It took such a tremendous act of courage on Father Luis's part to do that. The people that were there were kind of overwhelmed. I think everybody felt it was a very historic event. And a very beautiful event. Of course there were other people there from other religions.

García: Do you remember what you said?

Huerta: I would have to think back a few hundred speeches.

García: Spoke to the issue of the sanctuary?

Huerta: Oh, yeah.

García: What did César think about Father Luis declaring sanctuary at La Placita?

Huerta: He thought it was great.

García: César would sometimes visit La Placita?

Huerta: Oh, yes. Definitely. Sometimes he was just doing political stuff down there, looking at elections, whatever campaign he was working on. He would go to La Placita.

García: You would just visit, have dinner with him?

Huerta: We would have lunch or dinner with him whatever time we got there.

García: You were always welcome.

Huerta: Absolutely. Our relationship with Father Luis was very strong. Also, when he did his Mass for the Virgen de Guadalupe there on December 12, it was a very big event. There were thousands of people that would go there at 4:00 in the morning; there were all these people there. Just incredible.

García: Did you go to the feast day there more than once?

Huerta: A couple of times.

García: Did César go as well?

Huerta: I don't know if César ever went to it. It was a very good crowd.

García: Did you ever speak at the church itself?

Huerta: I did for the sanctuary.

García: When he became ill with AIDS, what do you remember and what was your reaction?

Huerta: We were just really saddened. Of course at that time we didn't have all these medicines that they have now. For somebody who had done so much and had to be down there in Central America helping out and then to have to become ill from being down there. It was just very sad. We visited him, César and myself.

García: The funeral. Did you visit him when he was already at the Claretian house?

Huerta: Yes.

García: What do you remember?

Huerta: He maintained his dignity. He was the same person. He wasn't bitter or resentful or anything like that. He was someone that being with him you were filled with his spirituality and his goodness. Talking about this, I'm starting to cry over here.

García: Were you and César together on that visit?

Huerta: Yes. We went more than once. We went a couple of times.

García: César must have taken it pretty badly, too.

Huerta: Yes, he did.

García: At the funeral, did you attend?

Huerta: I'm trying to remember if I went or not. I think I did. I remember César spoke.

García: Any memories?

Huerta: There were a lot of people. A lot of people were there. Martin Sheen. One of the things that I regret is that when they demonstrated against U.S. policy in Central America down in L.A. and he invited me to come down there with him, but I couldn't because I was already committed to another place, and I feel bad about that now.

García: These were some of the protests against Central American policies.

Huerta: Yes.

García: Would Father Luis be on the picket lines with the union?

Huerta: Yes. He would come to our demonstrations.

García: Did he speak at your conventions?

Huerta: I think he did one of our very big Masses at one of our conventions.

García: This would be where?

Huerta: In Fresno. Father Luis being with us was like nothing unusual. If you had, say, somebody from the President's office, the bishop, or something like that, it would be unusual. But Father Luis was so much one of us that it would be more usual than unusual for him to have been with us.

García: How was he with the rank and file of the UFW?

Huerta: He was a very common person. He related directly to the workers.

García: Did he ever share with you or César about his relationship with Archbishop Mahony?

Huerta: I know he was very deeply disappointed because Mahony did not attend that Mass on sanctuary. It was advertised he was going to come.

García: Did he ever share his feelings about the archbishop?

Huerta: That he was disappointed. He didn't bad mouth Mahony at all. But for us that know Mahony well, that was not surprising. I think what hurt him the most was that Mahony said he would be there and then didn't show up.

García: When he became more involved with the sanctuary movement, did that mean he had less time to help out the UFW?

Huerta: I think that any time that he was in Los Angeles that we could count on him. He never really separated himself from the farm workers movement at all.

García: He always had time to help the union even though he was immersed with all these other activities?

Huerta: Yes. Of course, when he was out of the country he couldn't help us. But any time that he was in town, he would.

García: What do you think is Father Luis's legacy?

Huerta: His legacy, number one, is he really brought home to all the Latinos here in the United States, particularly the Mexican Americans, how important that struggle was in Central America. How we were directly linked to it. Because it was also our struggle, it was our cause. I think that's one of the biggest things he did. And to see someone of his stature taking leadership in this at a time when so many religious were ducking these difficult issues. He was out there, being right out front.

García: As a Latino priest, was his relationship with the UFW, César, unusual? Was there a particular quality that made him stand out?

Huerta: I think at the beginning it would have been unusual. I think towards the end, about the time that he got involved with the sanctuary movement, Fr. Luis was pretty much on our side by that time. But in the early days it definitely was.

García: He was easy to get along with?

Huerta: Yes. He was not pretentious at all. He was very accessible. You never felt you were intruding on him although he was very, very busy. Turning La Placita Church into a sanctuary was no easy thing. He did that and he also handled all the problems that came with it. He was always under a lot of pressure.

García: Do you remember seeing the refugees there?

Huerta: Oh, yeah. You'd go down there at night and see all the refugees there. They were sleeping in the church. I know a lot of people were very critical of what he was doing.

García: Any other anecdotes about Father Luis?

Huerta: Probably when he was with César, and the two were together alone, it was probably different than when I was with Father Luis. Sometimes I saw Father Luis myself without César. I would go visit him when I was in Los Angeles and ask for help on stuff. We had all these problems. His place at Soledad Church was actually our official campaign office, not political campaign, but for the boycott.

García: When he was at Soledad Church he would house some of the farm workers there at the church?

Huerta: Right.

García: Where?

Huerta: I guess they had a hall or something over there.

García: That's when his connection with you and César and the union started.

Huerta: I think it was before that. It might have been then, but might have been a little bit before that. I can't think chronologically in terms of years.

33

"Our Fight Is Your Fight"

*Civil Rights Leaders Dolores Huerta &
Julian Bond Speak Out Loud and Clear
for GLBT Equality*

Julian Bond and *Dolores Huerta* are true American heroes. From the back roads of Georgia to the California growing fields, the two have been on the cutting edge of social change for decades—through organizing, protest, lobbying and voter registration campaigns—often risking their lives along the way.

Fortunately, Bond, the chairman of the board of the NAACP, and Huerta, co-founder of the United Farmworkers of America, really get the fact that "civil rights" are rights shared by all. They really get the fact that as more people are able to have equal rights and protections and can live and work free from discrimination, the stronger this country is and the stronger all Americans are. For years, the two have stood with us in the fight for gay, lesbian, bisexual and transgender equality. Bond and Huerta recently took time out from their busy schedules to speak with the Human Rights Campaign.

Legendary labor leader Dolores Huerta is definitely someone you want on your side. Fast-thinking, fast-talking and fearless—she is more than ready to act. Decades ago, Huerta co-founded the United Farm Workers of America with César Chávez, and she's been making history ever since as a leading advocate for immigrant workers' rights. She's also a mother of 11 and grandmother of 14 and heads her own foundation for community organizing.

One recent morning in downtown Los Angeles, Huerta, 76, addressed a crowd of reporters, denouncing racist and sexist remarks

Originally published in Human Rights Campaign's (HRC) *Equality* magazine, Fall 2006.

by California Gov. Arnold Schwarzenegger. An hour later, she's seated next to you, quietly talking about organizing, lobbying, religion and her love of dancing.

Huerta has supported GLBT equality for decades, marching in early pride parades, testifying against discrimination and previously serving as an HRC board member. Here are excerpts from her chat with *Equality*'s Janice Hughes.

Equality: Early in the farm worker movement in California, I understand that you knew several gay men who were activists.

Huerta: Yes, there were farm workers who were gay and lesbian. César Chávez had a "comadre," a lesbian who baptized his oldest son, Fernando. She owned a little bar called People's. For the strikers, that was our hangout because there was so much discrimination against us—People's was a place where we all went because there was never any hostility. In fact, it was part of our movement.

Equality: You've said often how much your mother influenced you.

Huerta: One of the most important lessons I learned from my mother— one of her principles—was to help others when they needed help and not wait to be asked. When you saw someone in need, help them, and do not expect anything in return.

Equality: The Dolores Huerta Foundation focuses on helping others— through community organizing.

Huerta: It's about meeting with people, showing them what they can achieve by giving them successful examples. These are lessons I learned from the farm workers' movement. Before the movement, farm workers didn't have toilets, cold drinking water, hand-washing facilities in the field or a rest period. They have them today because farm workers went out and marched and worked in the political campaigns to get their supporters elected.

Equality: You've worked so hard for a variety of groups—for rights of women, immigrants and others. Can you talk about the role of coalition work?

Huerta: It's extremely important. We live in such a segregated society and we don't always know what other groups are doing. We can make our movements a lot stronger if we learn how to work together. For instance, the environmental movement does not have a real strong presence among Latinos, even though Latinos are the fastest growing population and are very adversely affected by environmental degradation—pesticides in our food and in the ground. If groups were more integrated, we would be a lot more powerful.

By the way, I remember a hearing in San Francisco in the 70s or early 80s on the issue of discrimination against gays and lesbians. When I arrived to testify, no one had any idea what I was going to say and they were nervous. When I testified and said it was wrong to discriminate against people because of their sexual orientation, the opposition forces were shocked. It was something I felt strongly about—so much so, that I went on my own to that hearing.

Equality: I bet that made a big impression.

Huerta: When I was political director for the union, we joined the first gay marches both in West Hollywood and in San Francisco. We had the farm workers come out in droves to come and march. My daughter Lori de Leon participated in the one of the first marches for gay rights in New York City. She actually got hit by [a] policeman in the back and to this day she still has scars.

Equality: I understand one of your daughters identifies as bisexual.

Huerta: My daughter, Juanita. She's a teacher in L.A., and has been active in the movement. While she was teaching in San Francisco, she set up a resource center for any of the kids who happened to be gay and lesbian. When she was teaching at a charter school near Los Angles, some parents took up a petition for her to get fired because she told the class she was a lesbian. She kept her job.

Equality: Thank you for your work on marriage equality in the California State Legislature. How has the presence of Latino/a support for marriage equality influenced the Latino/a community at large?

Huerta: Well, a couple of people who voted against the marriage equality bill lost their elections. Incumbents who supported marriage equality all got re-elected. A number of Latinos who voted in support of it were also re-elected.

Equality: How do you think the presence of you and others in your community in such efforts affects the Latino/a perception of the gay, lesbian, bisexual and transgender community?

Huerta: We do influence when we stand up. When I'm speaking to the public or to colleges or community organizations, I like to quote a president of Mexico, the first indigenous president of the Americas, Benito Juárez. He said a Spanish phrase that every Latino family knows: "El respeto al derecho ajeno es la paz." Or in English: "Respecting other people's rights is peace." No matter how many children you want to have, that's your constitutional right. The right of privacy, whom you want to marry, whom you want to live with—is your constitutional right. You need to respect the rights of others. When I say that to Latino audiences, they understand. They get it. So it's important for political leaders and civic leaders to speak out. Very important.

Equality: When you lobbied lawmakers in Sacramento on marriage equality, did you find that some arguments resonate more than others?

Huerta: I'll tell you this little story. One legislator voted against the equality of marriage bill. And afterward, the president of the Democratic Women's Club—she's Latina, Sara García—wanted a meeting with him. And he said, "You know, I vote my religion." Her response: "We didn't elect you to vote your religion, we elected you to represent us." Isn't that great? He got defeated in the next election.

Equality: You've spoken out about the need to put fair-minded judges into the system, to make sure everyone is treated equally.

Huerta: And politicians. I think we have to be a lot more assertive. Anybody who is not supportive of gay and lesbian rights is against human rights. We've got to be more assertive in running candidates against those who are against you.

Equality: How do you see the struggles for fair treatment by field workers and immigrants compared to the struggles by the GLBT community?

Huerta: Both are extremely similar because both involved discrimination. The farm workers faced racial discrimination and never received respect for the job they did—until they organized, educated others and organized for change. The GLBT community also has had to do outreach and education and organize for change.

Equality: Some leaders dislike when we say that the GLBT fight is a civil rights fight. What do you say to people who say to us, "Your fight is not our fight"?

Huerta: The civil rights struggle was a human rights fight to end segregation under Jim Crow and end racism against African-American people and other minorities. Just like the struggle for GLBT equality, we must end discrimination and recognize gay and lesbian rights as basic human rights.

Equality: Recently, very prominent Hispanic leaders like Los Angeles Mayor Antonio Villaraigosa and members of Congress Linda Sánchez and Hilda Solis of California and Charlie González of Texas have joined with you in support of equality because they see it as discrimination against a specific group. What do you say to leaders who fight discrimination yet do not support equality for the GLBT community?

Huerta: It's time for leaders of the entire community to take a stand. Leaders cannot represent their constituents if they do not represent and educate all of their community on GLBT equality.

34

Respect, Spanish, and Unemployment Insurance

Dolores Huerta founded the United Farm Workers with César Chávez. At 76, she's still fighting for social justice, running a foundation that recruits and trains community organizers.

Huerta taught elementary school in Stockton, California, in the 1950s. Her daughter teaches third grade in Los Angeles.

Huerta talked recently with *NEA Today*'s Alain Jehlen.

NEA Today: What do educators need to understand to help farm workers' children learn?

Huerta: They need to understand that these children are very intelligent even though they don't speak English. If you don't speak Spanish, you need to get an assistant who does.

It's very difficult now for Latino children who don't speak English in California and other states that have eliminated bilingual education. The children will learn English eventually, but if they are made to feel guilty for speaking Spanish, that leaves a terrible mark that's very hard to get over.

NEA Today: How can we help them gain confidence and learn?

Huerta: They shouldn't be made to feel inferior. They should be proud of their parents. Farm workers do the most important work in the world: they feed the nation. I often ask people, if you had to be on a deserted island—like on Survivor—who would you take with you, a farm worker or a lawyer?

And the second person I would take would be a teacher.

Originally published by the National Education Association, http://www. nea.org/neatodayextra/huerta.html.

NEA Today: When students move so often, how can a teacher connect?

Huerta: In states like California where farm workers can get unemployment insurance, the family can stay after the harvest is over and the children can go to school.

Education is so important. You know, César Chávez only went as far as the eighth grade, but he always had a book under his arm. He was always learning and always promoting education.

A farm worker's daughter told me that when she was a girl, her father went to a Farm Workers rally and heard César say, "Your children need to go to school. They don't belong in the fields, take them out." The next day, her father sent all his children to school. Today, that daughter is a community college president.

Dolores Huerta with Virgen de
Guadalupe in background, circa 2000s.
© Victor Alemán/2 Mun-Dos.Com.

35

Dolores Huerta on Spirituality

Interview with Mario T. García, June 1, 2007

MG: How important has religion been in your life?

DH: It has been extremely important in my life. Especially when you start doing things like organizing a union with no money and seven children. Talk about faith. It takes a lot of faith.

MG: Would you say that from your early childhood to today that religion has been central?

DH: Like everybody else, you grow up in the Catholic culture and religion, going to all of the sacraments and everything, but I think you don't really grasp onto the faith until you are in situations like I have been in in organizing, both with the Community Service Organization and the union. I remember when I was lobbying in Sacramento to get the bills passed—we had a bill to get pensions for non-citizens, so people who were legal immigrants would be able to get pensions— before I would go to the capitol to lobby I would go to the cathedral right there by the capitol and I would light all my candles and say my prayers. Then I would go to the legislature hearings. It's really funny because Sal Alvarez who was my assistant later on when I was with the union—I was a lobbyist with CSO—Sal is a deacon and very religious. I would call Sal about people on the committee and he would say, "Well I lit all the candles," and I would say, "No, Sal, that's not going to do it, you have to light the candles and work the committee too. Lighting the candles isn't enough."

There was a time when my mother was dying of cancer and I was in Sacramento and responsible for passing not only that bill but several other bills that I had, like driver's licenses in Spanish, getting unemployment insurance for farm workers, disability insurance, I had a whole ton of bills, being able to register voters door-to-door, I had a whole plate of legislation I was carrying, and my mother's dying.

I guess my prayers were continual. I would lobby Sacramento and then jump in the car and drive to San Francisco, my mother was in the hospital at the University of San Francisco, and then drive back to Sacramento. Then my husband, who I was in the middle of a divorce with, took my kids from the babysitter. I had no idea where my kids were. All of this was going on at the same time. Talk about the need for prayer and faith. It was tested. That's your consolation, that you go there and you have that support.

MG: Now when you were growing up . . .

DH: When I got my kids back just before my mother died. We were all together when she passed away. My bills all passed in the state legislature.

MG: What year did your mother die?

DH: '61.

MG: When you were a child growing up in New Mexico and later when you came to California, what role did religion play in your life?

DH: I always say when people ask me where did you get your values from, I say I got them from religion. Especially in the Southwest where people are very devoted to St. Francis Xavier, to again follow the same values as St. Francis of Assisi about helping others and doing good for other people and not expecting gratification or rewards for what they do; if you see someone in need you should help them, don't wait to be asked. All those core values I did get them from religion.

MG: There is a concept that some theologians use called "abuelita theology." How did that play in your life, in terms of your mother or grandmother's influence?

DH: Not really because my mother's mother died when my mother was a little girl. She was raised without a mother. My aunt raised her. My mother's aunt was pretty strict and not a very loving person. My dad's mother was sort of senile. I look just like her—La Indita—but not too much direction from her. But my influence came mostly from my mother.

MG: How religious was your mother?

DH: She was very religious. My mother was a very hard worker; she had to work two jobs because she divorced my dad and this was right after the Depression, during the '30's. We came to California in 1936. My mother had to work two jobs just to keep us fed. I call her the Horatio Alger type, she would never take anything from welfare. She wouldn't take anything she said that was for people who couldn't work. She always worked two jobs until she saved up enough money to set up a business. Although she didn't go to church every Sunday she made sure we went to church every Sunday. I went to confession. She would go to church for the holidays and holy days of obligation. She usually had to take her Sundays to catch up on her rest.

MG: In your home with your mother, did you have particular religious icons in the home?

DH: Yeah, we always had the Virgin of Guadalupe, of course, and crucifixes and the Santo Niño de Atocha. This is a New Mexican influence.

MG: Did your mother have a home altar?

DH: No, we didn't do altars. I guess that's more Mexican than New Mexican. We didn't really have an altar. I do remember when visiting relatives in Mexico some of them had altars. I remember visiting one family that every afternoon they would stop and pray for a woman's husband who had died and I asked when did he die and they said a year before and they were still mourning and wearing black.

MG: What do you remember about your First Communion or confirmation?

DH: I remember the church in New Mexico in Las Vegas, it was Nuestra Señora de Dolores. I remember going to church there all the time. In Stockton we went to St. Mary's, that's where I had my First Communion, Confirmation, and my first marriage. I was very active in the choir. I sang in two choirs—at St. Mary's and at St. Gertrude's, another Catholic church. I would do the midnight Mass at one church and the morning mass at the other. St. Gertrude's had more of the Latino community. I started going to that church also. A lot of my friends went to that church. I became part of the youth group called Santa Teresita. We used to do different activities. There was a folk dancing group.

MG: Would you say that you were devout as a teenager?

DH: I can't say devout. I had a really good family, my mom was really great in giving me a lot of freedom. I was very active in the church. I knew all the priests by their first names. When I became older I became very active. My cousins always went to Catholic school but I couldn't go because we couldn't afford it. It's interesting because my cousins went to Catholic school and once they got out they didn't go back to church. I used to get mad at them. One of my cousins, she passed away a few years ago. I stayed with her one time and I asked where's the nearest church, I want to go to Mass, and it was down the block. I said I could fall out of bed and land in the church. I noticed that the kids that went to Catholic school were all bad. They were much more naughty than my kids who all went to public school.

MG: Did you raise your own kids as Catholics?

DH: Yes I did. It was great because when I started with the union, we used to have Masses, we had our own priest. We had Mass every Sunday and it was awesome. That doesn't exist anymore.

Before we had the strike I used to go to Mass every Sunday with Helen Chávez. When the strike broke out the priests were all related to the growers and they were telling people to break the strike and go back to work. César started having Masses in his home every Sunday.

Before the union I worked very closely with some of the priests, Father McCullough, Father Dugan in Stockton. Before the union with César I organized another organization called AWA, Agricultural Workers Association, and I worked very closely with Father McCullough and Father Dugan.

MG: Is Father McCullough still alive?

DH: No, he died.

MG: Getting back to when . . .

DH: I have to tell you something. We kind of broke our relationship. I was organizing AWA and then it became AWOC. They sent somebody over from AFL-CIO to see what we were doing and when they saw how many people we had organized they were blown away. They sent an organizer out and it became the Agricultural Workers Committee and I was working with them. I was trying to get them to bring César because he had a lot of success in Oxnard where he was organizing another group for the packing house workers' union. They didn't want to. I was hoping that Father McCullough would support me on this but he didn't. We were at my mother's house—this was after we had been working together for three or four years—he says to me, "Well, you really should stay home with your children, this is not a good place for women." Can you believe that? I remember this because I was so close to him. I lived in the housing projects, went to his church every Sunday. I even named one of my kids after him. I was shocked. But luckily my mother said to me, "Don't pay attention." She always had really good liquor for company and she pulled out a bottle of tequila and we had a shot of tequila.

I didn't see the Father again. We used to talk every day. I didn't see him again until we were doing the boycott in San Francisco. One of my comadres who was also from Stockton said, "Guess who's at the church across the street from my house, Father McCullough." I went over there to see him. He was like, "What can I do for you, do you need any help?" I said "Yeah, I could use a couple of tires for my car."

When I was beat up by the police he went to see me in the hospital. He died shortly thereafter.

MG: Had your mother sent you to CCD classes?

DH: What is that?

MG: To religious classes, even though you went to public school?

DH: Yeah, we all had to go to Communion. We had to go to catechism to get our First Communion.

MG: Did you do the same thing with your children? Did they go to catechism?

DH: Actually, my older kids did. I had my kids in Catholic school in Stockton. Once I moved to Delano I put my kids in Catholic school too. But once the strike broke out they actually asked me to take the kids out of school.

MG: Are you serious?

DH: I'm serious.

MG: The nuns did?

DH: Yeah. The growers all had their kids there because all the growers are Catholic.

MG: How did you react to that?

DH: Well they had to come out. It was funny. My son Fidel, his best friend in school was Bruno Despoto, the son of one of the growers. The Church was very political. They told Father Alovar when we had our big strike meeting, they forbid him. They wouldn't let the union have any more meetings in the parish hall.

MG: There was only one Catholic church in Delano then?

DH: There were two. St. Mary's and Our Lady of Guadalupe. Usually all the growers went to St. Mary's and that was where the school was at. Guadalupe was on the other side of town, on the west side.

MG: You had your kids at St. Mary's?

DH: Yes. I didn't have any money hardly. The little money I had I was using to pay their tuition. They told me to take the kids out.

MG: The year the strike began in 1965 was also the years of Vatican Council II. What was your reaction to the changes of Vatican II and did it have any relationship to the strike itself and the struggle?

DH: Not really. I thought the changes were great. Some of them started before we came to Delano. What year did the changes start? I remember this one lady, an older woman, I was asking the priest at St. Gertrude, is where all the Latinos went to church—she said, "I always wanted them to say the Mass in Spanish, but they didn't want to." But then after Vatican II, they brought a Franciscan to take over St. Mary's church in Stockton and they started having Spanish Masses. The Father at St. Gertrude's told her, "Well, if you want the Mass in Spanish go to Mexico." She told the Father, "Well I don't have to go to Mexico, I can just go to St. Mary's."

MG: Did Vatican II make the Church attempt to be more relevant to social issues and did it have any impact on the farm workers' struggle?

DH: Not immediately. In terms of when we went out on the boycott it did. But the valley was so controlled by the growers and the growers were Catholics. Up until recent history when the Pope came to Salinas, we were all excited because we got the word because César was going to take the offering. The growers put pressure on the Pope so at the last minute it was not César, it was a farm worker. We ended up not going.

MG: This was John Paul?

DH: Yes. It's probably still going on.

MG: What effect did your divorces have on your Catholicism?

DH: I went to confession about that and told the Father. I still take Communion, even though I've been married again.

MG: But it didn't alienate you from your faith?

DH: No. The thing about being a Catholic, you've gone through the whole mill, you've had the priest who would stand up at the front of the church and say, "Give us your money." I remember in Stockton, he'd say, "I don't want any pennies in the collection box, I want only dollars." Some of my cousins raised money to build a gym at the Catholic school at St. Mary's in Stockton. What they did was they used the money to build another church. My cousins got mad and left that church. They started another church, they raised money to build another church. They were so angry with what they had done with the money.

MG: You had a critical view of the Church?

DH: I still do. I'm very much in support that we should have women priests and they should be allowed to marry.

MG: What did you think about how César employed religious symbols in the farm worker's struggle?

DH: It was very important. He did it sincerely, it wasn't a gimmick. The one great thing was that he always had the priest give absolution to people when we had these giant rallies and Masses with a thousand people. Then people could take Communion. César always promoted the people taking Communion.

MG: What were your own thoughts on things like fasting?

DH: It's very important. Fasting is very important.

MG: Did you participate in fasting the way César did?

DH: All the time. In fact I just fasted 14 days for the immigration bill. It wasn't a total water-only fast, we had one meal a day. I fasted one meal a day, with no snacks, nothing in-between, for the whole Lent of last year, for forty days. I lost fourteen pounds and my wrinkles got deeper. You can't win.

MG: You, like César, connect fasting with your faith?

DH: Absolutely. I promote it. I tell people it's very important. It's got to be an offering, not coercive.

MG: What are you thoughts on things like pilgrimage?

DH: Definitely. We did the pilgrimage to Sacramento more than once. Actually César had promised a pilgrimage to the Virgen de Guadalupe at the basilica in Mexico City, but we never had the time to do it.

MG: Like César, do you have a special devotion to Guadalupe?

DH: Definitely. To the Virgin Mary in general. I've had some experiences—when you talk about the faith—I had been negotiating in Yuma and I was going camping . . . and I was traveling down the highway from Yuma to Calexico and there were no exits on the road. The alternator went out on my car. I thought nobody could see me from behind and there were a lot of trucks behind me because they take that road moving the produce from Calexico to Yuma to go back East. I just started saying rosaries all the way because I was driving without lights, luckily there was the moon and I could see the road. I didn't have any taillights and thought nobody can see me. My car went all the way and it stopped just as I was getting off the exit at Calexico, but that was almost sixty miles. Just as I got to the end of the road, a truck was starting to come off and I ran up to him and he was a farm worker and he helped me push my car off and sure enough there was a big ol' truck coming up right behind me. Not only did the farm worker help me but he had an extra battery to put in my car. I was able to move my car and get an alternator.

I have had so many, when I was beaten up by the police—I've had so many close calls and I always start praying the rosary right away.

MG: Do you pray the rosary on a regular basis?

DH: Definitely, yeah.

MG: Almost daily?

DH: Well, if I can. Last year I prayed it every day. That was one of my New Year's resolutions.

MG: Do you have particular religious icons in your home?

DH: Tons.

MG: Like what?

DH: Everybody. Icon of Guadalupe in the basement of a house in New York City when we were on the boycott—during the boycott by the time we got our first contracts the church stepped in. When we signed the first grape contract we got the bishop of Los Angeles supportive. By the time we finished the boycott after several years the bishop of Los Angeles was supporting us. For the second grape boycott the Church really went all out. They supported the boycott, they opened all the seminaries all across the country where farm workers could stay at. They had a very active peace network all over the country involved in the boycott.

We had a committee of the bishops that was very involved in the boycott including Bishop Roger Mahony. The bishop was later on the ALRB (Agriculture Labor Relations Board), he was pushed around by the teamsters, so he's had a lot of experiences. When César died he wanted to do the Mass. There were a lot of priests that had been a lot closer to us, like Father Kenny, Father Boyle, that were still alive.

MG: Do you carry a rosary with you?

DH: Yeah.

MG: Do you wear anything like a cross or anything else?

DH: No I don't, I just carry a rosary.

MG: What are your own thoughts on nonviolence?

DH: Nonviolence is very important.

MG: Do you see it in connection with your faith?

DH: Actually no. I think the nonviolence goes back to Gandhi. I read Gandhi when I was very young, even before we started the union.

MG: On the Church's position on—you had mentioned women as priests—what is your position on birth control and abortion?

DH: I've gotten a lot of hate mail on this—someone just sent me an e-mail yesterday comparing me to Lucifer. My feeling is this, I have eleven children and it was my decision to have eleven children. But I don't think I can impose my values on somebody else. That is for somebody else to decide. It's total hypocrisy because if people did not use birth control, like the Church prohibits, everyone would have twenty kids. From day one even native peoples and indigenous peoples, they always had some way of birth control and abortion. But the bad thing is that if you don't have a safe procedure for women who do need to have an abortion then you put the woman's life in jeopardy. Unless women can control their own bodies then women will always be suppressed.

You look at the history of the Church, it's very negative on women. They wouldn't even let women come onto the altar. I think it's inevitable that the Church will eventually have women priests. The Church is in so much trouble right now, with the pedophilia.

MG: What about abortion?

DH: On abortion it's the same. I don't think any religion or any legislature should be able to dictate to women what they do with their bodies. When you look at the other side of this, what does the Church do? You want women to have a lot of kids, do we provide day care for the children? Do we provide parenting classes for families? We really want to make sure that the fetus is born, but what about after they're born? They take these negative positions and even promote people to vote against their own economic interests. The antigay marriage is another thing. How many priests are gay? That's another hypocritical position. Some of my cousins are very devout—I was with them in Colorado recently—these are women who would never miss Mass. On Sunday they don't even want to go to Mass anymore. I couldn't believe it. "Why aren't you going to go to Mass?" "Oh, we don't want to give our money to priests who pay off their lawsuits on pedophilia." I was shocked. You find that people are really fed up.

MG: Dolores, have you been influenced by other religions or other spiritual movements in your life?

DH: When I was in college, I went to other churches. I studied other religions. I read the Qu'ran. I was thrilled to see that they recognize Mary and Jesus in the Qu'ran. I think in the Qu'ran they mention Mary more times than the Bible does. I think it's 129 times or something. They had a *Life* magazine that came out about Mary, I saved that magazine. In that magazine they had Mary on the cover. They said that the mentions of Mary in the Bible you can put on one page. The Qu'ran actually mentions her more than the Bible does.

MG: I didn't know that.

DH: I explored other religions. But I came back and it all stems from the Catholic Church.

MG: You were just kind of exploring?

DH: Yeah, I was just exploring. I also think that the Catholic religion, we threw a lot of the good values of the Jewish religion out. Like the Seder, most Catholics don't even know that the Last Supper is the Seder. In the Jewish religion, because of the Seder, because of the Hannukah, the social justice values are engrained into Jewish children. We don't have that in the Catholic religion.

MG: Do you think we should go back to that kind of tradition?

DH: That was what Christ was about, feeding the poor. All of Christ's life was about that. It's painful to go to Mass sometimes. The priest rants and raves about gay marriage and about abortion, but not one word about farm workers around here not being paid for their work because they're undocumented, or social justice issues. The incarceration rate is going up, the poverty rate is going up. I almost got into a fistfight with a priest on Palm Sunday last year. I was in Northern California and I was putting the foot to the pedal so I could get to Mass on time on Palm Sunday. I finally made it in time and the priest was telling people that Senator Kennedy should be excommunicated.

The Kennedy family is one of the most Catholic religious families that exists. He was saying they should be excommunicated because they were talking about the Schivel case. I got mad. He was Latino and to top it all off he was gay. When they were going to give Communion, a nun in a habit—which is a rare thing to see these days—she gets up to go help him to serve Communion and he told her no. Then he goes over to the front row and picks this real *guapo* (handsome), this young Latino dude to come up.

MG: So you confronted him after Mass?

DH: I sure did. I didn't confront him about being a hypocrite, but I asked him, "How can you stand there and attack Kennedy who does so much for poor people? He's been behind all of our health initiatives, he's standing up for the rights of immigrants, he's always supported Latinos, how can you stand there and attack him?" We were standing there yelling at each other.

MG: How much have you studied liberation theology?

DH: I actually met Paulo Friere, Fr. Miguel Discoto, he visited us because he wanted to know about our nonviolent movement. He did this just before he organized the women's march in Nicaragua. I haven't really studied it but I know about it. Father Juan Romero and Father Luis Olivares, both liberationists. I was very close to Father Bill O'Connell, who passed away, he's an incredible person. He just passed away. He was on the board of my foundation. He was put in prison for protesting the School of the Americas. He spent six months in the federal penitentiary at Atwater. Father Louie Vitali is another person who's always supported farm workers in terms of the peace movement. He just finished his third stint in prison, because of protesting at the School of the Americas in North Carolina where the U.S. military teaches torture techniques.

MG: How do you practice religion or spirituality today?

DH: By prayer, going to services.

MG: Do you go to Mass daily?

DH: No. I go weekly. Once in a while I'll miss it if I'm traveling. I used to be really pained about it if I missed Mass because I was traveling, but

Father McCullough said, "Don't worry, as long as you're doing what you're doing, that's as good as going to Mass."

MG: I understand that you have some Christmas family traditions around Los Reyes Magos and Las Posadas, can you tell me a little about those?

DH: We try to do the Posadas every year, we don't always make it but we try. I always have All King's Day, I have a party for my grandchildren. We talk about the kings. They look forward to it and they remember it. The one problem we're having is we're running out of kids. They're all grown now.

MG: How many grandkids do you have?

DH: Fourteen grandchildren.

MG: Great-grand?

DH: I have five. It's interesting because one of my nephews is into theater and lives in New York City. He worked at the Metropolitan Opera as the technical director there. He worked at Carnegie Hall, at the Wang Theater, and now he has his own company. He always says, "Auntie Dolores, you're the one who got me started in theater when I was one of the Three Kings."

MG: So you organize Las Posadas around your family then?

DH: Yes.

MG: Do you actually go from home to home?

DH: We try and go to each others' houses.

MG: What church do you go to now in Bakersfield?

DH: St. Francis and St. Phillip's. St. Phillip's is more of an upscale church. I always try to go to St. Phillip's for Christmas and Easter Mass because their Mass is just incredible.

MG: St. Francis in Bakersfield . . .

DH: The Father is Craig Harrison.

MG: Is it more of a Latino parish?

DH: No, they've been trying to get a Latino Mass in there. They do a bilingual Mass, which is interesting because they've been trying to get a Latino Mass. The furthest they've gotten is a bilingual Mass. They do have a Vietnamese Mass.

MG: What is your general reaction to the sexual scandal in the Church?

DH: I feel sorry for the Church. I think it's pretty disgraceful because of their position on gay marriage and abortion rights.

MG: How do you think it's hurt the Church?

DH: I think it's hurt the Church a lot. It's worse than hypocrisy, it's opportunism. When they had the Parent Notification Bill, Prop 85, in 2006, this is where the teenager has to get permission from a parent or a doctor before they can get an abortion. The Fresno diocese has a radio station. They interviewed me on this because I was doing a lot of work gathering support against Proposition 85. I said that it was hypocritical for them to take a position on this because it doesn't say eliminate abortion, it just says that a teenager needs to get a parent or doctor's permission to get an abortion. It still doesn't say it's against abortion. But why do they do it? Because they have a lot of money. That's a totally hypocritical position for them to take.

MG: How much do you think the sexual scandal has affected the Church's social role?

DH: I think that the Church is losing people. When I'm in Los Angeles I go to St. Thomas Church on Pico and Normandy. It's a wonderful church. There were 900 people at the Mass. My daughter lives down there, she's a teacher, I stay with her when I'm in Los Angeles. I'm driving to her house and I notice another storefront religion, just a block away from St. Thomas. I figured out what it is. There are a lot of immigrants and they have no community. So they put up little evangelical churches for the immigrants and form a community for them, so they have a support system. That's what the Catholic Church should be doing. And they are in some places, but it should be a policy of the Church to be doing that everywhere.

MG: Cardinal Mahony and the Church in California have a pretty strong position in support of immigrant rights. Do you think the sexual scandal hurts the Church's credibility?

DH: I think it leaves the Church very vulnerable to criticism. I mentioned to you, over at my primos, my cousins—those cousins of mine were so religious. We would have conversations about abortion. They never missed church. My cousins and I are the same age. I told them you can't blame your church or your priest for what's going on. You can't take it out on the religion. We know that from day one that the Church has taken bad positions on certain issues.

MG: Dolores, last question. César often said that what kept him going all those years wasn't politics or economics, but it was his faith. Would you say the same about yourself?

DH: I think so. Because you have so many setbacks in what you're doing.

MG: Did you and César ever talk about religion and spirituality?

DH: Yeah, definitely. When César was doing his first fast, many people, including Father Dugan who had by then left the Church, were very upset about the fast. A lot of people were very angry that César was doing this. They thought he was trying to play a saint or God. César was very pragmatic. He really respected religion, he was devout. Some people would criticize him about having the image of Our Lady of Guadalupe in our marches. But that's what Guadalupe is about. That's what religion is about. He would criticize people who just went to church and prayed but didn't do anything to help anybody.

Mario T. García and Dolores Huerta in
Santa Barbara, California, early 2000s.
Photo by Mario T. García.

Bibliography

Sources Cited

"A Life of Sacrifice for Farm Workers: Dolores Huerta." Archives of Labor and Urban Affairs, Wayne State University. Jul. 1990.

"An Interview With Dolores Huerta." *El Chicano* 25 Jan. 1973.

Baer, Barbara L. "Stopping Traffic: One Woman's Cause." *The Progressive* Sep. 1975: 38–40.

Baer, Barbara L. and Glenna Matthews. "'You Find a Way': The Women of the Boycott." *The Nation* 23 Feb. 1974: 232–38.

Carranza, Ruth. "From the Fields Into the History Books." *Intercambios Femeniles* Winter 1989: 11–12.

Clemmons, Nelda. "Dolores Huerta mothers 11 kids, one labor union." *Tampa Times* 1 Feb. 1978.

Coburn, Judith. "Dolores Huerta: La Pasionaria of the Farmworkers." *Ms. Magazine* Nov. 1976: 11–15.

del Castillo, Richard Griswold and Richard A. García. "Coleadership: The Strength of Dolores Huerta." *César Chávez: A Triumph of Spirit*. Norman: University of Oklahoma Press, 1995, 59–75.

Etulain, Richard W., ed. "Dolores Huerta Recalls, 1975." *César Chávez: A Brief Biography with Documents*. Boston: Bedford/St. Martin's, 2002, 42–43.

———. "Dolores Huerta Recalls, 1975." In Jacques Levy, ed., *César Chávez: Autobiography of La Causa*. New York: W. W. Norton & Co., 1975, 277–78.

Felner, Julie. "Woman of the Year: Dolores Huerta, For a Lifetime of Labor Championing the Rights of Farmworkers." *Ms. Magazine* Jan/Feb. 1998.

Floersheim, Ryan. "Campus Workers Urged to Unite." *Daily Lobo* 30 Oct. 2003.

Foley, Eileen. "'Sorrow in the Orchards': Her Life for Years." *Detroit Free Press* 16 Sep. 1974: 1C–2C.

Forter, Scott. "UFW Official Operated on After S.F. Beating." *Daily Californian* 16 Sep. 1988.

García, Mario T. "Interview with Dolores Huerta on Fr. Luis Olivares." 5 Apr. 2005.

García, Mario T. "Interview with Dolores Huerta on Spirituality." 1 June 2007.

Harding, Vincent. "Excerpts from an Interview with Dolores Huerta: Early Family Influences." The Veterans of Hope Project: http://www.veteransofhope.org/show.php?vid=51&tid=46&sid=77.

"Hearings of the Fact Finding Committee in Labor and Welfare: Testimony of Dolores C. Jerta [*sic*]." *California State Legislature Senate* 15 Jun. 1960: 117–22.

Huerta, Dolores. Debate between the Teamsters and the UFW. UFW Archives, Archives of Labor and Urban Affairs, Wayne State University. 1973.

———. "Dolores Huerta Talks about Republicans, César, Children and Her Home Town." *Regeneración* II 1975: 20–24.

———. "Dolores Huerta Talks about Republicans, César, Children and her Home Town." *La Voz del Pueblo* 25 Jan. 1973: 3–4.

———. Letters from Dolores Huerta to César Chávez. Archives of Labor and Urban Affairs, Wayne State University.

———. Speech. Transcription of tape cassette recording labeled "Dolores Huerta 2/22/78." Campus Farm Worker's Support Committee 22 Feb. 1978.

"Interview with Dolores Huerta: Community Leader and Activist." *Teaching to Change LA*, Vol. 4, No. 1–3, Issue 2: 2003–4. http://www.tcla.gseis.ucla.edu/equalterms/dialogue/2/huerta.html.

"Interview with Dolores Huerta: Respect, Spanish, and Unemployment Insurance." National Education Association: http://www.nea.org/neatodayextra/huerta.html.

"Keynote Address before the Annual Convention of the American Public Health Association, New Orleans, La." Archives of Labor and Urban Affairs, Wayne State University. 21 Oct. 1974.

"Labor Heroines, Dolores Huerta." *UNION W.A.G.E.* Jul/Aug. 1974: 6.

"Leadership and Popular Movements: The UFW Experience." Center for the Study of Democratic Institutions. 12 Mar. 1985.

Lobaco, Julia Bencomo. "Dolores Huerta: The Vision and Voice of Her Life's Work." *AARP Segunda Juventud* Fall 2004. http://www.segundajuventud.org/english/nosotros/2004-oct/dolores_huerta.htm.

Murphy, Jean. "Unsung Heroine of La Causa." *Regeneración* Jan. 1971: 20.

"News from UFW: Statement of Dolores Huerta." Archives of Labor and Urban Affairs, Wayne State University. 15 Jul. 1969.

Orozco, Samuel. "Bush's 'Cowboy Mentality': Interview with Dolores Huerta." *War Times, Tiempo de Guerras*, 2002.

Ortega, Frances. "An Interview with Dolores Huerta." *Voices from the Earth*, Vol. 5, No. 2, Summer 2004: 6–7.

"'Our Fight Is Your Fight': Civil Rights Leaders Dolores Huerta & Julian Bond Speak Out Loud and Clear for GLBT Equality." *Equality* Fall 2006. http:// www.hrc.org/Template.cfm?Section=Home&CONTENTID=34630&TEM PLATE=/ContentManagement/ContentDisplay.cfm.

Rainey, James. "The Eternal Soldadera: To Her 11 Children, She Was an Often Absentee Mom. To Those Who Crossed Her, She Was a Harsh Foe. But to the Thousands of Farm Workers She Still Fights for, Dolores Huerta is the Ultimate Warrior." *Los Angeles Times* 15 Aug. 1999: I-12.

Rose, Margaret. "César Chávez and Dolores Huerta: Partners in 'La Causa.'" In Richard W. Etulain, ed., *César Chávez: A Brief Biography with Documents*. Boston: Bedford/St. Martin's, 2002, 95–106.

———. "Dolores Huerta: The United Farm Workers Union." In Eric Arnesen, ed., *The Human Tradition in American Labor History*. Wilmington, Del.: Scholarly Resources Books, 2004.

———. "Traditional and Nontraditional Patterns of Female Activism in the United Farm Workers of America, 1962 to 1980." *Frontiers: A Journal of Women Studies*, Vol. 11, No. 1, 1990: 26–32.

Torres, Maria Luisa. "Labor leader Dolores Huerta credits family and faith." *The Tidings* 31 May 2002.

Additional Sources

Dalton, Frederick John. *The Moral Vision of César Chávez*. Maryknoll, N.Y.: Orbis Books, 2003.

Day, Mark. *Forty Acres: César Chávez and the Farm Workers*. New York: Praeger Publishers, 1971.

Dunne, John Gregory. *Delano: The Story of the California Grape Strike*. New York: Farrar, Straus and Giroux, 1967.

Ferriss, Susan and Ricardo Sandoval. *The Fight in the Fields: César Chávez and the Farmworkers Movement*. New York: Harcourt Brace & Company, 1997.

Jenkins, Craig. J. *The Politics of Insurgency: The Farm Workers Movement in the 1960s*. New York: Columbia University Press, 1985.

Kushner, Sam. *Long Road to Delano*. New York: International Publishers, 1975.

Levy, Jacques. *César Chávez: Autobiography of La Causa.* New York: W. W. Norton & Co., 1975.

London, Joan and Henry Anderson. *So Shall Ye Reap.* New York: Thomas Crowell Co., 1970.

Majka, Linda C. and Theo J. Majka. *Farm Workers, Agribusiness and the State.* Philadelphia: Temple University Press, 1982.

Matthiessen, Peter. *Sal Sí Puedes: César Chávez and the New American Revolution.* New York: Dell Publishing Co., 1969.

Meister, Dick and Anne Loftis. *A Long Time Coming: The Struggle to Unionize America's Farm Workers.* New York: MacMillan, 1977.

Nelson, Eugene. *Huelga: The First Hundred Days of the Great Delano Grape Strike.* Delano, Calif.: Farm Workers Press, 1966.

Rose, Margaret. "Women in the United Farm Workers: A Study of Chicana and Mexicana Participation in a Labor Union, 1950–1980." Ph.D. Dissertation: UCLA, 1988.

Ross, Fred. *Conquering Goliath: César Chávez at the Beginning.* Keene, Calif.: El Taller Grafico, 1989.

Taylor, Ronald B. *Chávez and the Farm Workers.* Boston: Beacon Press, 1975.